# Preface

During the Victorian era the conservatory was principally a show place for exotic plants of every description, it being quite common for the wealthy owner to sponsor plant-hunting expeditions to distant parts of the world in order to seek out as yet undiscovered plants. Plants of special merit would be used as *prima donnas* to excite and add further interest to the already splendid collections of plants. The conservatory owner of today is much better placed in respect of plant supplies as exotic plants, both flowering and foliage, are readily available from any number of retailing outlets.

*The Complete Book of Conservatory Plants* covers all aspects from laying the foundations, erecting the building, and choosing fixtures and fittings. The importance of heating, shading, ventilation and insulation are also covered with recommendations given for the most suitable materials and products.

Detailed information on all aspects of plant care forms an essential part of the book with details given on all the problems in the way of pests, diseases, and such like, that the conservatory owner is likely to encounter. Watering, feeding and potting on are essential to the well being of one's plants, and these practical tasks are explained in simple terms.

The book will appeal to both the beginner and the more experienced grower of plants, with the A to Z section offering an extensive range of both exotic and familiar plants. Here will be found plant descriptions and solid information regarding their care and suitability as subjects for the modern conservatory. The modern conservatory is often an extension to the living quarters of the house and the plants will have to compete with all sorts of activities; this aspect has not been neglected in *The Complete Book of Conservatory Plants*. By reading the book the authors feel sure that the conservatory owner will be enthused and encouraged to ensure that attractive plants become an essential part of the conservatory scene.

W.D.
J.B.

D1443615

# PART I

## THE HARDWARE

# CHAPTER 1

# *Which Conservatory?*

So you have decided to build a conservatory. Fashion alone has created an enormous market for them and you will be spoilt for choice. Making this vital decision can be quite a headache. The market has something for everyone and is constantly expanding. With the recent recession, all these factors have been very positive for the buyer. Market forces have dictated that to stay in business the conservatory manufacturer has had to develop well built attractive conservatories at a fair price. Those that have lost sight of these criteria may well have dropped by the wayside.

At one end of the spectrum you will find manufacturers producing beautiful, ornate designs, which can regularly be seen in the glossy magazines. At the other end there are products which have more in common with an, albeit smart, greenhouse. What do you go for? The choice can be quite bewildering.

## Preliminary selection

A preliminary selection may be made from the handful of better known manufacturers simply because you recognize their name. Their conservatories are usually easy to view as they can frequently be seen at the big trade exhibitions and flower shows. This does not necessarily mean that their product is any better than that of a local designer/builder, and of course because they are local you can easily go and view the finished article. Personal recommendation from a satisfied customer might also give you some peace of mind at this early stage. You should now arm yourself with some of those seductive brochures to find out whether what is aesthetically pleasing is also financially viable.

Whatever your ultimate choice your budget will dictate it to a certain extent. Therefore the first and most important decision you have to make is how much money you want to spend.

This can vary considerably. For example, a modest double-glazed conservatory measuring approximately 4.2 m × 3.9 m (14 ft × 13 ft) will cost about £4000; the mass-produced more traditional modular conservatories will follow at around £7000, obviously becoming more expensive as their size is increased. As a general rule the more individual the design, the more expensive the end result will be.

It is also a good idea at this early stage to decide upon how you are going to pay for it. A straight cash payment is easy, but Building Societies can be notoriously slow at lending money, so if it is a matter of extending your mortgage, find out early on just how much they are prepared to loan.

## Will it add to the value of my house?

When house prices began to rise appreciably in the mid 1960s, house owners began to think in terms of extending their homes rather than undertaking the huge capital expense of moving. At this time the need was filled chiefly by bricks and mortar, but within ten years technology began to produce very cheap aluminium glazing extrusions in kit form. To begin with there was very little difference between these glass extensions and a lean-to greenhouse but they were an extremely economic way of expanding a living area, and considerably less expensive than moving house. The tide was turning, and the public gradually became more adventurous and required less utilitarian and more attractive glazed structures.

Whether a conservatory will add to the value of your home today depends very much on its original cost and its degree of sophistication. For example, a well insulated, centrally heated extra living room in the form of a conservatory would represent further living space at any future valuation, whereas a single glazed lean-to sunroom, with use restricted to the warmer months of the year, would be less likely to be an appreciating asset. The cost of a bricks and mortar extension can be calculated at approximately £50 per square foot. The price of a conservatory depends on the manufacturer and the product he sells you.

One very real financial benefit of a conservatory is the contribution it makes to energy conservation. Situated over house doors a conservatory provides a buffer zone, rather like a porch. Adjoining house walls will absorb heat (Fig. 1.1) thus insulating the house, and of course the better your house is insulated the more significant will be the passive solar benefits of a conservatory.

After purely financial considerations, a welter of other basic criteria, many of which are connected with the construction materials, should be studied.

## Legal aspects

### Planning permission
In the UK, conservatories generally come under the umbrella term of 'permitted development'. This very simply means that the building of a conservatory is allowed without formal planning permission provided that the extension is not more than 70 m³ (50 m³ in conservation areas), that it does not extend beyond the existing building lines, and that it does not intrude upon the amenities. This usually means that the potential conservatory must not take light from neighbouring properties. It is always worthwhile just to check with your local planning office, because a previous extension to your house may mean that your conservatory will take you over the limit of your allowed 70 m³.

### Building regulations
Since 1985 these have not been required, as long as the conservatory is no more than 30 m², that it is situated at ground level and it poses no hazard or fire risk to adjoining buildings or property. If you live in a listed building, none of these rules applies to you, as you must always apply to your planning authority for permission to extend.

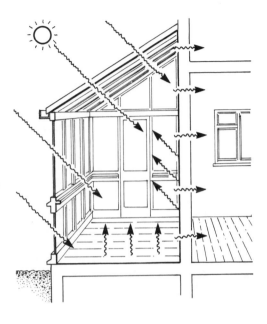

Fig. 1.1 A conservatory is rather like a buffer zone as it traps free heat. House walls absorb this warmth and adjacent rooms benefit from it.

Wherever you live the conscientious manufacturer will take care of all the above for you as part of their service.

## How long will my conservatory last? Man-made vs wood frames
If asked that question one manufacturer might reply: 'Barring acts of God, forever. The superstructure is extruded aluminium covered with an ultra high specification uPVC making it totally maintenance-free, and the glass is not glass at all, but triple thickness polycarbon, which is practically unbreakable.' A manufacturer of a more traditional product would probably reply: 'Looked after in a recommended way, barring acts of God, forever! The superstructure is made of hardwood, sourced from reforested plantations; it has been treated with preservative and given four coats of microporous paint. The roof is hardwood, made maintenance-free with low profile aluminium capping. It is double glazed. Each double-glazed panel has integral

condensation channels, and is made with toughened glass which is strong enough to withstand rain, wind, gales and snowfalls.'

The brochures of course are full of this kind of jargon. Most products have built-in longevity. This is partly because the market place has become so competitive and also because the conservatory designer is innovative. Products are constantly being upgraded and improved with conservation very much in mind.

Without a doubt, man-made products such as extruded aluminium, uPVC, and fibreglass are, as the manufacturer claims, totally maintenance-free. With modern technology, it is becoming difficult to tell, other than by close inspection, the difference between wood and plastic or aluminium (Fig. 1.2). In addition, these man-made structures are considerably cheaper than wood.

Taking all these factors and conservation into consideration, why is it that wood is used at all in the construction of conservatories? Aluminium is cold to touch; it conducts the heat to the outside in winter and lets the cold in. To improve the insulation factor the aluminium product you are considering should have a 'thermal break'; this minimizes the conductivity of aluminium, preventing internal condensation and reducing heat loss. uPVC is strong and lightweight, but although it is maintenance-free in the general sense of

**Fig. 1.2** Type of building materials and durability must come high on our list of priorities. The man-made materials used in conservatories 1 and 2 will have an indefinite lifespan, but will their fine lines suit your house? All these conservatories have a maintenance-free roof; make sure yours has too.

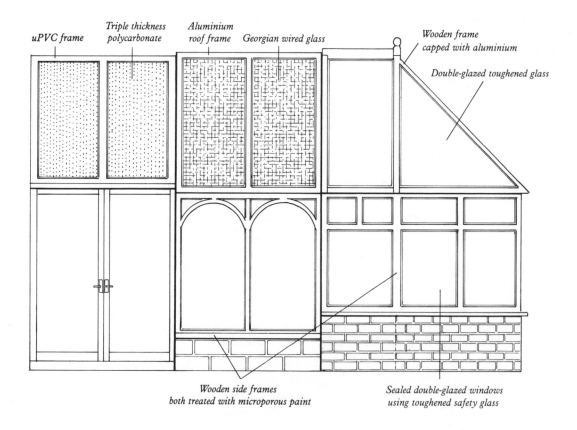

uPVC frame

Triple thickness polycarbonate

Aluminium roof frame

Georgian wired glass

Wooden frame capped with aluminium

Double-glazed toughened glass

Wooden side frames both treated with microporous paint

Sealed double-glazed windows using toughened safety glass

the word, it does get marked, or scuffed just like any other plastic surface and this type of damage is irreparable. Despite their inherent strength, both aluminium and uPVC look frail; some manufacturers are countering this by producing aluminium in boxed sections and fashioning uPVC to look stouter. However, the very real drawback of these man-made fabrics lies in their fine and rather delicate looking lines. The lightweight look they create which generally works well on houses with similar modern design, often looks insubstantial and out of place on an older house of more stature.

Thus, aesthetically speaking, wooden frames do have that added appeal of appearing traditional, although the Victorians often built their superstructures out of cast iron. Perhaps it is more important that they are aesthetically pleasing and wood has natural insulation properties. Wood feels good to touch and any unintentional damage is easy to repair. Also conservatories with wooden frames can be fashioned to echo the shape and design of the house to which they are attached.

Great pains are taken to use the best types of wood for the job as the timber for a conservatory must be able to withstand enormous stress. Therefore the responsible manufacturer will ensure that all woods are well seasoned and treated with preservatives and layers of special microporous paint — this does not need stripping before reapplication every four to six years. Conservation alone has dictated that the responsible manufacturer uses hardwoods derived from reforested plantations.

It is vital that the traditional conservatory manufacturer knows his wood. I once visited a very attractive little conservatory, which had been fashioned in complete harmony with the heavily beamed cottage to which it was attached. It was an individual design and cleverly linked one side of the cottage to the other, and the views over the rolling countryside were quite breathtaking. However, the builder involved with the construction had used young unseasoned timber, with the result that the conservatory was extremely well ventilated — it had been completed barely four weeks and the glazing was already parting company with its support!

### The maintenance-free roof

The conservatory roof is also very important. However much your manufacturer insists that it is strong enough to walk on — and thus easy to maintain — the average odd job man will probably not be prepared to take it on.

Some conservatories are designed with wooden side frames and an aluminium roof structure. Others have wooden roof framework which is capped with aluminium. Both these designs would therefore have a maintenance-free roof. Consider this aspect at the design stage; it may well be worth your while.

## Glazing

In the search for the perfect solar conductor, manufacturers have gone well beyond the simplicity of single or double glazing. There are now several possibilities — clear sealed double-glazed units, Georgian wired glass, laminated glass, toughened glass, low E glass, solar-controlled glass and polycarbons.

Although glass intensifies the rays of the sun, it is a relatively poor insulator, and it is for this reason alone I would strongly recommend double, as opposed to single, glazing every time. However, when the sun shines, the rays pass through glass easily. Floors and walls will absorb this heat so the conservatory will remain warm long after the sun has moved on. So, we could say that the area inside is solar heated, and will be so even on gloomier days. Therefore to gain the maximum benefit from this free source of warmth, ways have been developed to improve the insulation value of glass.

*Single glazing.* If used at all this must be toughened or laminated glass; never consider cutting your costs by using horticultural glass, or annealed glass. Neither is strong or safe enough to use in a conservatory.

*Double glazing.* As its name suggests there are two sheets of glass. These come in different thicknesses, not less than 4 mm, depending on the degree of strength and safety that is required. The two sheets of glass sandwich a sealed air space, providing further insulation. The thicker the air sandwich the greater the insulation value. Double glazing starts to insulate when the sandwich exceeds 5 mm and improves up to 20 mm. More glass obviously

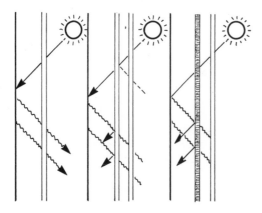

**Fig. 1.3** Glass is a relatively poor insulator; we can improve upon its insulation qualities by using double or triple glazing. Although initially more expensive, glazing using Low E glass will improve the insulation value of the conservatory by a third.

means greater expense although the saving in energy costs means that the increased initial outlay is quickly recouped. Another advantage is the fact that it makes an excellent noise shield (Fig. 1.3).

Double or triple glazing using *Low E* glass is a still more efficient way of insulation. Ordinary glass has a high emissivity and loses heat quickly; some metals have a very low emissivity and retain heat well. Low emissivity, or Low E, glass is treated with a special metallic coating. The coating behaves like a mirror reflecting warmth back into the conservatory, thus improving the insulation value of the conservatory by a third.

Finally, how do you keep all that glass clean? Elbow grease or a patient window cleaner are both time consuming and expensive. You could use the *Clear Shield 'non-stick' glass* in your conservatory. Clear Shield Glass is a unique high quality glass with exceptional clarity, visibility and cleanliness. It resists staining and discoloration and is always easier to clean. Clear Shield Glass can be purchased with your conservatory; alternatively glass can be converted in situ. Once installed Clear Shield Glass will need cleaning less than half as often as normal glass.

## Glazing alternatives

The very latest is polycarbon, a carbon development. It is virtually unbreakable — 200 times more resistant to impact than glass — and it is fabricated in layers. As the number of layers increases so does the insulation value. By using triple thickness polycarbonate sections you will be provided with three times the insulation value of double glazing or put another way, cut your heating costs by 50%. It also has the advantage of diffusing the sun's rays so the glare factor is reduced; it can also be tinted, reducing glare still further.

Perhaps the most valid reason for its success is the fact that it is considerably cheaper than glass. It can also be altered on site when fitting tricky corners unlike glazed units which are usually fitted together away from the immediate site. Any errors in initial measurements cause delays, as new glazed panels have to be specially made. On the minus side, it is very noisy. When it rains you can hardly hear yourself speak and when the sun shines it creaks and groans, just like PVC guttering. However, a real drawback of a roof glazed with polycarbon is the fact that it lacks the clarity of glass. My conservatory is almost a part of my garden; the glazing and heating mean that I can grow plants that I would otherwise only dream about. I can sit among my exotic beauties, look up and see the sky, just as though I was outside on the patio (Fig. 1.4). Under a polycarbon roof the edges would be slightly blurred reducing the feeling of space and freedom.

## Safety

Although solar conduction and heat conservaton must come high on our list of priorities, the strength and safety of the glazing must surely be just as important. Once again we must rely on the ingenuity and integrity of the manufacturer. Very simply the thicker the glass the stronger it is, but there are different methods of ensuring its strength.
*Laminated glass.* This consists of two or more sheets of ordinary glass between which there are interlayers made of a tough resilient plastic material. Bonded together under heat and pressure, they make one transparent plate. If this glass is broken the fragments remain in place, adhering to the interlayer.

*Toughened glass.* This is four to five times stronger than ordinary horticultural glass (the type commonly used for a greenhouse) of the same thickness. It has been strengthened by heat treatment to resist impact and has been stressed so that when it breaks it should shatter into relatively small harmless pieces.

*Georgian wired glass.* Here a wired mesh is either sandwiched between two layers of glass, or pressed into one face during the manufacturing process.

## Siting the conservatory

It is usually only the fortunate who have a choice of site for their conservatory; the manufacturer will refer to this subject as orientation. The facts behind this are fairly simple but the practical application is often more complicated. Your conservatory will effectively be a

**Fig. 1.4** Despite its inherent safety and insulation value uPVC is slightly opaque. This conservatory has a traditional glass roof, you can see the sky, it feels spacious and light, you could be in the garden outside.

buffer zone between your house and the outside world. Depending on the sort of glazing you choose it will insulate you to a lesser or greater extent from the rigours of the weather. Therefore, from a purist's point of view, you must attempt to gain as much as possible from passive solar radiation and if you are living in the Northern Hemisphere you must align the central axis of your conservatory along a north–east, south–west line.

This sounds fairly simple. If you have more than one possible site for your conservatory it

**Fig. 1.5** Typically conservatories are fitted where they will gain as much heat and light as possible. Tucked into a corner site they can be accessed from more than one room and could be more economical to fit as there are only two new walls to build.

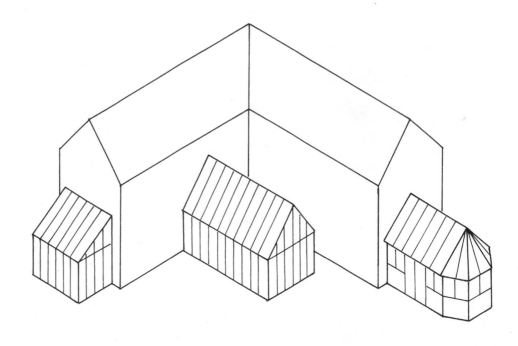

**Fig. 1.6** Although there is a great deal to be said for perfect orientation, as far as the plants are concerned it is not of great significance. Of course, you must choose the right plants but the glass will intensify what light there is and warm the air around them, and the plants will flourish.

is quite likely that you will be able to orientate it perfectly. However, future use may also influence where you want it built (Fig. 1.5). If your conservatory is to be used purely as a sun trap on a rectangular house, the end result will probably be as near perfect as possible. Even then you will also have to consider the view. Where the potential usage is more clearly defined, as a dining or family room for example, it would perhaps be best if it were positioned with access to the kitchen.

A conservatory tucked into a corner site may be the obvious solution for you. Built in this way it will also be more economical as there will only be two new walls 'to buy'. The house will gain more from passive solar heat as the surface area contact is extended. More rooms will adjoin the conservatory, and they too will gain from the free heat as it diffuses through doors and windows. Finally if this corner site is perfectly orientated, the solar gain will be outstanding as the conservatory will be sheltered, to a certain extent, from the cooling effect of the wind. In reality, do not worry unduly; with plants in mind, it is the quality of light that really matters (Fig. 1.6).

## Cost

Most manufacturers will happily provide you with their brochure and price lists. As many of the conservatories are modular it is relatively easy to ascertain an approximate budget without a salesman or architect coming to visit you, but a cursory glance at half a dozen brochures advertising what amounts to a very similar structure will show you just how much the actual prices can vary. Why should this be?

It is all down to how a particular product is packaged and marketed. A manufacturer may function on a variety, or combination of different levels. His price may look appealing because he is simply selling the pieces, leaving you, the purchaser, with the expense of foundations, erection and glazing. In fairness, where this is the case, he will often provide you with a list of recommended builders to help you out.

Another potential package is the manufacturer who expects you to provide the foundations and basework; in this respect he claims to avoid expensive errors by forwarding detailed drawings for your own builder to follow, and some may provide you with a surveyor to liaise with your builder. Once this is complete he will erect the superstructure, and allow you to apply those final coats of paint, before he glazes and finishes the conservatory.

Within these two modes of operation there are many variables, but basically a conservatory can appear fundamentally cheaper, because the real building work and related labour are not included in the price. Foundation work alone can represent 20% of the final cost and obviously, any brickwork involved will increase the percentage still further. So unless you are a really handy DIY person you should not compare the cost of these partly packaged conservatories with the more sophisticated.

However, even if you opt for one of those manufacturers who increase the cost but cushion the client as far as building headaches are concerned there is still more to be considered. The building costs will only cover the structure of the conservatory itself. Any structural alteration to necessitate access from house to conservatory, for example, may well be outside the original quote, so that cost must also be included in your budget.

Finally, a cautionary note. As in any other walk of life there are a few conservatory manufacturers who give the majority a bad name. Putting up a jerry-built conservatory represents a relatively easy way of making money, the results of which can be disastrous. I once visited a conservatory built on the side of a lovely old English manor house. The unsuspecting owners had relied purely on the integrity of the manufacturers as far as construction was concerned. They had carefully chosen their site and had it vetted and checked by their local authority for theirs was a listed building. Unfortunately, the chosen site was over the top of a disused well. The builders, however, said nothing of this, although it must have become obvious that something was amiss, when they found the ground unseasonably saturated whilst digging the foundations. When I arrived the conservatory was all but finished and the result was appalling. The retaining walls and scree floor were heaving with damp, and the consequent condensation on the glazing made waterproofs statutory equipment. You may say that this was purely the result of poor liaison between the builder and manufacturer, or insufficient attention to detail on the part of the architect. Whatever the cause, the only real solution was demolition and rebuilding. An expensive and disappointing mistake, difficult and extremely time-consuming to rectify.

There is, in fact, a form of protection for conservatory owners — The Conservatory Association. Unfortunately not all manufacturers are members, and some of the major manufacturers are notable by their absence. This national watchdog has an almost impossible task if only because of the number of trades involved in the construction of a conservatory. There are few quality controls in operation in respect of conservatory structure. Therefore your only real insurance is in the 'good name' or 'good will' of your manufacturer.

## Foundations, sills and basework

As with any extension to your home a conservatory has to have a concrete base and dampproof membrane. In the case of fibreglass conservatories, which are impervious to water, it is as simple as that, but most conservatories

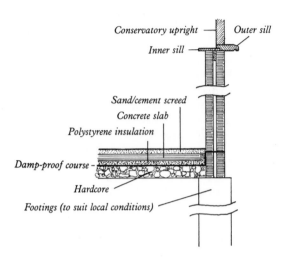

Conservatory upright — Outer sill

Inner sill —

Sand/cement screed

Concrete slab

Polystyrene insulation

Damp-proof course -

Hardcore

Footings (to suit local conditions)

**Fig. 1.7** Basework of a typical conservatory. Note the inclusion of a polystyrene insulation layer.

constructed with other materials need standard foundations and a damp-proof course.

The depth of the preliminary footings will depend on local conditions. The way in which the foundations are prepared and constructed varies from one manufacturer to another to suit his product. Some incorporate drainage systems which link up with the existing drainage facilities or construct rainwater soakaways. Others may include a polystyrene insulation layer which isolates the floor from the ground below thus helping to retain the heat absorbed during the day (Fig. 1.7).

The term basework also embraces the retaining walls on which the glazing rests. The material used in their construction is very much a matter of personal taste. Often the standard module includes an insulated timber, dwarf wall which will make the end product more economical, and some conservatories are fully glazed, i.e. the walls are entirely glass, or an equivalent. Many manufacturers offer you the alternative of opting for stone or brick basework as opposed to wood. You may conclude that the alternative is more in keeping with the external structure of your house. If this is the

case you must make sure that the basework will be well insulated.

The critical height of all these retaining walls is often neglected. Your conservatory will be in a unique position between your house and the garden. Imagine your distress, when, for the first time you are seated in your beautiful new conservatory, you realise that you cannot see the garden because the retaining walls are too high.

There are often both external and internal sills built into the framework of a conservatory. Beware the artificially wide internal sill; it is frequently cosmetic fine tuning. In conservatories where internal sills are negligible, or absent, the framework between vertical glazing panels can provide the perfect position for climbing and twining plants in their scramble upwards. The wide indoor sill will present an obstacle to this ascent. You can avoid it by using the sill for pots but not many plants will enjoy such a permanent position where they will have to endure the direct and intensified rays of the sun.

## Drainage, soakaways and water-butts

By adding a conservatory to your house you could be posing yourself quite a problem. Few manufacturers consider it seriously enough. Normally the water which falls on the roof of your house, passes down the drainpipes and disappears into soakaways or drains. Where will the water from the conservatory roof go? Are your existing soakaways man enough for the job?

We had two new soakaways to cope with this extra water and they were not sufficient. True it was a very wet spring, but there were days when I felt like Noah as the water lapped at the dwarf walls of the conservatory. There were other contributory factors, like a new patio surrounded by a small retaining wall, and the problem was eventually solved; the fact remains we did not give drainage careful enough consideration. What we should have done was alter existing house downpipes before the conservatory was constructed so that the house roof water was fed in another direction. How easy it is to be wise after the event. Of course I ensured that the drop on the

**Fig. 1.8** Save soft rain-water from the conservatory roof in nearby butts or tanks.

## A room with a view

Your orientation may be perfect, but does this mean that you are looking at the new motorway instead of your beautiful garden? This question of panorama is all too often neglected until the conservatory is finished, and by then it may be too late. Have you got a view that is worth looking at? Why not position the conservatory so that you can really appreciate it? Imagine, for the first time you will really be able to enjoy the glory of your early spring garden in comfort.

Maybe the word view is rather too expansive — you do not really need wide open spaces. Perhaps what you need is a focal point, or simply a calculated arrangement which leads the eye away into the distance. I well remember the planning stages of my conservatory. It came almost simultaneously with a new house and garden. Fortunately for me the garden itself was fairly uninteresting, no noticeable focal points, so the garden plan was all made with the conservatory in mind. Your new conservatory could well alter your whole perception of the garden, as it did mine. Flower beds changed significantly in both shape and appearance, plants that I had rarely glanced at stood up to be noticed.

conservatory guttering led to the water-butt (Fig. 1.8) situated conveniently out of sight near the conservatory. If possible you need more than one. As I write we are well into winter and both my water-butts are full. This was not so during the drought of June, July and August when my conservatory plants needed watering and misting twice a day.

## Flashing

While on the topic of water, I must mention that without lead flashing your conservatory will leak. It is a simple way of sealing the gaps either between the fabric of the conservatory and the bricks and mortar of the house to which it is attached (Fig. 1.9) or where glazing meets the superstructure at angles in the roof. Done properly, it takes time. Many manufacturers regard this as part of their job, but not all. I have seen conservatories leaking like sieves, closer inspection revealing a lack of flashing in the right place.

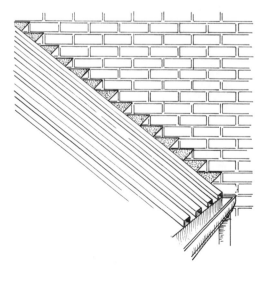

**Fig. 1.9** The lead flashing seals the conservatory roof superstructure where it meets the masonry of the house.

**Fig. 1.10** The patio can be a real conservatory extension. Its shelter will provide the perfect environment for those slightly tender climbers, giving you something interesting to look at outside all the year round.

I had a small pond in the foreground and an expanse of north-facing border further in the distance. I started with the pond as it was the obvious focal point. I concentrated on interesting, but not too pervasive peripheral planting. I used architectural, eye-catching plants, grasses to provide interest all the year round, bulbs and corms for early spring, *Rheum palmatum* and *Symphytum rubrum* to carry the interest through the summer. I curved the lines

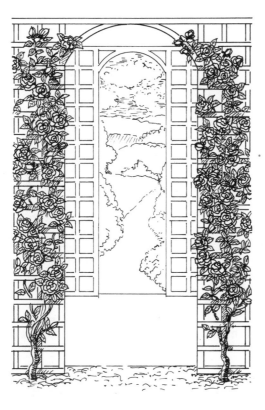

of the north-facing border so that it appeared to sweep away from the conservatory, and filled the gaps with autumn foliage plants and evergreens, so that there would always be something to look at. Your focal point may be animate or inanimate, relatively nearby, or in the distance. Eventually you will be able to arrange the seating in the conservatory in order to appreciate fully your self-made vista.

Carefully orchestrated, a patio (Fig. 1.10) can become a real extension to the conservatory during the summer months. Pot and tub planting can take on a whole new dimension. Shelter is provided from the winds for fuchsias; a new piece of wall is free for that climber you have always dreamt of such as *Wisteria sinensis* or *Campsis radicans*; either will love a calm warm south-facing position. Many frost-tender plants such as *Cestrum fasciculatum, Coronilla glauca, Fatsia japonica* or exotic-looking *Cordyline australis*, can adorn your patio during the summer, for at last you have a safe place for them to spend the winter.

**Fig. 1.11** Some conservatories have no real 'view'. Why not create one using clever treillage?

If you have no possibility of a view at all, do not despair. I've seen one created within a conservatory (Fig. 1.11). It was done by using a blank wall, clever treillage and a hand-painted mural. The effect was fantasic, you really felt as though you could walk right through the archway and onto the lawns beyond. I have also seen a similar effect created with a wall of mirrors; the illusion of space they gave was remarkable. They reflected a cleverly planted bed, filled with rampant climbers and beautiful orchids. Instead of standing in an enclosed corridor you were surrounded by a living picture which appeared to go on and on.

You should by now be beginning to understand just a little of the world of conservatories. Although actual planting is still in the realm of fantasy, you must also plan for plants now.

# CHAPTER 2

# *Planning Ahead for Plants and People*

Having dealt with the very practical aspects of choosing and building a conservatory, you should now consider what it might contain. Obviously you will buy accessories according to your needs, but you must not forget that you are planning for plants too. There are some horticulturalists who declare that people and plants cannot live side by side in a conservatory. I would disagree — for on the surface our requirements are very similar. Therefore we shall here consider them in tandem, our aim being to plan for the benefit of both.

## Heat in the conservatory

How do you intend to use your conservatory? If it is to form a permanent and integral part of your living area you will undoubtedly need some form of supplementary heating. Whereas if the conservatory is simply a luxurious way of extending your days and enjoying the winter sunshine, probably only the meanest amount of winter back-up will be necessary. When you have made this very human decision, you have to a certain extent already selected a group of plants (see Chapter 5 for details). Of course whatever your anticipated usage the need and supply of any form of supplementary heating will effectively be reduced by the presence of double glazing, Low E glass and insulated floors.

As far as methods of heating are concerned they are as variable as any domestic heating. Your choice is only limited by the power source you have available. Almost all the conservatories I visit are heated by some form of extension to the domestic system. There is nothing wrong with this at all, provided you make certain allowances. First of all make sure that your boiler can cope with the extra capacity. Secondly, but just as important, most domestic systems are programmed to turn off at night, and with plants in mind this is when their need for heat is at its greatest. Therefore your conservatory heating system should definitely be on separate thermostats and possibly on an independent pump.

You may of course need somewhere to hang the radiators. This may seem rather a pedantic and obvious statement, but in a conservatory the best position for any radiator is under the glazing. Placed there, their heat will rise in front of the glazing and form a block of warm air. Often, however, the retaining wall is too low. Skirting radiators are a useful alternative but the bottom line is that no radiator is particularly attractive. From a horticultural point of view the heat provided by radiators is very drying, and plants thrive in a humid atmosphere; thus, while considering radiators, also consider the amount of extra time you will have to spend maintaining adequate humidity levels.

In order to get around these problems you might like to consider underfloor heating. This is probably the most acceptable method of maintaining temperatures in a conservatory. It is simple to install by means of coiled pipes laid onto an insulated sub-floor. Thermostatically controlled it can be powered by most types of boiler, and it reacts quickly to changes in air temperature. Although installation time is short it does need to be synchronized carefully with the rest of the building work.

The Victorians used independent solid fuel boilers to heat the pipes which warmed their enormous glasshouses. Banks of pipes ran the length of the structure. When they became damp their effect was enhanced as they added warm moisture to the atmosphere. It is still possible to heat a conservatory in this way. The boiler can be sited inside or outside the conservatory. Maintenance and installation in a system of this sort will be expensive, but it is probably the most economical to run.

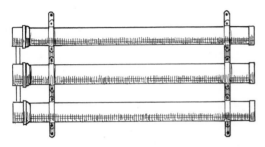

and both produce a large amount of water vapour, which leads to unacceptably high levels of condensation.

## Orientation vs heat and glare

Many potential conservatory owners are quite unaware just how much of a problem an excess of heat can cause. In fact the heat and glare in a mid-summer conservatory can make it quite uninhabitable for three or four hours every day. Of course there are methods of controlling this but often their importance is very much understated at the outset and both need budgeting for.

In a closed conservatory, heat build-up is alarmingly fast: turn your back for an hour on a sunny morning and the temperature will have

**Fig. 2.1** Although tube heat is a perfectly acceptable way of maintaining temperatures, and installation is a relatively simple DIY job, do follow the manufacturer's recommendations for both siting and fitting.

**Fig. 2.2** Wooden or cast-iron grilles are an effective way of hiding the aesthetic shortcomings of radiators.

A modern variation on this theme is tube heat, simply banks of aluminium tubing run by electricity. Provided it is correctly sited, tube heat (Fig. 2.1) is an extremely efficient form of heating a conservatory. It is most important that the pipes are evenly distributed, and if you are fitting banks of pipes, say three of four, the lowest must be 23 cm (9 in) from ground level. As with radiators, their only drawback is their lack of aesthetic appeal. Some innovative conservatory manufacturers hide these shortcomings behind ornate and attractive cast iron or wooden grilles (Fig. 2.2).

Another possibility for smaller scale, or back-up heating, is an electric fan heater. Their steady movement of air promotes healthy plant growth as it imitates the warm breezes of a plant's habitat. Designed for greenhouses they can be thermostatically controlled and made reasonably economical to run if you use off-peak electricity.

What about Calor gas and paraffin heaters? For me these are non-starters. Both need an open window for ventilation in order to remove the fumes which are potentially toxic,

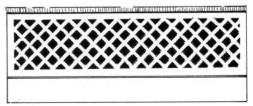

reached impossible levels. If you have followed all the rules, adjoining rooms will also benefit from this heat build-up. This sounds fine on a cold winter's day, but what happens when the weather warms up? Your unventilated conservatory and all adjacent rooms will literally shimmer with heat, rendering them tempor-

arily unusable. As for plants, their systems will literally shut down under such circumstances and your return will be greeted by an array of poor wilting specimens.

Adequate and efficient ventilation and shading will undoubtedly make your conservatory appear more expensive at the outset; their inclusion will make it infinitely more adaptable, so both must go into your budget.

**Fig. 2.3** Whatever shape, style or fabric, all conservatories need proper roof ventilation.

### Ventilation
I cannot overemphasize the need for efficient and effective ventilation (Fig. 2.3). Lack of

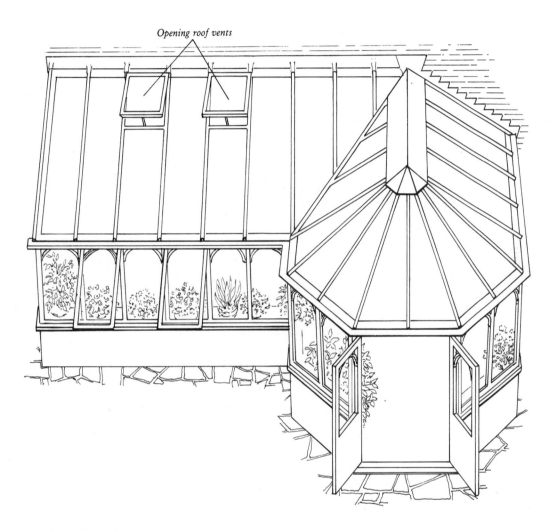

*Opening roof vents*

**Fig. 2.4** Roof vents can be fashioned to perform manually or automatically. Forced ridge venting usually contains an extractor system which draws air up and out.

proper ventilation is one of the greatest causes of heartache I come across, as once the conservatory is complete it is extremely difficult and expensive to remedy. Many manufacturers still erect their conservatories with no form of permanent ventilation at all.

Ventilation on the simplest level means opening roof vents (Fig. 2.4), side vents alone are inadequate as left open while you are away they present a security risk. Roof vents may be portions of lean-to roof glazing, ridge vents or lanterns (Fig. 2.5). Most can be fitted to perform manually or automatically. Automation

here does not necessarily mean enormous financial outlay. You can purchase automatic ventilating arms to attach to your roof vents once you have discovered just how fickle temperature can be; they operate spontaneously with no power source. Once fixed onto an opening roof vent, the wax cased

**Fig. 2.5** This conservatory has opening lights in the lantern section which form its ventilation system.

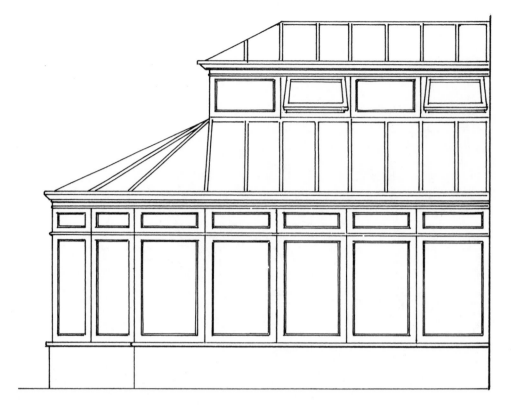

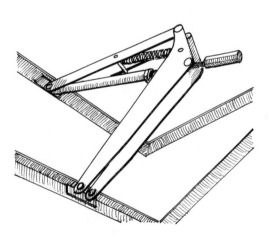

**Fig. 2.6** Venting arms like these can be fitted to almost any vent, whatever its weight. They open and close according to variations in inside temperature.

within the arm expands as it gets warmer causing it to extend. Thus the vent opens and closes according to the inside air temperature (Fig. 2.6).

This very simple, but effective, system only takes account of the inside temperature. There may well be those among you who do not want to see expensive centrally heated air escaping through open vents on sunny mid-winter days, or alternatively getting wet during a hot summer storm. If this is the case, there are motor controlled ventilating arms which operate according to pre-set thermostatic sensors, fixed both inside and outside the vent.

Ridge vents and lanterns can also perform manually or automatically — the automatic variety operate by thermostatic controls and are often aided by extractor fans which suck the warm air up and out.

Check these factors in your manufacturer's package. Consider a manual or automatic system. Although automatic opening vents may mean increased initial costs, those sudden sunny hot days are out of your control, and you might not be there to crank open the vents.

There is another possibility: HVR — heat ventilation and recovery. On a very basic level such a system draws heat from the conservatory and ducts it to another site. It could represent free heat in the second bathroom or the spare bedroom.

Finally, a word about ceiling fans. They have nothing to do with actual ventilation. They can be very attractive and often add a Colonial air to a conservatory, but they do not introduce fresh air: they only move the air about (Fig. 2.7).

The exceptions to this rule are perhaps those conservatories which receive at least some natural shade in the form of nearby trees or large shrubs. Provided that the roots or top growth do not represent any sort of hazard, take advantage of this. It could improve your aspect, and at the same time provide just the right sort of dappled shade your plants need.

The variety of artificial shading is gradually increasing, and becoming more versatile and durable. I have seen very effective and attractive exterior roof blinds on lean-to conservatories made from willow. Cedar lathe (Fig. 2.8) is used in interior and exterior situations.

**Fig. 2.7** Although attractive these fans do not introduce fresh air, they only move the air about.

### Shading and blinds

Temperature control also means efficient shading and although this will not be fitted until completion you must think about it now, if only because it can represent a large amount of money. They very idea of shading a conservatory may seem quite ridiculous to the uninitiated. Many folk think 'We are buying this conservatory so that we can enjoy what sun there is'. It will only take two or three sunny days before they are begging for the name of a shading company. In the long term, furnishings will dry out, upholstery will lose its colour, and from a horticultural point of view, direct sunlight means death to some plants. I know that the reason for all that glass is to intensify the rays of the sun and help you abolish winter, but there are very few conservatories which do not need a certain amount of artificial shading.

**Fig. 2.8** Cedar lathe blinds, although expensive, produce a beautiful dappled effect when used for shading conservatories.

**Fig. 2.9** Glass intensifies the rays of the sun. Although some plants love it, there are many which prefer shaded light.

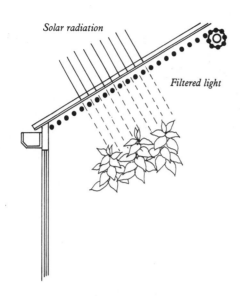

Solar radiation

Filtered light

More commonly used are pinoleum and fabric blinds (Figs. 2.9 & 2.10). For me the most important criterion is that they are not too densely woven. I must be able to seek the sky.

As with ventilation, a shading system can be tailored to function automatically in accordance to temperature; you can even purchase remote controls, keep cool and protect plants without leaving your seat.

Considering longevity, blinds are expensive. Wherever roof blinds are sited they will be under enormous stress from their mechanism alone. Add to this high temperatures, intense

**Fig. 2.10** Pinoleum is a good, natural looking alternative, but fabric blinds are quite acceptable. However they are made, conservatory blinds must filter the light, not block it out altogether.

ultraviolet light and possibly high levels of humidity and you have a recipe for disaster. You may decide to purchase fabric and make your own blinds, a viable possibility if you have the skill and the patience. When making your choice of material, remember that it will suffer from the extremes mentioned above. Select fabric which has been treated to withstand them.

Your blinds' supplier will be keen to tell you that full shading also provides a layer of insulation to your conservatory which is perfectly true, but it is often unnecessary to shade the entire conservatory, so with economy in mind, it may perhaps be better to wait until the conservatory is built so that you can discover where the hot spots are. Some manufacturers offer blinds as part of their total service; this is a good idea as these blinds will have been tailored to fit their conservatory. Before you decide on this course, ask to see some in action — you may not like the look of them 'en masse'.

The underlying and understated fact is that whatever you choose — internal or external, fabric, louvred wood or pinoleum, manual or automatic — shading is expensive and is often as vital as the glass that to most people 'makes' a conservatory.

While you are considering internal and external views think a minute about the conservatory at night. Lit from within, the glass acts to reflect the contents and it is not only uncanny to be able to see a constant reflection of yourself in those black panes of glass, but also rather frightening. Although you can see nothing, the outside world has a clear view of every detail of your life in your conservatory.

Blinds in the conservatory will obviously eliminate the problem, but a more interesting way of avoiding the goldfish bowl effect is to spotlight a feature in the garden. It need only be as simple as a tree, but in providing light outside the conservatory it no longer seems so isolated and of course your neighbours will no longer be privy to your most intimate secrets.

## Watering

For me, watering is part of the daily conservatory routine; it does take time, but it is my way of keeping in touch with what is going on.

While walking round attending to the needs of my plants, I keep a close check on them, especially in respect of small, but extremely damaging pests (see Chapter 9 for details). However, there are some conservatory owners, who perhaps do not have the time, or inclination, to be tied to such a task. Some form of automatic watering system must then be the answer to their problem. There are such systems available, but they are either very basic or highly sophisticated.

*Drip feed* consists of source water coming direct from the domestic supply and reaching the plant through a system of tubes and adjustable nozzles (Fig. 2.11). The 'drip' is finely adjustable and can be individually closed off. The system can be permanently connected to the mains, the water running continuously with the mains tap turned low. Alternatively the water can be turned on for a set period each day, either manually or with the aid of a 'tap timer'.

**Fig. 2.11** The drip-feed system.

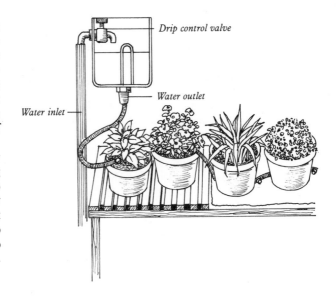

Drip control valve

Water outlet

Water inlet

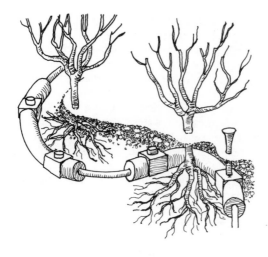

**Fig. 2.12** A system of tubes and reservoirs has the advantage of being almost invisible.

Alternatively, in permanent planting areas, you can install a simple system of *tubes and reservoirs* (Fig. 2.12). These have the advantage of being almost invisible as with the exception of the top-up tube, they are buried within the bed. The reservoir is filled, and the water within gradually seeps out into the composts.

For complete automation, there are computerized systems, in which amounts of water and time of watering can be programmed, taking mean air temperature, light intensity and relative humidity into account.

You will have gathered that I do not really approve of any of these systems. The modest systems do not take into account an individual plant's needs; the pre-set interval can make no assumption for variable temperatures and in my experience those at the end of the line sometimes receive an insufficient supply. In addition, mains water is often very cold and hard, when conservatory plants prefer soft water at room temperature (see p. 39). Tubes and reservoirs are slightly better as you can at least fill the reservoir with soft rainwater, and it will be at the right temperature, but, once again the system does not take account of the individual, and all the water is at the bottom of the bed, the top compost quickly forms a hard

dry crust with no healthy evaporation taking place. Complete automation sounds like fun, but I suspect that only those with very large heavily planted conservatories would consider the capital outlay worthwhile.

Forward planning where watering is concerned dictates a nearby water source either inside, or outside the conservatory.

## Permanent planting areas

However keen you are, the idea of creating permanent planting areas often gets forgotten about until the conservatory is complete. By then it may be too late.

Permanent beds mean that you can give your plants a real chance to grow. In addition, treated like this plants last longer and look more natural. The Victorians were masters of the technique: although there were always some visiting potted varieties, the majority of their plants were permanently sited in beds that were flush with the floor of their conservatories.

These days we are anxious about damp problems; the very suggestion that we might like planting areas which 'bridge the damp course', could make your manufacturer hold up his hands in terror. I have seen it successfully accomplished, but a useful compromise which troubles no one, is the installation of raised beds. These do not bridge the damp course, and have their base at the scree floor of the conservatory.

### Raised beds — design and construction

A raised bed can be any shape or size, the most permanent being built with bricks and mortar, but to suit your conservatory you may wish to echo the material of the dwarf walls and use wood or some alternative for their construction. Your only criteria should be future rigidity and strength (Fig. 2.13). Their height and width is also a matter of taste, but remember that you might want to plant some mature specimens, so do not be too mean. A good working minimum width and height would be 35 cm (14 in). I designed the shape of ours by drawing with chalk on the screed floor of the conservatory. In this way, I discovered what would be a realistic working depth as well as how much the finished bed would intrude

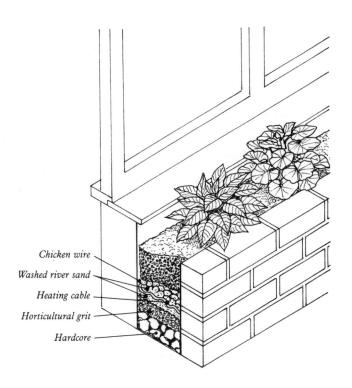

**Fig. 2.13** A cross-section of a permanent planting site showing layered drainage and possible position of heated cable.

Chicken wire

Washed river sand

Heating cable

Horticultural grit

Hardcore

on the floor area of the conservatory.

Whatever their fabric, permanent beds should be entirely sealed within with heavy duty polythene, or a bitumenized paint. Once this job is complete the base of the bed will need lining with a layer of graded drainage material. This might consist of crocks or rubble, horticultural grit and sharp sand; in total this drainage layer should be about 10 cm (4 in) deep.

### Raised beds — drainage
Planned well ahead, drainage tubes can be led from a proposed planting site and through an outside wall, More simply, the bricklayer can be asked to leave weep holes along the base of the bed as he builds it.

### Electricity and wiring
You really have to be clever to get this installed in the right place at the right time. It is most unobtrusive when laid within the cavity walls, so think ahead. Where will you want sockets, table lights and spotlights (Fig. 2.14), wall

**Fig. 2.14** Spotlights are a versatile method of lighting. Their position can be altered to highlight a particular plant or feature; they are easy to keep clean too.

lighting and light switches? Perhaps you have a water feature in mind — you will need a power source for the pump.

Any electrical installation must primarily be safe. As there is frequently water in a conservatory, and water with electricity can be potentially fatal, it is most important that all wiring is of the heavy outdoor variety. In order to avoid unforeseen electrical accidents it is really essential to have all conservatory wiring on a separate circuit, with a voltage control breaker built into the system.

**Fig. 2.15** The type of flooring you choose will depend on the style and future use of your conservatory. Remember that flooring with a highly ornate pattern will tend to detract from the beauty of your plants.

## Interior decor

### Light fittings

There is no special sort of lighting for a conservatory. From a personal point of view I dislike seeing outdoor light fittings in a conservatory: they seem too heavy and consequently out of place. You have to make your selection from what is available from many high street stores. Choose plastic or glass, as both are easy to remove and clean and will not fade in the sunlight.

### Floors

As with any room in your house, you choose the flooring to suit the use of the room, your lifestyle and your pocket. I have seen conservatories that are fully carpeted, others which have vinyl or a pine-sprung floor. None of these three is particularly suitable for a 'planted' conservatory. Water will mark the

carpet and the sprung floor and make vinyl dangerously slippery. Any highly patterned floor will detract from the beauty of your plants. I choose plain terracotta with a slate inset. It looks good and doesn't mark or get slippery and it gives the conservatory a warm Mediterranean feel. Brick sets, quarry tiles or York stone have a similar effect which is both practical and natural (Fig. 2.15).

### Furnishings

The type of furniture depends entirely upon the use of the conservatory itself, but remember that whatever you put within a conservatory will suffer adversely through the intensity of light, the high temperatures and the degree of humidity (Fig. 2.16). Choose upholstery fabrics with care; many of them are designed specifically to endure. As with floors, any strong patterns can interfere with the impact of the plants.

### Security

Unpleasant as it may seem, this subject, although brief, is important enough to mention on its own.

For obvious reasons, it is unwise to rely upon opening side vents as part of your permanent ventilation system. Once locked shut, the laminated or toughened glass, which represents the side glazing will pose an immovable barrier as far as an intruder is concerned. It would be easy enough to depart through the conservatory if the party doors are not toughened, or double-glazed, and if the locks on the exterior door are not mortised. The most effective method of protection must be some form of alarm system, linked with the rest of the house.

### The 'on-site' visit

By now, you should have whittled down that handful of manufacturers to three or four. You

**Fig. 2.16** The natural colours of wicker and basket work furniture will complement any conservatory; it also weathers the extremes of temperature and humidity well.

are fairly sure that these match your financial criteria. You like the look of their product, and you are in agreement with the materials they use. You have viewed and compared the finished products and possibly talked to former clients about their conservatories, and the service they received. You are ready to request your on-site visit. These preliminary discussions are usually free of charge and should be wholly without obligations. It is your opportunity to use the expertise of the conservatory manufacturer, or his representative, to find out whether or not your dream conservatory can be realized.

You may think you know where you want to site the conservatory, and have very clearly defined ideas as to its future use: your professional should question you closely on both these aspects. Most modern conservatories form an integral part of the house. The ultimate design should not just fit in with the house's structure. It should also reflect your lifestyle. It has the potential to improve both. Therefore, the designer should consider your anticipated usage within his brief. Unfortunately, not all do.

Very few people realize just how much a conservatory can improve the way living areas are used. Sympathetically designed they tend to become the focus of attention, the quality of light alone drawing both friends and family towards them. Single access will diminish the rest of your house. The most successful conservatories I know are multipurpose — everyone wants to use them. You can have a relaxing family room by day and the perfect venue for romantic dinner parties by night. So do not be surprised when your manufacturer suggests a dual access for your conservatory, or at the very least he should encourage you to have your conservatory extending from the room you use most.

With lifestyle still very much in mind, he should be able to provide you with extensive information covering heating and conservation of energy, ventilation, possible shading and preparation for planting all in relationship to his product. He should be able to recommend specialists where necessary, and be prepared to incorporate their work into his building programme.

Any conservatory will be in a unique position between house and garden. Well integrated means the transition must appear as natural as possible. The innovative conservatory designer should not neglect this fact, and if necessary suggestions and future plans could well encompass patio design, even subtle alteration of the garden itself reflecting the need for views from within the conservatory.

After this marathon of decision-making, your manufacturer will send you preliminary plans and costings for your consideration. The drawings should include all the features you discussed as well as his suggested finishing touches. Many of these may appear purely cosmetic to you, but to his tutored eye they are vital specifications, made to ensure that his conservatory fits perfectly with your house. Are the walls rendered, or is the brickwork exposed? The width and height of sills should be covered — too high, or too low may create an imbalance between the conservatory and the rest of the house. Natural or painted finish, the shape and height of doors and windows, his selection should complement what exists (Fig. 2.17). His finished product should match the stature of your house. The embellishments which will make it unique should not be unnecessary additions but reflections or enhancements of existing features within its structure. This icing on the cake will make your conservatory look as though it has been there for ever.

Don't let your dreams turn into a nightmare. Choose a manufacturer whose name you recognize. Make your preliminary selections at leisure: you have plenty to choose from. Do not be hassled into early site visits by aggressive salesmen on the strength of a request for a brochure. Finally be aware that buying accessories for a conservatory is an expensive business: flooring, heating, wiring and shading, could add thousands to your bill.

A final word of warning before your manufacturer visits the site. Is there any routine maintenance work that needs to be done on your roof? I must admit that I thought that our job was finished when we had one chimney removed and the other rebuilt. My trusty builder did mention a snowguard, but our manufacturer said that his conservatory roof was strong and there was no danger from fall-

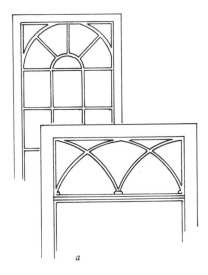

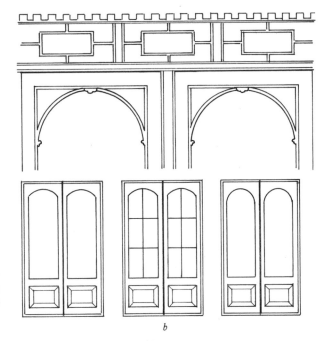

Fig. 2.17 (a) The shape and height of doors, both internal and external, is important. (b) The shape and decorative features on glazing should complement that which already exists on your house.

ing tiles. The conservatory had been complete about three months when a tile came scuttling down the roof onto the conservatory. Most satisfying was the fact that the glazing was strong enough to withstand the tile: it didn't shatter, just split. We now have a snow guard.

So, you are now in a position to make your choice. One point I will emphasize however, is that you must look around; do not feel pressurized. If you were going to buy a car, you would look at plenty of alternatives, perhaps test drive some to see if one in particular suited you better than the others. Do the same with the conservatory manufacturers, for their conservatories will cost you 'car money'.

## What are you actually paying for?

Within one contract I saw the words 'skirting throughout'. I assumed, just like my client, that this meant just what the words suggested. In reality, it meant skirting throughout the conservatory, omitting the house walls to which the conservatory was attached.

In another instance, I visited a newly completed conservatory, with no internal access. The manufacturer's detail was complete, to the last letter of the contract. Plans for the knock through had been omitted; my clients had to organize their own builder to do the work and order expensive extra doors — the resultant doorway was wider than standard — from the manufacturers so that they matched those in the conservatory.

## Checklist
- Decide upon your financial criteria.

- Make your preliminary selection through brochures alone: compare and contrast completed conservatories; talk to conservatory owners; find out if they are pleased with their conservatory and if they were satisfied with the service they received.

**Fig. 2.18** The building of a conservatory can be a long and complicated job involving many skills; the most important thing is that you, and your plants, are satisfied with the result.

- Consider building materials and longevity — traditional wood and glass or aluminium, uPVC and polycarbons, or a combination.

- What is your guarantee of safety as regards glass? Is it laminated or toughened? Is safety glass used as a norm?

- The maintenance-free roof must be a high priority — how is it going to be achieved?

- How well insulated will you be?

- Is roof ventilation part of the standard package or an optional extra?

- How much is the manufacturer going to do for you?

- At the on-site visit do you feel that the manufacturer is paying sufficient attention to your existing house, garden and lifestyle? Do not be coerced; salesmen can be pretty clever at persuading you to part company with cash.

- Finally, when your plans and estimates arrive, study them carefully. We failed to check the measurements — a slip made between the preliminary and final plans meant that our conservatory might have lost over a metre. It only became clear when the builders were digging the foundations; modifications had to be made on site, and extra side panels ordered.

Having signed on the dotted line you can relax and begin to think about plants. Where completion dates are concerned, do not get too despondent if they overrun: remember all building work causes headaches, and a conservatory is no exception (Fig. 2.18). It is especially difficult when outside trades are involved. The most important thing is that you and your plants are satisfied with the result.

# CHAPTER 3

# *The Conservatory Environment*

Your conservatory is finished — the heating, ventilation and shading have been selected and installed with plants in mind. To me the most exciting thing about any conservatory is that you are lord and master of the climate; by adjusting the heating thermostats or the shading, you can move from the Mediterranean to the jungle regions of the equator. Provided you choose the right plants and care for them correctly they will behave like botanic supermen.

What do plants specifically need? Would plants grow in a completely unventilated conservatory? We all know plants need light but why is it that artificial shading is mentioned so frequently? The answer to all these questions is found within their method of growth and the fail-safes that are built into the system to help ensure their survival.

Green plants have evolved an ingenious method of providing sustenance for themselves; it is called *photosynthesis*, which, given a literal translation, means building by light. Thus, plants absorb light, and with its energy combine water and carbon dioxide to make the carbohydrates they need to grow. It is not by chance that we provide that carbon dioxide in the air we exhale. Plants absorb it, use the carbon, and release the oxygen we need for life, back into the atmosphere (Fig. 3.1).

Inside your plant-filled conservatory, you and your plants need one another in more ways than this, some more obvious than others: it is simply a matter of slight adjustment. Success in caring for conservatory plants lies chiefly in creating the right environment for them. In many ways you are like Nature in her most benign form: you set the minimum temperature, adjust the ventilation and sunlight factor, provide water, humidity, and a suitable place and medium in which to grow. All this sounds easy, so why do so many people find it difficult? Mostly because they choose plants that do not match the total environment of the conservatory they are working in.

## Temperature requirements

The preliminary environmental consideration is temperature and the level which you are going to maintain: it is the minimum temperature that is really important. Broadly speaking plants occur naturally in particular places where the climatic conditions suit them. For convenience sake conservatory plants are divided into four basic groups according to the minimum temperature they require.

Cold house plants have a minimum temperature requirement of 0°C (32°F), a cool house minimum will be 7°C (45°F), a warm house a minimum of 13°C (55°F) and a hot

**Fig. 3.1** All green plants absorb light; with this energy they combine carbon dioxide and water to make the carbohydrates they need to grow.

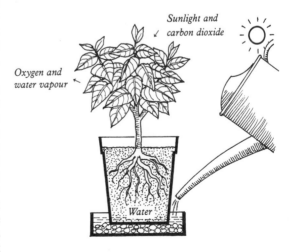

Sunlight and carbon dioxide

Oxygen and water vapour

Water

house a minimum of 16°C (61°F). Of course this is all very simplistic, because within each temperature band you will find subgroups of plants which require more or less water, and varying degrees of ventilation, sunlight and different humidity levels. Always remember

**Fig. 3.2** Movement of air through a conservatory. (*a*) When the sun shines the warm air inside the conservatory rises.
(*b*) The ventilators open and the warm air escapes, reducing the temperature and ensuring a gentle movement of air around the plants.
(*c*) We use blinds to prevent heat build-up and to ensure that plants do not get scorched.
Properly cared for plants will thrive in this atmosphere.

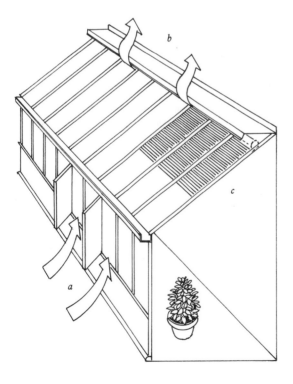

that you are dealing with fairly adaptable living things. You will often find a plant that will defy the rules and either settle down at temperatures well below or above their recommended minimum slot.

I have seen many plant-filled conservatories, but perhaps the one that stays most firmly in my mind was filled with the most inappropriate plants. The minimum temperature was just frost-free and strictly speaking this was a cold house. The plants had been haphazardly placed, some in beds, others in pots. The time of my visit was late February, a notoriously tired time of year for the frost-free conservatory, and the place was like a jungle. The remains of last year's *Lapageria rosea* was on the trellis, still threatening to flower. Fantastic *Hoya carnosa* had escaped the walls and was cascading from the roof rafters. There were dozens of varieties which you would normally expect to find in a conservatory of this temperature but few were resting as they should be; most were living life to the full. A notable exception to the minimum temperature rule was an *Aeschynanthus parvifolius* (syn *A. lobbianus*), a rather lovely trailing plant, recommended minimum temperature around 10°C (50°F). Admittedly it was not in flower, but it certainly wasn't showing any signs of stress either. The only explanation for this sort of plant behaviour was that they had all adapted themselves to thrive in a supposedly alien environment. However, at the outset, the novice needs a set of rules to follow; the urge to experiment grows with confidence.

## Ventilation
Carbon dioxide passes into the plants through tiny apertures called stomata. These are found all over the green parts of the plant, but are at their greatest density on the underside of the leaves. Once inside, the carbon is retained and the resultant oxygen released. Thus the need for a gentle movement of air (Fig. 3.2): if this air is too hot or too cold the stomata will close, and temporarily the plant system will shut down.

## Water
Although all green plants rely on water as their means of support it also forms part of the

photosynthetic process. They absorb water from the medium in which they are planted, and it moves up the plant to the leaves by a knock-on effect, which is known as the *transpiration stream*. While the plant is photosynthesizing, the stomata will be open. If the atmosphere around the plants is too dry, or the temperatures too high, the water needed for photosynthesis will begin to evaporate dangerously fast — once again the stomata will close, checking the transpiration stream before too much damage is done (Fig. 3.3).

## Hard or soft water

Provided you do not live in a highly polluted area, plants undoubtedly prefer soft rainwater.

**Fig. 3.3**
(*a*) Healthy plant – with the stomata open and an adequate supply of water the plant will be photosynthesizing at its optimum rate.
(*b*) Unhealthy plant – if the temperature is too high or the air too dry the stomata will close to prevent water loss. This checks the transpiration stream and the root hairs will stop taking up water, with the result that photosynthesis stops, and the plant wilts.

This should be gathered from the roof of the conservatory and collected and reserved in covered water-butts or tanks close to the conservatory. (The water collected from a house roof, whether thatched or tiled, may already be tainted with algae.) If you are concerned in any way about the possibility of your local rainwater being contaminated, there are water-testing kits, widely available from garden centres.

Mains water might be an alternative; this is acceptable, provided you realize that hard water will leave an unsightly chalk residue wherever it dries on the aerial parts of the plants. Mains water which has been artificially softened by chemicals is quite unacceptable, however. The chemicals used for the softening cause an adverse reaction in green plants.

You can of course purify mains water by using a water filter. This action will remove much of the lime and reduce high levels of chlorine.

## Water temperature

Conservatory plants prefer their water at room temperature, so be prepared to keep a couple of cans inside ready filled for future use. This is particularly necessary during the winter months when water from the outside butt is really cold; if you find you have to use this, add a little boiling water to it first.

## Watering technique

Getting this right takes time and experience. My first advice has to be 'watch your plants, feel their compost, and do as they ask'. Symptoms of both too much and too little are very similar: any flowers will drop prematurely; leaves will lose their colour and gradually begin to look slightly mottled; some may drop off altogether; wilting is almost instantaneous. The latter is not necessarily caused by lack of water; look for other reasons before adding more water to a compost — is the plant too hot, in too sunny a position or in a draught? Perhaps you are providing too much water.

The amount of water a plant will require will alter according to season and temperature, the degree of sunlight and ventilation. Press the compost with your fingers before adding a fresh supply. It may look quite dry on top, but still feel moist to touch; this is especially true of resting plants. They do need significantly less frequent attention when they are in this phase but they still need a good soaking from time to time. Therefore, my second advice has to be: 'don't mess about when watering — really soak the compost.' How do you know when they are resting? My conservatory has a high minimum and my garden plants rest as the days shorten and the temperatures drop. What would happen if the temperatures never dropped? They rest just the same — as the days begin to shorten noticeably, my summer-flowering plants begin to lose their strength of colour and their composts remain damp for longer periods of time; I react by extending the period between waterings. The resting period does not last long: new growth starts appearing in late January when I gradually start to supply more water. In cooler conservatories this resting time could be expected to be longer, but not by much for day length seems to be the key.

It is easy in summer, when mean temperatures are higher, and plants are growing and photosynthesizing at their optimum rate. Their uptake of water will be relatively high, excess moisture evaporates quickly, so daily, or even twice daily attention is required. The trick is in reducing and increasing amounts according to an individual plant's needs. Once again, think about the plant's origins. Mediterranean summers are hot and dry, whereas plants from the tropics are used to and need a regular drenching.

Plants kept permanently in pots, will need close scrutiny every day, especially if they are planted in unglazed clay or terracotta pots which are extremely porous (see p. 46 for more details). When you water these plants, give them so much that the water leaks out of the bottom of the pot, and fills the drip tray. Never let these plants stand in full drip trays for longer than an hour.

In addition, the type of compost a plant is growing in will also alter the amount of water you must provide. Loam-based composts drain a great deal faster than those based on peat and if you have added extra drainage materials to a loam-based mix, you can expect it to dry out faster. (See pp. 46–7 on Composts and Drainage.)

## Emergency measures

Plants can dry out or be overwatered; the plant reacts in the same way, whatever the crisis. With too little water the potting mixture will eventually shrink away from the side of the container. Too much and the system becomes waterlogged — the fine root hairs will stop absorbing moisture. Whether or not a plant actually dies depends on its variety; some are a great deal better than others at surviving either feast or famine.

Some will be irredeemable, but as a general rule I would prune out some of the top growth. Those that are waterlogged should have their pots removed to let the compost drain freely; if the mixture smells rancid the plant can be re-potted in a fresh compost as soon as it is dry enough to handle. It should then be placed in a cool, shady spot to recover.

Where a plant has been allowed to dry out, treatment alters slightly according to the type of container. With unglazed clay or terracotta leave the plant in its container and submerge the pot in a bucket of water, removing only when the mixture and pot are quite saturated (Fig. 3.4). If the container is plastic or fibre-

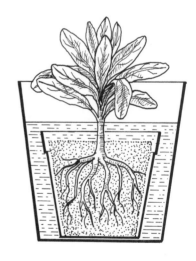

**Fig. 3.4** If a plant has been allowed to completely dry out, submerge the pot in a bucket of water.

glass, the mixture may well have shrunk away from the edge of the pot. In these cases remove the plant from its container and submerge the root ball until it is fully wet. (This may take time, according to its size and the degree to which it has dried out; to begin with you may have to wedge the root ball in the water as it will tend to bob up to the surface.) Once the root ball has absorbed the maximum amount of water, remove it from the water and allow the compost to drain freely, before replacing the plant in its container.

It would be dreadful to walk back into your conservatory after your annual holiday and find that your beautiful permanently planted specimens had been given insufficient, or incorrect attention. (In my conservatory the damage would very probably have been caused by drought, as I deliberately instruct my carer to underwater.) First, having ensured full shading and ventilation I water all plants thoroughly. If the temperature is very high, I also douse the floor. Then weak and withered stems can be removed along with scorched foliage. Depending on the condition of the composts within the beds I may water again a couple of hours later. Plants are amazingly tolerant; although drought slows them all up, and it takes time and care to re-establish normal growth patterns, I find it a rare occurrence to lose something altogether.

Given adequate drainage materials (see p. 47) and drainage tubes or weep holes, water-logging should not occur in permanent planting areas. Too much water will certainly affect some plants: *Bougainvillea*, for example, is very quick to react to too much water; I have known a *Ficus benjamina* lose the majority of its leaves, but provided the water is draining away and the roots are not swamped their arrest will only be temporary.

## Light and shade

Plants have adapted their lifestyle in relationship to light intensity over thousands of years. Some are designed to make the most of really strong direct light, right in the roof of a south-facing conservatory, whereas other more delicate ones would quickly shrivel and die if forced to live under such circumstances. Too much strong direct light for these shrinking

violets will cause scorching and photosynthetic arrest. Environmental control as far as light is concerned means efficient shading (see pp. 27–9 for more details). Of course, hot sunshine also causes heat to build up; 29°C (85°F) is about the maximum allowable temperature for any conservatory.

In some conservatories the problem may be insufficient light. Where this is the case you can artificially increase the light intensity with the use of Gro-lights in order to give the plants that require more the correct amount of sunlight. It is often a very tempting idea to boost daylight hours during a long gloomy winter. However in a conservatory it is both unnecessary and unwise, chiefly because it encourages plants to come out of their resting phase prematurely. Plants that need a winter rest will do so quite naturally as the days shorten, and as they lengthen again they will regain their vigour. Many plants subjected to unwarranted extra light make foliage at the expense of flowers. Normally, leave Gro-lights to the commercial growers who know what they are doing. It may be better to come to terms with what light you have and grow plants which like those conditions.

The plants that will be most vulnerable as far as direct sunlight is concerned are those with green foliage, and delicate foliaged plants such as the caladium. Even rhoicissus which is a notably tough sort of plant will quickly develop hard, yellow leaves if exposed to direct sun for any length of time. Shade is a term that simply indicates that the plants under consideration need some sort of protection from direct sunlight. For a single plant it could be nothing more than a sheet of newspaper that will prevent the plant becoming damaged.

Where flowering plants are being grown in quantity there should be varying degrees of shading. Poinsettias, for example, will require very little but the plants grown in pots for the Christmas trade will have seen very little direct sunlight, with the result that inevitable damaged leaves would result if plants were left totally unprotected. Considerable care is needed to ensure that the right degree of shade is applied, whether it be on the outside of the glass or controlled by screens inside the conservatory.

Cyclamen on the other hand, besides needing cool conditions, require a dappled shade. Foliage plants belonging to the *Maranta* and *Calathea* groups will simply shrivel up and die if they are exposed to direct sunlight, and it need only be for a very short length of time. Philodendrons are similar in their need for fairly heavy shade, but they will tolerate light that is a little brighter.

Shading is obviously a compromise where a mixed collection of plants is concerned. The important things to remember are that the majority of foliage plants need to be in the more shaded area of the conservatory, and that flowering plants need the lightest location. Some of the variegated foliage plants, such as the croton, will have to be grown in a lighter location if they are to retain their colouring.

In the small hot-box type of conservatory it will be difficult to do anything other than expose all plants to the same conditions as it is almost impossible to segregate them in a small

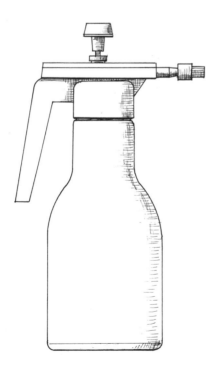

**Fig. 3.5** The mist sprayer – a most important piece of equipment.

area. Erecting a sheet of thin material as a temporary measure over the plants that are more at risk will be helpful, but the best advice really is to choose the right sort of plants for the situation at the outset. Introducing plants to the sunny conservatory that have been grown in shaded conditions at the nursery where they were reared will be a futile exercise that is almost bound to end in failure. Similarly, the plants that were reared in sunny conditions will not like being deprived of the light that they had become accustomed to.

## Feeding

With the exception of newly planted conservatories all container grown plants need supplementary feed. Although there is a certain nutrient value in all composts it only lasts a limited period of time. After this time has elapsed you must provide these elements in the form of liquid or powdered feed. It is easiest to feed plants in conjunction with watering. There are various commercial feeds available, some with a chemical base, others organically formulated. From a purely personal point of view I select those which are organic, or natural.

The only shortcoming of these packet feeds are their quantity recommendations. Once every 10 or 14 days during the summer is not enough; it is better to feed once a week. While plants are resting they need no feed at all, but watch out for new growth; then it is time to gradually reintroduce feeding regimes.

## Mist spraying and humidity levels

Plants thrive in a humid atmosphere; however good your watering technique, there is a need to add extra moisture to the air around them. This is not just another routine, time-consuming conservatory job. Mist spraying is fun. Do it in the morning, before the sun really warms up, to give the foliage a chance to dry slowly as the sun can scorch dampened leaves. Spray all the plants thoroughly, except those with densely furred foliage, with soft water. When you have finished they will look marvellous and repay you with the heady scents of moist compost and perfumed flowers.

The mist sprayer (Fig. 3.5) is a most vital piece of conservatory equipment. Keep it filled in the conservatory and only ever use it to spray plants with water. I use a hand-held sprayer, with a capacity of 2 litres, not too heavy to hold aloft. It has a pump action and an adjustable nozzle, so that the mister can be primed to produce a fine spray around the plants.

You can also use a horticultural aggregate, or peat to increase humidity levels (Fig. 3.6 a & b). Both these readily absorb water and as the temperature rises the moisture they contain gradually evaporates. Use an aggregate in drip trays, peat where you are using a large pot containing two or three others.

## Cleanliness

Quite apart from the facts that plants like it humid, and that they look good when you have misted, there are two other very good reasons for taking time to spray.

First of all, conservatory plants get dirty — tiny particles of dust will clog up the pores, so spraying helps to keep them clean. If you really want to make your plants look squeaky clean you may consider using a plant cleaner. Beware those sold in aerosol sprays,

the effect of these used in sunlight can severely damage plants. A white oil cleaner, if you find it, will perform the dual task of cleaning leaves and ridding the plants of pests.

Secondly, maintaining adequate humidity means that conservatory pests are less likely to find your conservatory plants appealing. Pest control is covered in detail in Chapter 9, but a good primary line of defence is found in misting.

Finally, keep your conservatory plants tidy: dead head them regularly; do not let dead leaves and flowers litter the floor or composts — here they present perfect dry nesting places for malicious insects. Remove any too vigorous or sickly growth in spring. Rake over any planted beds to keep them fresh. Stepping stones can be useful in these areas.

**Fig. 3.6** (a) Increase the humidity levels around plants by using a horticultural aggregate in drip trays or (b) by plunging potted plants in peat.

a

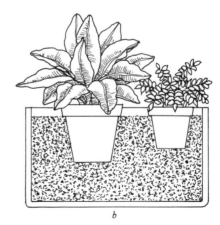

b

Give your conservatory interior a thorough clean out on a regular basis, especially during the winter months — its warmth makes a haven for tiny spiders and hibernating moths and butterflies. The spiders will fabricate a fine network of webs throughout the plants in no time at all. Butterflies and moths pupate: the emerging caterpillars can do terrible damage to foliage.

Although you may be surrounded by plants all day long it is not until you begin to handle them physically that you often realize that they are not as bright and cheerful as they might have seemed. This is a good reason for giving them a good clean up in spring and autumn. This will mean, wherever possible, taking plants out of displays so that they can be placed on a table and given a thorough examination. You will find all sorts of dead and dying pieces, and it is quite normal for the majority of plants that produce a lot of leaves to lose some of the older ones as new develop.

It is also beneficial to clean around the soil on the top of the pot and to use a pointed stick to remove the top layer, replacing it with a fresh mixture. This is known as top-dressing the plant; not only will this improve the plant's general appearance, but also will provide some new nourishment.

You will find that routine conservatory chores will become a form of relaxation therapy. The family I most remember in this particular instance had led a high-powered globetrotting life. Their conservatory was to be a pure indulgence and the plants had to be geared to easy care and low maintenance. Gradually their enthusiasm grew. The underlying, gentle, but inevitable march of the seasons was predictable, and their patient care was quickly rewarded by flourishing plants. What to begin with looked just like another daily task, had become a joy, a revelation of the beauty and permanence which they had helped to create. When I last visited them their enthusiasm and excitement was touching, each plant in their conservatory had taken on a personality of its own, each flower was a personal triumph.

# CHAPTER 4

# Getting Started

Now that you have decided on the type of conservatory you want, you must decide where you are going to put the plants. You will want them to look spontaneous and natural, as though they belong, like a real garden under glass. There is no shortage of pots and containers in enormous variety; almost any material can be pressed into service and formulated into a container for plants. Some pots are beautiful and will fit in perfectly with the picture in your mind's eye. However you see your conservatory, it can be infinitely more successful if you display your plants effectively.

The obvious way to create a completely natural look, is to build flower beds for your plants within the conservatory (see pp. 93–5).

Plants like to be grouped together — it enables them to create a humid microclimate around themselves which enhances their ability to grow naturally.

## Pots and planters

A quick glance around the garden centre, DIY or hardware store or even the garage forecourt will tell you that everyone is in the business of selling plant pots and containers. Salesmen have made sure that there is something to suit everybody's pocket, but what is most suitable? All the different varieties have their advantages and disadvantages and the decision must rest with you and the style of your conservatory (Fig. 4.1).

**Fig. 4.1** There is a wide variety of containers available for displaying conservatory plants.

45

### Clay, terracotta and stoneware vs plastics and polystyrene

Points to note are:

- Look for pots with drainage holes at the bottom and for containers that will not dry out too fast. Unglazed clay and terracotta pots lose their water to the atmosphere while plastic is completely impervious.

- Many of your plants are going to need re-potting quickly, so you are going to need pots that come in graded sizes.

- While considering plant growth, remember that some root systems adhere to the sides of their containers and the pot will need breaking in order to release the root ball; other root systems are so strong that they actually break pots. Terracotta and stoneware is not cheap — are you prepared for breakages?

- Some of your larger plants will have a great deal of top growth and will need containers of appropriate size. Plastic and poly-styrene pots are not really strong enough for this task; clay or stoneware is more appropriate.

Plastic pots are by far the most adaptable and economical, but they are not very attractive. I use them all the time but hide their aesthetic shortcomings inside prettier containers. By selecting an outer container a full size larger than the plastic pot I can increase the humidity levels too. The space between the two pots can be filled with an aggregate or peat, which if kept damp will slowly release moisture into the air around the plant.

### Self-watering pots

These are quite effective provided they contain plants which each require the same amount of water. They do not take account of the plants like *Ficus benjamina* or *Schefflera arboricola* which like to get quite dry in between water-ings, or resting plants (see pp. 39–40). The compost in a self-watering pot will be moder-ately damp all the time. The user fills a small reservoir at the base of the pot with water about once a week. The moisture is fed into the compost through a wick. A quick look at the

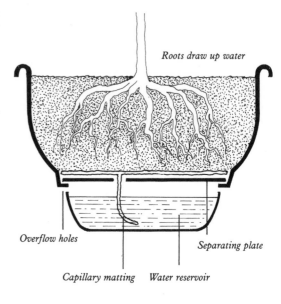

*Roots draw up water*

*Overflow holes*

*Separating plate*

*Capillary matting*   *Water reservoir*

**Fig. 4.2** Construction of a self-watering pot.

reservoir will tell you how much water the plant is taking up, and the pot should be topped up accordingly (Fig. 4.2).

## Composts and potting mixtures

These are many and varied, each having a very specific purpose. I refer to them as the bulk ingredients. Even though my conservatory was set up and planted a long time ago, I still keep small quantities of all of them in a cool dry frost-free place.

### Loam-based composts

These are generally known as John Innes Composts. They contain sterilized loam, peat, sharp sand and a John Innes base which can be chalk or ground limestone and a good supply of plant nutrients. Anyone can make them up and although they should conform to the basic recipe, some are better than others; it all depends on the quality of the main bulk ingredient, loam.

John Innes mixes come in three grades; as the number gets higher the loam becomes less refined. For example, John Innes 3 is chunky and eminently suitable for more mature plants and trees, but is not appropriate for cuttings and young plants.

Loam-based mixes tend to be free draining. Use them for plants that are used to thin soils, Mediterranean varieties, South African and Australian plants.

'My garden is full of loam, packet composts are expensive — why can't I use what's free outside the back door?' This is a very reasonable question that I have been asked hundreds of times. My answer is always very direct: 'Never use garden loam in your conservatory'. Pre-packed loam-based mixes are sterilized; they are heated to a pre-set temperature which kills all the harmful bugs and predators it naturally contains. A handful of garden loam contains thousands of harmful micro-organisms. Imagine what damage they could do to the plants in a carefully controlled warm environment of your conservatory.

## Peat-based composts

As their name suggests these are basically peat, with sharp sand and a few short-term nutrients. It has a lovely rich colour and it feels good. Its most important quality is that it retains moisture. It is a perfect medium for those plants from the tropics which are used to living in the litter of the forest. It has two drawbacks. First, it contains very few nutrients — plants growing in it will need feeding sooner than in loam-based composts. Secondly, it is very lightweight in comparison to loam which makes it unsuitable for big potted specimens.

## Drainage aids

I use both washed river sand and horticultural grit to increase the drainage capacity of a compost mix. It really depends on the plant in question. *Bougainvillea* and *Allamanda* both seem to like a handful of each mixed into a loam-based compost. The more you add the faster a mix will drain. Some plants hate water lying around the base of their stems; for these I

**Fig. 4.3** The conservatory 'storehouse'. This need be no more than the corner of a garden shed, but make sure it is dry and frost free. Always keep any pest controls and plant feeds well out of the reach of children.

scatter horticultural grit on the surface of the compost all around the base of the plant.

## Moisture retention and conditioning

Both perlite and vermiculite absorb water and the minerals it contains. These are the tiny white specks you sometimes see in peat-based mixtures. Charcoal keeps the soil sweet by absorbing excess mineral salts. Most plants are fairly easy going, but some, like *Lapageria rosea* and *Gardenia jasminoïdes* will use its absence as an excuse not to grow.

Fig. 4.3 shows the main items that need to be stored in the garden shed, which are used regularly in the conservatory.

## Preparing beds for planting

Once drainage materials and possibly heating cables are in place (see p. 66) you are ready to fill your permanent planting sites with a basic mix. Use a combination of John Innes No. 2 and peat-based compost in equal quantities. Combine it in bucketfuls and use a handful of perlite per bucket. Once it is well mixed gradually fill the bed to within about 20 cm (8 in) of the top. When planting time comes you can prepare a site for an individual plant by adding more of the main bulk ingredients, peat or loam, and fine tune with sand, grit or perlite and perhaps a bit of charcoal.

Whatever sort of conservatory you have there must be a place within it for some climbing plants. Not only do they provide a foil for those smaller varieties but also their height will

Fig. 4.4 All conservatories have some space available to grow climbers. Secure climbers to trellis and add height to your planting displays.

provide a balance in your planting displays. Prepare for these climbing plants by providing trellis where necessary (Fig. 4.4). Its installation is a simple DIY job, but it must be attached slightly proud of the wall, so that there is a ventilation gap behind it. Use discreet garden wire on glazing bars and get ready for the hardy sun lovers like *Clerodendrum thomsoniae* and *Hibiscus schizopetalus* to escape the trellis and decorate the roof space.

## Choosing and buying plants

Since I have been growing conservatory plants, there has been a transformation in the market place for them. Plants which I only ever saw in the glasshouses of a botanical garden, or on the pages of my horticultural dictionary, have become freely available. *Lapageria rosea* is a good example. Those lovely, drooping, deep crimson blooms looked wonderful in glossy photographs. It was grown by specialists but considered a rarity; I spotted it recently at my local garden centre, outside among the tender climbers.

There are now many specialist conservatory plant nurseries. Being experts, any of these growers are well worth a visit whilst you are deciding upon your conservatory plants, because they really know their plants and are generally prepared to share their knowledge to help you make a suitable selection.

When buying from these nurseries, I tend to buy young plants for three reasons. They are cheaper; they grow and mature very fast in a conservatory and when young they are a great deal more adaptable to change. As a general rule, all plants react adversely to changes in their environment. During the acclimatization process, growth may check, foliage may wilt for two or three days and a flowering variety may lose all of its buds or flowers. Buying conservatory specimens from a garden centre is usually more expensive.

In such collections you will inevitably find a selection of grape vines and citrus trees ranging widely in quality. When purchasing different plants for the conservatory, it is wise to inspect the plants first. Look for fullness of growth, potential in the way of developing fruits and for the presence of pests. Citrus trees in particular are a popular resting place for

A well-insulated, centrally heated extra living
room in the form of a conservatory would
represent further living space at any future
valuation.

By planting in permanent beds you are offering plants a more natural way to grow. They will repay you by performing better and lasting longer.

*Below:* A room with a view – almost all conservatories have this potential, so position your new conservatory in such a way that you always have something interesting to look at outside.

Although a fully planted conservatory takes time to maintain properly, the beauty and permanence of flourishing plants are surely sufficient reward.

Here is a
successful marriage
between house and
conservatory, they
look as though
they belong
together.
Unfortunately
some new
conservatories look
as though they
have just landed.

Plants grow just as well when kept in pots and when grown in this way their size, to a certain extent, will be controlled.

*Opposite:* Much is said about growing plants in pots, but providing the final container is large enough there is no reason why a tree should not reach maturity when grown in one.

A 'cold house' in summer. Despite having its use restricted to the warmer months of the year, this conservatory provides a most satisfactory site for the right plants.

scale insects; their presence is indicated by black sooty mould on the upper surfaces of the foliage. The pests themselves hide on the undersides of leaves immediately above those that have the mould covering. Any plants that show signs of disease or pests should be passed over as they will only create problems when placed among other plants in the conservatory.

When visiting the garden centre in search of plants for the conservatory do not restrict yourself to those that are on offer in the special collection, as there are likely to be many more suitable plants in the houseplant section. Here you will find a wide choice of suitable miniature plants for growing on to fine trees that may well fill the conservatory without need for other plants!

Great care must be taken during transportation and acclimatization. Make sure they are packed adequately and carried in the main part of the car, not in the boot, where they will suffer from extremes of temperature. Once you have reached the safety of your conservatory, water them well and place them in a cool shady spot for at least two or three days, while they get used to the light intensity and temperature of their new environment. The environment in a hot house at the garden centre will usually have been very well controlled, with heat, ventilation, shading, watering and humidity regulated and controlled automatically. Your conservatory environment may be perfectly balanced, but it is almost bound to be different. Secondly, in respect of the plants themselves, those available at the garden centre have been grown to be sold as 'house plants'; this means that many of them will have been acclimatized to expect a relatively low degree of light intensity, such as that which you might find in your living room. Your conservatory is light and bright, a perfect place to grow, but the plants need time to adapt to this more natural type of light.

## Seeking the unusual

It is said that money can buy anything, but this is not always so when it comes to the purchase of plants; they often take many years to develop. Generally speaking, however, if you have the money and the necessary contacts you can buy almost anything in the plant line. It may have to be shipped in from abroad and it may take some time to get to you, but if you have the right contacts you can buy 50-year-old olive trees, black bamboos, or quite magnificent plants of *Magnolia grandiflora* with glistening copper-coloured leaves and large creamy white flowers. Any expensive plant might seem ideal on paper, but do view it first before any cash changes hands.

When seeking the unusual you have to visit the places where such plants are likely to be displayed, such as important flower shows in Philadelphia in America, Ghent in Belgium and Chelsea in London. These are the places where the nurserymen will be showing off their best and most unusual products, and where you can see the actual plants and perhaps chat to the person responsible with whom you can work and obtain supplies in the future.

However you go about obtaining plants, it is wise not to go for the largest plants that are available with the intention of having an immediate finished effect in the conservatory. In warm and agreeable conditions the majority of plants will grow at a surprising rate, and mature plants that are bought in will well outgrow their allotted space in a much shorter time than one might have imagined. It is also wise not to be too ambitious at the start — learn how to manage the easier plants and think about the more exotic and difficult ones once you have found your feet and feel that you can cope with something that is more challenging.

## Seeds, bulbs and corms

These will be the least expensive source of material that may be suitable for bringing into the conservatory. It is not necessary to have specialized growing conditions for rearing much of what is being offered within the pages of a good seed catalogue.

Seed of annual plants that will give a fine show over the summer months will not be difficult to germinate. Use a bright windowsill of a warm room indoors for the initial stages of development. In the same way corms, such as those of *Begonia tuberhybrida* (of which there are many varieties) can be started into life on the windowsill indoors. These, and their related pendulous types, can be bought at any good plant shop during their dormant season and should be planted in shallow boxes filled with fresh, moist peat to get them under way.

Besides the bulk-produced tubers that are freely available at almost every plant retail shop over the winter months, there are also available from specialist growers named varieties of tuberous begonia. These will be much more expensive, but they will also be infinitely superior in terms of flower size and colour. However, it does pay to be cautious and the beginner should not rush into purchasing expensive named varieties of begonias at the outset. It would be much more sensible to try out the less expensive tubers to begin with. When well grown there are few plants that surpass tuberous begonias. These are plants that

**Fig. 4.5** A basic selection of tools and equipment you will need for planting in the conservatory.

are at their best during the summer months of the year, and when grown by the expert for major flower shows the blooms are more perfect than one could possibly imagine. As a step in the right direction it could well benefit the interested person to make a point of visiting such a show and perhaps chatting to a few of the exhibitors to get some indication of what is involved. You may well discover that it is a time-absorbing business that could occupy all your leisure time — dedication requires time! In the end it might be better to settle for the cheaper, less demanding plants, which will also provide an excellent display either as plants in pots, or as hanging basket subjects. The latter will need fairly large baskets to give of their best.

Less demanding and more reasonably priced bulbs will be the general range of daffodils and tulips available in early autumn. These, with very little effort, can be guaranteed to give a wonderful early spring display in the conservatory — nothing beats a crowded potful of daffodils in the conservatory and perhaps a month or more ahead of those outside in the garden. Similarly, there are many wonderful lilies that can be purchased through spring and autumn to be grown in pots to give colour and fragrance to the summer or autumn scene.

## Ready to plant?

Make sure that your conservatory is really clean. If it has just been built remove all plaster dust and ventilate freely. If you have moved to a house with a conservatory it would be a good idea to disinfect thoroughly.

Tools and equipment (Fig. 4.5) you will need include: trowel and small fork; secateurs; bucket or bowl for mixing; canes; pea sticks; plant ties; watering can with long spout and fine rose; mist sprayer; a selection of pots and drip trays. Plant food and remedies for possible pests and diseases must be kept in a cool safe place, such as the garden shed.

### Planting

Having selected your plants according to the minimum temperature of your conservatory, you should position them according to their habit and possible height, the degree of light intensity they require and more aesthetically you should plant them so that they will be shown off to their best advantage. See Chapter 8 for more information on planting displays.

Consider the position of your conservatory, which areas, for example, receive the hotest direct light for the longest periods. Many sun lovers need this type of light to ripen their wood before they will flower for you, whereas some need a degree of direct light, but not for sustained periods. Place these where they will receive early morning sun since this is not as strong or hot.

Use the A–Z list to ascertain potential height, light and compost requirements and position your plants in the bed. Where possible use taller plants to provide shade for those that need it. As you plant, prepare the final mix for each individual plant. As a general guideline for mixes, study the plant's current compost. You will be able to see the specks of perlite which will have been added to make the mixture more moisture-retentive. Generally peat-based mixtures have a much darker colour. When a mix is more loam than peat it tends to be light and slightly granular. If extra sand and grit has been added the mixture will crumble more easily.

When mixing, concentrate on small quantities, adding just enough water to make the compost damp. If you are adding perlite, dampen it first, while it is still in the bag as it is extremely dusty.

**Potting on**

This is a real horticultural tease, almost guaranteed to cause arguments! The plants you buy will be potted; some will be planted into permanent sites, others will remain in pots. The instructions for fast-growing annuals are simple and mostly common sense — if a plant is pot-bound, i.e. the roots are coming out of the bottom of the pot, and/or spiralling densely around the perimeter of the root ball — it is telling you that it needs more root space and fresh compost (Fig. 4.6. a & b). Water well first, mix a compost that looks similar to the last, or use a specially prepared compost for potted plants. Choose a pot not more than one size larger, very gently tease a few of those precious roots away from the

_a_

**Fig. 4.6** Take care when removing a plant from its pot. (_a_) Support underside of pot with one hand, using the other to support the main stem as shown. (_b_) Turn pot upside down and plant-and-rootball should dislodge as shown. (If plant is reluctant to drop out, tap edge of pot gently on edge of bench, when pot is in upside-down position.)

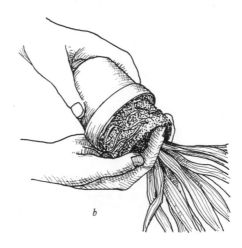

_b_

spiral, and pop the plant into its new pot and backfill with the freshly mixed compost, pressing down gently so there are no air holes.

What about those plants that the books say like to be pot-bound? Why shouldn't we treat them all the same? All our conservatory plants have near relatives that grow naturally somewhere. Without exception their roots spread out, or down, their foliage and flowers reach for the sky. Since there are no pots here, we should not insist that some plants should stay in the same size pot forever. It would be true to say that in restricting the roots you are also restricting the size of the plant in question. Also by giving some varieties too much root space they will busy themselves in making lots of roots at the expense of top growth. There are indeed some varieties which really object to being tampered with at all.

**Fig. 4.7** Provided you have the space there is no reason why you should not encourage your plants to grow tall, but to do this they will need annual re-potting.

Heated conservatories are almost protected tropics and in these plants do make enormous amounts of growth. Given the space and height some plants look attractive growing tall. I would strongly recommend a palm, *Caryota*, for example, a variety which regularly suffers from recommended potting neglect, be annually repotted into a pot one size larger until your plant has reached its required height; only then will it need its roots restricted (Fig. 4.7).

Free-standing plants that do not need their roots restricted are easy; you just have to keep an eye on that root ball and pot-on accordingly throughout their growing season. It is when you are planting permanently in beds that the problems arise. In this respect, I really envy the Victorians: they had teams of gardeners and extensive greenhouses in which to nurture their immature specimens. Nothing was ever planted in the conservatory until it was good and ready. Not having the prerequisites, I have found that I can do quite well with peat pots instead. These are readily available in a variety of sizes, and by using them I find that I can temporarily restrict the roots, while the young plant is growing on in its permanent site. This has not been horticulturally proven, but it seems to work.

## Hydroponics

The leisure gardener with a stylish conservatory might well approve of plants that enhance the surroundings yet offer little trouble when it comes to their maintenance. The same gardener may also be attracted to plants that are going to be clean to handle, causing few if any problems when it comes to watering. Plants that are grown on the hydroponic principle and plants that are similarly managed on what is known as a half-hydro system (see p. 61) will suit this purpose admirably.

Hydroponics is a method of growing that has been experimented with for many years but, although very successful when properly managed, it has not become as fashionable as it ought to be. There are numerous trade names which apply to plants that are grown hydroponically, a term that simply means the plants are growing in water only with no soil whatsoever around their roots. Among commercial growers interest in this form of growing has been very spasmodic, with most operators being put off by the high initial cost of growing such plants compared to the setting up of a growing area that caters for plants conventionally grown in potting soil. It must be said, also, that there has been a certain reluctance, perhaps suspicion of hydroponics on the part of the consumer, and the consumer is the person who will dictate the success or failure of all plant products — if there is not sufficient demand then there is no point in stepping up production.

Plants, however, do grow well with this method and, perhaps more importantly, such plants require less on-going maintenance compared to plants grown in soil. One way of raising these plants is to start them conventionally in soil in pots until they have developed a strong root system before being converted to growing on what are known as their water roots. The latter are very much fatter and more fleshy than roots that are produced conventionally in soil.

Following the development of conventional roots in soil, the plant has to be converted to growing in water; this is done by washing off every vestige of soil from around the roots in running water before relocating the roots in an inert medium, such as prepared clay granules (Fig. 4.8). The latter supports the plants and, being open and porous, ensures that the roots of the plant are well aerated. The next step is to place the lower third of the pot in water on a specially fitted greenhouse bench. The bench is in effect a watertight channel with a slow rate of water being pumped among for the six or so weeks that it takes for the plant to re-establish as a hydroponic.

When established the plant will go into a decorative watertight container in which it can live for virtually years without any need for potting or handling, other than to provide fertilizer every six months and to top up the water supply at monthly intervals. All such plants will have an explanatory leaflet with information on how it functions and what is needed in the way of attention.

For the casual gardener there could not be a less demanding kind of plant. They will generally grow very freely once established, but will

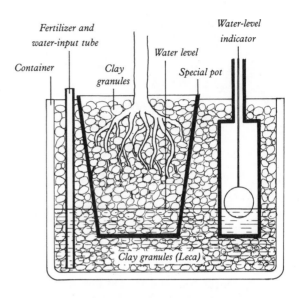

**Fig. 4.8** Construction of a hydroponic pot. Excellent results can be obtained using this method of growing plants which needs no soil whatsoever.

still have the same problems in the way of pests as conventional plants. They will also require the same consideration in respect of temperature and protection from direct sunlight.

**Half-hydro system**

More popular with many of the professional handlers of plants for decoration is what is known as the half-hydro system of growing. It is also favoured by the growers supplying these outlets as the costly business of converting plants does not apply. In the main, the interior landscapers use large fibreglass containers for most of their work as these are attractive and can be supplied in almost any colour or size. When such containers are utilized for half-hydro about one quarter of the container is filled with clay granules on top of which is placed a covering piece of capillary matting before the container is completely filled with houseplant potting soil (Fig. 4.9).

During this operation a funnel is inserted so that it goes through the matting (a hole of appropriate size being cut) to rest on the

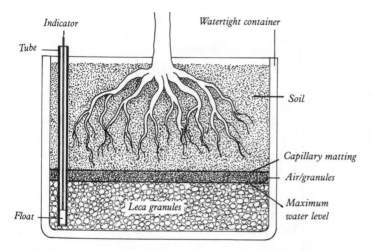

Labels on figure:
Indicator
Tube
Float
Watertight container
Soil
Capillary matting
Air/granules
Maximum water level
*Leca granules*

**Fig. 4.9** The half-hydro system. Plants are established in soil then placed in a much deeper container with an aggregate such as Leca in the bottom section. There is a gap between the soil and the Leca which the roots will bridge before finding their way into the lower section where they will develop their lush water roots.

bottom of the container. The funnel is nothing more than a piece of plastic piping, the top of which protrudes above the soil in the containers, and its function is to enable one to check the water level in the bottom of the unit. The water level should never be more than half the depth of the granules, and is monitored by use of a dipstick lowered through the plastic funnel. The most important point is that the water in the reservoir and the soil should not come into direct contact, as capillary action would result in the soil becoming totally saturated.

The chosen plants are planted in the soil in the normal way and will first root into the soil and subsequently they will penetrate the matting in search of moisture. The plants that are grown in this half-soil, half-hydroponic system tend to grow extremely well and could very easily be utilized for growing in the conserv-

atory. Individual plants or a general assortment can be grown in this fashion, and it will be found that they do very much better than plants that are growing conventionally in the same environment. Experimenting in this way will add considerable interest to the growing of plants in the conservatory, as well as offering an interesting talking point when visitors call.

## Holiday care

Holidays can be a difficult time for the owner of a conservatory full of costly plants. There is no doubt that someone will have to be appointed to do the watering, even if they do nothing else. They should be fully briefed about their duties! Avoid vague instructions — if need be write them down on paper and attach the note to the plant with a copy for the caller telling them precisely what the plants need in the way of watering and feeding. This to some degree obviates the tendency for the inexperienced to flood everything in sight every time they visit the premises. Knowing the needs of your plants in the way of watering and feeding is knowledge that is gained with practical experience, and not from reading a book on the subject!

A really worthwhile temporary custodian would also be pleased to receive directions in relation to the opening and closing of any ventilators or windows, morning and evening, having paid due regard to the weather. The fact that someone is seen around the premises will also help considerably with the security factor. There are all sorts of devices available for the automatic watering of plants but there is nothing that compares with an intelligent human when it comes to caring for a variety of plants in a wide range of pot sizes.

# PART II

THE PLANTS

# CHAPTER 5

# *Plants for Specific Environments*

To discover what plants need ask yourself where they occur naturally. The south of France, Florida, perhaps the Far East? If you were to think about the conditions which exist where the plants occur naturally and then echo this environment as closely as possible in your conservatory, this should work well, despite the fact that this can only be considered in the broadest terms. There will be many places with the same basic minimum temperature but with dramatically different rainfall patterns which thus alters both the scale of temperatures and humidity levels.

*J.B.

However, it is an interesting idea and it has often worked well for me*. I wanted cerise *Bougainvillea glabra* like the ones I had seen growing in Portugal. Having been in high summer, I knew nothing of winter minimums, or indeed rainfall, but my experience dictated arid growing conditions, hot direct sunlight, constant sea breezes and low humidity levels. I planted my young bougainvillea in a south-facing position, with its back to a warm wall. I prepared the planting site well, and mixed plenty of sand and grit into the surrounding compost, finally dusting the area around the

**Fig. 5.1** The unheated conservatory environment can cater for a wide variety of plants. Many of the half hardy shrubs, such as pittosporum, make fine winter plants for the unheated conservatory.

whole plant with more grit, for even better drainage. In February, three years on, I have just pruned it hard back in preparation for this year's proliferation of magic pink bracts.

## The cold house environment

If this is the conservatory of your choice you will have decided to install no supplementary heating at all. Your permanent plants will be what horticulturists refer to as frost tender. Many of them will grow happily outside in the relatively warm far south and south west of the British Isles. Here *Acacia dealbata* and *Camellia japonica* will be in flower by late winter and daffodils finished by early spring. On cold winter nights the temperature could well dip below freezing point, but because the air will be dry, the majority of the plants dormant (thus minimally watered) and all of them protected from the added chill factor of the wind, your chosen plants can continue to thrive.

Because of their origins this group of plants is unused to temperatures above 26°C (80°F), therefore keeping the temperatures down for them in summer can be a problem; so good ventilation and shading are vital. These frost-tender plants very often defoliate during the coldest months, giving them added protection from the cold, but spring will start sooner and autumn will last longer for you and your plants. The protection and warmth provided by solar radiation alone in your unheated conservatory (Fig. 5.1) will mean that simple pelargoniums and fuchsias which can be annually introduced in early spring, will become quite precocious and start producing flower buds long before they should. They will continue to flower throughout the summer and autumn.

Many of the *Citrus* family are quite happy to live permanently in the cold house. Given plenty of tender loving care they will not only provide gorgeously scented flowers but some fruit as well. Fresh figs (*Ficus carica* Brown Turkey variety) adapt well to life in the cold house; unlike their European relatives which flower and produce mature fruit in one season, their tiny offspring go into hold for the winter and mature the following year. Tumbling *Passiflora edulis* (passion flower) will grow

**Fig. 5.2** Abutilons are vigorous plants for the more spacious interior and reasonably easy to manage. They will benefit from an outdoor location during the summer.

rampant and adorn the walls. Lofty *Abutilon* (Fig. 5.2) will grow into a real tree if it has the root and roof space, and although it is really deciduous I have seen it in full dress and still flowering in mid winter.

You could try growing the extremely provocative but poisonous *Datura*. Even when potted these plants will grow into small branched trees in a season; their great drooping flowers come in a variety of colours and they are often hevily scented. Some will not like the coldest part of the winter, but strike easily from cuttings. The easy going *Plumbago auriculata* (syn *P. capensis*) is extremely accommodating and will tolerate almost any minimum. In your conservatory it may well die back during the coldest months, and it really appreciates a good hard prune in the spring. This species is not for the tidy minded; fixed gently to its support it will grow through all its neighbours and by mid summer be covered in never ending flushes of wonderful, powder blue corymbs of flowers.

The serious gardener may not be able to resist growing some fruit. It is perhaps the grape vine which is the most rewarding, for not only will it produce fruit but a dappled shade to benefit those plants growing underneath. They are fast growers and should be encouraged upwards by training the stems onto wires: once established they will need frequent pruning and training if fruits are to be produced in any quantity.

I think it is the camellias which have the strongest appeal for me when included in the cold house. Every year well seasoned gardeners anxiously watch the weather as their camellia buds approach maturity in case the frost attacks. In your conservatory most of your worries are over. Camellias so love this frost haven that often they produce many more buds than the plant can maintain, and with plant health in mind you should pluck half of them off!

Although the winter minimum temperatures are lower than those in heated conservatories, remember that the summer temperatures are going to be the same. Therefore many more tender plants can be introduced into the conservatory for a summer holiday. If you have one, use a heated greenhouse as a feeder unit and protect your more exotic conservatory stock while the cold weather lasts. Those without a greenhouse can winter plants inside, but do remember that day/night temperatures will fluctuate wildly in a centrally heated environment; the light will not be nearly as good as the plants are used to; the air will be relatively dry. Do not expect your plants to grow vigorously in their winter quarters; they will simply survive until conditions improve.

Many cold house plants prefer to spend the warmest summer months outside; their ventilation requirements are a great deal higher than you would expect to find in any conservatory. Therefore, keep the winter visitors, varieties such as *Citrus limon*, *Cassia corymbosa*, *Coronilla valentina* ssp. *glauca* and azaleas in containers which are easy to move.

Both skill and patience are necessary in winter to maintain the required fine environmental balance. Except on unexpected sunny, clear winter days you will rarely sit within its confines at this time. Plants kept in this conservatory will be resting. Many will defoliate, but the evergreens will almost glow in this still cold atmosphere. Despite the fact that the deciduous varieties seem to have shut down altogether, all the plants will need a little water from time to time, if only to prevent their compost from drying out completely. Remember that day length dictates growth patterns; here you are sheltering plants from the worst of the winter, their new shoots will appear much sooner than those outside.

The installation of a heated cable can be a very appropriate addition to a cold house. The cable itself is placed on top of the standard drainage materials (see p. 31). Once these are in place you must ensure a level, 5 cm (2 in) top layer of sand on which the cable is secured — according to the manufacturer's instructions — then it is held in place with a further layer of sand. I would recommend that this cable sandwich is protected with a layer of fine chicken wire, before the final composts are added to the bed. This is simply to ensure that the cable does not become dislodged or damaged by planting.

The extra warmth at the roots will protect just over 1 m (about 4 ft) of the top growth. Obviously the plants grown in this area can be slightly more exotic as the minimum temperature will be higher. You can further improve their viability by covering the entire bed with bubble plastic. Where you decide to do this, you *must* remember to ventilate the protected bed as often as possible, as the slightly warmer damp air contained within could well cause fungal attack.

## Checklist for cold houses

- *Temperature* Minimums are out of your control, but make sure that there are no draughts: use old newspapers or rugs at door thresholds and make sure windows and vents are shut securely. Alternatively proprietary draught excluder may be purchased. Don't allow dramatic swings in temperature: ventilate the conservatory well when the weather is relatively warm, or when the sun is shining. (This will also help to alleviate condensation build-up—cold damp air is more damaging to plants than cold dry air.)

● *Ventilation* This is still vital. Plants such as evergreens are growing, and a camellia will flower in February. They need that gentle movement of air around them as often as is feasible.

● *Watering*
  • NEVER let the composts dry out completely.
  • NEVER provide too much water.
  • ALWAYS water during a warm, or sunny morning, so that the plants have a chance to use what you have recently provided before the temperatures drop.
  • ALWAYS ventilate freely after watering so that excess moisture has a chance to evaporate before nightfall.
  • REMEMBER that the aerial parts of a plant can survive a frosting, but if the compost is too wet, the contained roots will inevitably freeze, and this will kill the plant.

These rules apply to all plants kept in this type of conservatory, whether they are planted in pots or beds.

## The cool house environment

Some form of additional heating will have been installed in this conservatory, as cool house plants come from parts of the world where the minimum temperature is between 7°C and 13°C (45–55°F), so your thermostat will have to be set within this range. The plants you will choose are accustomed to winters which tend to be wet and relatively mild. Their summers are long, hot and dry. Often the soil will be poor and very free draining.

The conservatory will need to be well venti- lated, except in really cold weather, through- out the year. Hot dry summers mean that many of these plants thrive in low humidity levels, and many of them will enjoy three or four hours strong sunlight a day. Watering requirements are slightly more specific. To counteract the poor soil, and lack of summer water, many of these plants naturally produce extensive root systems to aid the search for deep soil water and nutrients. In a conserv-

atory, there will be no deep soil water and of course the root systems will be restricted by the container within which the plant is growing, so be careful to water according to the needs of each plant.

Even though your conservatory is destined to be a daytime only pleasure during the winter months, there are plenty of plants which will thrive all through the year at your chosen mini- mum temperature. For example, with minimal heating you can insulate yourself from the world outside and luxuriate among elegant palm fronds in mid winter—many of them are indigenous to North Africa and the southern Mediterranean. In the last decade many of us have become well seasoned European travell- ers and the environment in your conservatory will be perfect for the flora from this part of the world. Why not be adventurous and reproduce your favourite taverna right outside your back door?

Just think about those balmy evenings you spent there surrounded by superb bougain- villeas. The air can be heavy with the scent of *Nerium oleander*, which produces large clusters of pale pink flowers over a lengthy period.

Pots and tubs can be filled with the extra- ordinary succulents which grow like weeds on little more than sand. You could try a less well known, but just as rewarding small shrub called *Brunfelsia pauciflora* (syn. *B. calycina*) (Fig. 5.3). It has its origins in South America but it seems to acclimatize quite happily to your minimum temperature. Its common name is the yesterday, today and tomorrow plant, as its fabulously scented flowers last three days, on the first they are deep blue, almost purple; by day two the flower has faded to very pale blue and by the end of its third day the blooms are white. In the right environment it will flower almost continuously. *Lantana camara* has flowers of several different colours on the same plant at the same time.

My favourite for this conservatory has to be *Lapageria rosea*. In pictures this lovely plant has the appearance of being quite delicate; do not be deceived—its appearance belies its toughness. It is found growing naturally in Chile, where it suffers great extremes in temperature and heavy winter rainfall. If the top growth dies back during cold or drought, it

**Fig. 5.3** *Brunfelsia pauciflora* has the interesting common name of 'yesterday, today and tomorrow' which relates to the manner in which flowers change colour from one day to the next. Colourful plants over many months in the early part of the year.

escape from the elements, all this living beauty literally at your finger tips.

## The warm house environment

If your conservatory is destined to be an integral part of your living area all the year round, it is likely that your heating thermostats will be set somewhere in the central heating range. With plants in mind we are moving into the subtropical area of the world where the minimum temperatures vary between 13 and 18°C (55–64°F). Your plants will have their origins in large areas of south-east Asia and Australia, northern India, Sri Lanka and South Africa. Despite the minimum temperatures the other climatic variations can be enormous. In some parts of South Africa, for example, the plants have had to adapt to seasonal drought conditions, whereas some of the Australian varieties have acclimatized to sporadic rainfall throughout the year. Generally speaking, the humidity levels are relatively high. Temperature control

quickly produces new stolons from its massive root system. In a conservatory, once established this root system really needs restricting within the confines of a large pot or planter. *Lapageria rosea* will climb anything, and given time it will also produce dozens of the most gorgeous pendulous, deep red, waxy flowers.

A couple of very tolerant house plants are the yucca, which tolerates much ill treatment and bright conditions, and the mother-in-law's tongue, *Sansevieria trifasciata* 'Laurentii'. The yucca does not like cold winter conditions with wet soil round its roots.

Finally, use this conservatory to bring your cymbidiums (Fig. 5.4) into flower. Despite their aristocratic connections these orchids need little more than a cool summer outside in some shade, and the protection and warmth of your conservatory during the winter. Their flower spikes will emerge from a mass of foliage. Although they are weeks coming to maturity, your patience will be finally repaid by their long-lasting exotic flowers.

For a relatively small increase on your heating bill, the cool house can provide a very real

**Fig. 5.4** *Cymbidium lowianum*. These are spectacular plants during the duller months of the year and are among the easier of the orchids to manage, but this does not mean that they are beginners' plants.

is fairly critical in this type of conservatory and even periodic dips below the recommended minimum will mean that your plants will suffer noticeably. Efficient ventilation is just as important, as the rise in temperatures coupled with increased humidity levels may mean that condensation becomes a problem. Shading begins to take on a more horticultural role as many of the plants in this group have evolved to *photosynthesize* in very poor light on the forest floor. Direct sunlight, of whatever duration, will make them scorch, shrivel and die.

Despite these conditions, this plant group is by far the largest, and on the whole most accomodating. Within it you will find many plants which are easily recognizable as house plants; your warm house will give them an energy boost and they will seem to grow before your eyes. Those which have formally scratched a living on your window sill, will thrive in your conservatory. You will be amazed by the ease with which luxuriant growth is made.

Beautiful *Allamanda cathartica* can adorn the walls; in a season, its huge growth will escape the trellis and decorate the roof space. Give it plenty of water and light while in active growth and it will repay you with masses of lovely yellow trumpets. If you want to be slightly more subtle you can try *Jasminum sambac*; this will grow more slowly, but its heavily scented clusters of white flowers make it really worthwhile. Gardenias can be fashioned into beautiful shrubs.

The temperamental *Ficus benjamina*, grown and sold by the hundreds as house plants, can totally defoliate in a matter of days if it does not approve of its position. In a warm conservatory it will really grow fast, it so loves this type of moist warm climate. Another super fast growing evergreen climber called *Tetrastigma voinierianum* will also thrive in this environment. Until recently it had gone out of fashion due to its bad behaviour. At the first hint of a change in temperature it has been known to shed whole branches — its common name is lizard vine. I planted three side by side in a conservatory once, my aim being to provide some extra shade. At planting time in mid summer they were 1.5 m (5 ft) high; by the time I went back five months later, each vine had made a mass-

ive amount of growth. They had escaped their trellis and were rambling, multibranched, among the rafters. As this particular plant produces no flowers to speak of, I had underplanted with a smaller, more delicate looking twining plant called *Ipomoea learii*. This close relation of morning glory is a good grower; it had used the vine as its support and its irridescent, bright blue, trumpet-shaped flowers completed the picture.

Carefully planned your plants can provide you with oriental scents and beautiful flowers all the year round in this conservatory.

## The hot house environment

Minimum temperatures have reached the top of the scale here. Most of the plants come from the tropical rain forests which line the equator. There tends to be little seasonal variation in temperature, the thermostats set somewhere between 18 and 26°C (64–80°F). High temperatures, no dry season and regular heavy rainfall causes high humidity. The need for constantly high humidity levels and temperatures will mean your ventilating technique needs to be highly refined. The conservatory still needs to be ventilated in order to refresh the air and reduce condensation, but the temperature must not be allowed to drop. Once again shading must take on its horticultural role, because those broad-leaved tall plants steal all the light from the forest floor and many varieties can only thrive in deep shade. Perhaps a word of warning here though — this is really a conservatory for the expert and for those with money to spare.

Recently I went to one of those enormous glasshouses maintained by our most august horticultural society. In order to achieve the required humidity levels a lad had the regular task of hosing the entire interior. The cool shower I received was quite a relief; the temperature was quite overpowering but the plants obviously loved it. Never having been there, I rather imagine that this is what life is like in Singapore's botanical gardens. Each plant has grown to monster proportions. The huge leaves of *Musa × paradisiaca* (Fig. 5.5) — banana to the uninitiated — spread upward and outward to catch as much solar radiation as possible in this dense forest. You

**Fig. 5.5** *Musa cavendishii*. The banana plant will add a touch of the exotic, and may well bear fruit in the warm and humid conservatory.

addition, you must select plants which are tolerant of high temperatures and low humidity.

With the large conservatory, there is obviously a great deal more scope when it comes to setting out planting areas, and in the selection of plants that may be used. As with the smaller establishment, however, one should decide at the planning stage what is to be done about creating plant displays. Will the entire floor be paved over, for example, or will certain areas be earmarked for free planting beds. There are good and bad aspects about both options; the least agreeable thing about free-planted areas is that they become permanent features that make radical change almost impossible. An alternative would be to free-plant the more important specimens and to arrange areas in the display bed that will accommodate other plants remaining in their pots. When opting for free-planted display beds and perimeter borders these ought to be clearly outlined on the plans for the internal area of the conservatory.

## Selecting plants

Given good soil, warmth and humidity you can then go ahead and plant a very wide selection of tropical plants, bearing in mind that they will require shaded conditions. This will preclude the possibility of including bougainvilleas and other flowers that must have much lighter conditions. In the long, terraced conservatory that is built against a house wall it will be possible to segregate shade and sunlovers by having a partition. This sort of arrangement is useful in respect of heat saving—you can have different temperatures in different sections of the terraced conservatory. There is nothing to be gained by providing a high temperature for plants that will do very much better in cooler conditions; in a high temperature most of them will only lose their normally compact appearance by becoming thin and straggly.

Visit a supplier some weeks in advance of the planting so that the plants can be reserved for you. The best kind of nursery will be one that combines home-grown products with more exotic imported plants. It is unwise to overdo the planting of specimens. Three, perhaps five

can try it if you have the space; once mature they are both interesting and attractive providing they receive enough water and feed.

You will need a conservatory of good size in both floor area and height, as many of the jungle plants will become very large if the conditions are to their liking; there will hardly be room for the human element at all. Perhaps the most likely situation for this type of environment is to be found within the bounds of a heated indoor swimming pool. It is possible, but worth a cautionary note. Given that the water temperature is high and the resultant condensation potentially damaging to the structure, efficient ventilation is usually built into the system which withdraws the moisture from the atmosphere. The air within, therefore, will be as dry and hot as a machine can make it—more like a desert than a jungle. Compensate by grouping plants together, plunging them in aggregate and, of course, by being really persistent with your mister. In plants should be adequate for most plantings, and these should be carefully spaced out so that other plants can thrive between them. An additional plant or two can always be added later if the planting seems too sparse, and this is easier than having to remove plants subsequently because they are too crowded together.

## Large specimens

Large specimens should be chosen from among the palms, philodendrons, *Ficus* and *Schefflera* (syn. *Heptapleurum*) as far as the bulkier plants are concerned, with members of the *Dracaena* tribe also offering more slender and graceful height. *Ficus benjamina* is the popular green weeping fig; its numerous variegated forms are of similar habit but with very bright foliage. One of the most elegant of foliage specimen plants when given ample space is the Norfolk Island pine, *Araucaria heterophylla* (syn. *A. excelsa*). The typical pine needles are an attractive soft green in colour and develop on elegant spreading tiers that protrude from upright stems. In nature this one becomes a giant, but in the cool, lightly shaded room it will be much more manageable.

Plant the specimens in generous holes with soil covering the complete rootball. Plants of this kind seldom do well when part of the rootball is exposed through the depth of soil being inadequate. When making the initial inspection of available plants at the suppliers it would be well for the depth of the pot in which the plant is growing to be measured as well so that one has clear knowledge of what is needed in respect of soil depth when the bed is being prepared.

Once the main plants are in position stand back and assess the scene in order to get some idea about the number and size of additional plants that will be needed. A professional would be able to look at the plans on paper and give an accurate assessment of what is needed, but a rough judgement can be made and certain plants acquired, on a piecemeal basis if need be so that the actual planting is done over a period of a few days, or weeks. Whatever else, it seldom pays to rush this sort of job, and there is much pleasure to be had from doing this job yourself.

## Intermediate plants

When intermediate plants are installed in the bed it is best to have them set around you in their pots and to try the plants in various positions in their containers before they are actually taken out and planted. As already mentioned, it is important not to overcrowd plants at this stage. There are plants, such as the tall and slender dracaenas, that will be more effective when planted in a group that is reasonably close. These are plants that do not expand laterally, but they do provide a pleasing effect when several plants of differing height are set together in a group.

While the bed is being planted it ought to be forked over as one retreats from each area so that a pleasing aerated surface is the result as opposed to one that is hard and trampled down. The sort of plants that will be most effective in the intermediate height area below the larger plants will come from the following — *Dieffenbachia*, *Aglaonema*, *Scindapsus*, *Fatsia*, large ferns, *Spathiphyllum*, *Dracaena*, *Ficus* and *Philodendron*. Plants of differing height and spread will always be available. The availability of the more unusual plants is changing all the time and one has to seek these out personally through suppliers' plant lists or, better still, by visiting the growing area to make a selection.

Although some groups of plants do have very specific high humidity needs, bromeliads and orchids for example, most of them will adapt to lesser degrees of humidity. Many of the shade lovers have beautifully variegated or striking foliage. You might like to try one of the varieties found in the *Calathea* family. Their name derives from the Greek, *kalathos*, meaning basket, as the flower clusters of this plant look like a basket of flowers. They are rarely seen when grown as a house plant but who knows what will happen in your conservatory?

You can grow all sorts of graceful ferns with ease — the gorgeous *Asplenium nidus* (bird's nest fern) with its bright green leathery leaves or the more delicate *Adiantum*.

As for colour, there are very few shrinking violets here. Bold fluorescent pinks, fiery reds and yellows are in abundance. The bizarre *Plumeria rubra* (frangipani) with its almost obscene thick trunk and stems makes a real conversation piece, but the tubular flowers are fantastic, 50 or 60 blooms held together in fragrant clusters. The varieties with white flowers are perhaps the most fascinating. You can also grow *Spathiphyllum wallisii* (peace lily), their waxy white flower spathes look almost ethereal in the gloom of their surroundings. Among the fragrant flowering plants there are few that can compare with the very heavy scent of the gardenia. These are plants that are occasionally available during the summer months as half standards — expensive, but guaranteed to add another dimension to the conservatory scene.

*Container plants*
The thought of dirty soil and planted beds could well be anathema to the owner of the swish conservatory that is more a leisure show place than a plant room. Large beds of soil for housing tropical plants are not to everyone's liking; the best answer here is to use fewer plants that remain in their pots. Often, fewer plants that are carefully selected will create a more elegant display.

The plants for this sort of setting can be the same as those suggested for the planted bed, you can also be more adventurous. Bananas are very desirable and can be appealing when carrying a reasonable amount of fruit. Clerodendrons are another possibility for gracing decorative containers in the spacious conservatory that offers very good light.

## One-type plant collections

### Cacti and succulents
Problems can be caused as a result of plants trying to grow in conservatories that do not offer any form of shade. Smaller units become virtual hot-boxes of heat in which little other than members of the cactus family can survive.

The cactus and many of the succulents are plants that have adapted to very arid conditions over the years and are able to store moisture in their thick leaves that will see them over naturally arid seasons in their natural habitat.

Cacti are not to everyone's taste, but they are low-maintenance plants once they have been put in position: virtually no water is needed during the winter months and plants will go for long periods at other times without showing too many signs of stress. During the spring and summer they will benefit from feeding, and there are specialist feeds available. Young plants that have the capability of becoming large specimens will need to be potted on during their younger stages as they fill their pots with roots. The best time to do this will be the spring and a specially prepared cactus mixture should be used for the job. The impression that cactus can go on for year after year without need for fresh soil is generally not true, although some have a remarkable capacity for survival when totally neglected.

These are plants that can be used in many different ways — as potted plants dotted about the room, as formal plants set out on a bench-style table or, more effectively, as groups in a display bed. Raising plants from seed is usually considered the easy option when it comes to building up a large collection of any particular group of plants, but it is in fact a slow business with cacti. One blessing with raising cacti from seed is that they will germinate fairly readily but develop very little growth in the first year, which usually means that the wee plants should remain fairly close together until they have matured sufficiently to be handled and potted. A properly prepared cactus potting mixture is needed at all stages of potting. This is best bought ready mixed and will contain all the ingredients that the plant is likely to need — in particular it will be well drained.

When arranging a display bed of cacti (Fig. 5.6), put them on the floor if the collection contains a selection of larger plants, but if the collection is small consisting of more choice plants, then they should be placed on a knee-high table, so that they can be seen, handled and inspected without too much difficulty. The man who is dedicated to his cacti will spend a lot of time simply looking at them.

The mixture used for planting such display beds should be fairly heavy and free draining — on the heavy side so that the soil is able to support more easily the taller, more top-heavy plants. Plants can either remain in their pots to be plunged to their rims in the bed, or they can be removed from their pots and free planted. There are reasons for and against both methods, but plants that remain in their pots can be individually treated in respect of watering and you can change the arrangement very easily.

The bed, on raised table or on the floor, should be landscaped to some degree before any thought is given to arranging plants — landscaping in this context relates to the contours, the mounds and hollows that the bed medium is made up from. A few weather-beaten stones placed here and there will further add to the landscaping in the hope of achieving a natural effect. The taller plants ought to be away from the front with the intermediate plants bringing down the height. With these plants it is very difficult to sit down and

**Fig. 5.6** A display bed of cacti makes an unusual and interesting feature in the conservatory. Cacti can remain in pots or they may be more effectively displayed in a raised bed. Provide cactus compost and use decorative stones to embellish the arrangement.

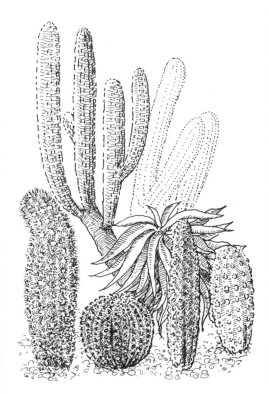

earmark precise locations on a piece of paper to indicate where the plants should be placed — it is much more a trial and error exercise, and a skill that is really learned through experience. One thing can be said, however, and that is that if there are several plants of one variety, it is very much better to plant these as a group rather than space them out all over the available area.

*Succulents and flowering species*

There are many succulents that share a characteristic with cactus in their ability to go for long periods without water and not seem to be harmed. The colouring of many of the succulents is unmatched by any other group of plants, and the metallic sheen on many echeverias is a case in point. There are many great rarities among the echeverias — a group of plants that could well prove to be a considerable fascination for anyone interested in specializing.

Among the succulents there are also many fine plants that are appreciated principally for their flowers. The Christmas and Easter cactus are well known for these qualities, but it is not always appreciated that mature plants of these make fine specimens in hanging containers. There are numerous others that are equally pleasing when suspended in mid air, notably the rat's tail cactus, *Aporocactus flagelliformis*, and the burrow's tail cactus, *Sedum morganianum*. The latter has pendulous stems to which are attached blue grey beads of leaves that are attractive in mature specimens.

Many of the cacti will take many years before they produce any flowers but there are others that flower when quite small — in the latter category there are rebutias and many of the mammalarias, both of which form neat mounds of compact growth. Many of the plants can be induced to flower by watering them as they would expect to receive water in the wild, i.e. keep them bone dry in winter, then in the early spring to give them a good soaking. The result of this is that buds appear and flowers of brilliant colouring soon follow.

The orchid cactus, *Epiphyllum*, is a good example of a plant that can lie around in an odd corner with little or no soil around its roots, often seeming to have died, only to produce a display of the most brilliant flowers during the summer and autumn. These are plants that could quite easily alter your view of the cactus family, as their flowers with long silky stamens are not only available in many remarkable colours, they are also fragrant. On top of this they propagate like weeds if stems are cut into sections and placed in a sandy mixture in reasonable warmth. However, it must be said that as they increase in size these become very ungainly plants. Varieties of *E. cooperii* produce their very large flowers during the night. Unlike most other cacti, they prefer a more spongy potting mixture containing a proportion of peat and leaf mould with good loam and a little sharp sand.

## Air plants

Air plants in recent years have proved to be remarkably popular; plants and the various pieces of equipment for their display are on sale in almost every outlet where one might expect to find indoor plants on offer. The common name, 'air plant', derives from the fact that many of the plants are, in fact, plants that will seem to survive on virtually nothing more than fresh air. They all belong to the family of plants known as Bromelaceae, and almost all the plants on offer are tillandsias. These are among the toughest of all, with an ability to tolerate very long periods of general neglect and drought without seeming to be unduly perturbed.

The strangest plant in this group is perhaps *Tillandsia usneoïdes* (Spanish moss); this has a capacity to survive when doing nothing more than hanging from a telegraph wire. In some parts of the world it has become an invasive weed that drapes itself from trees and other anchorage with the result that surrounding vegetation is virtually choked to death. The fact that this plant and many of its relatives will tolerate such harsh treatment should not give one the impression that a spartan existence is what is preferred. In fact, the opposite might be the case when plants such as Spanish moss are introduced to conservatory conditions for example that are very hot and dry. This is a plant that enjoys moistness in the atmosphere, and to be hot and dry for any length of time would simply be the end of it.

There are numerous other tillandsias (Fig. 5.7) used for decorating ornaments with apparently litle aesthetic feeling for the plant. Some are given a better chance by being planted in moss to form part of the general decoration, but others are simply glued onto the ornament, such as a shell, with very little consideration for its well-being.

Air plants are sold in vast quantities, so it is clearly a method of plant presentation that large numbers of people must like. In a smart conservatory, air plants could be arranged to better effect in a disused tropical fish tank so that they could be sprayed over regularly. The grey foliage of the small tillandsias is particularly attractive and most will also oblige with colourful flowers.

Wherever possible one should acquire plants that are planted in moss as opposed to those that are gummed to their anchorages. If nothing else it will make the potting of plants a

**Fig. 5.7 Air plants.** Fascinating bromeliads that have the common name of air plant and an ability to exist on little more than moisture and fresh air. Many interesting varieties are available.

much easier task when such an exercise is contemplated. When potting on, it is best to use an orchid potting mixture, as this will not be too rich.

### Bromeliad tree

Bromeliad trees can be tedious to assemble, but when carefully done can be one of the most exotic attractions of them all. Such trees can be part of a larger display of plants, or they can be made as individual features to stand on their own. The simplest form is to find an attractive branch and to anchor it in a large clay pot, either by wedging it in or, more satisfactorily, by concreting it in.

The bromeliad tree feature is invariably only as good as the person who did the work on the tree — some are so badly done that the plants have no chance of prospering. When badly done the tree branch is bare with the plants hanging forlornly to their perches with a piece of rough wire wound around their roots to hold them in position.

To do the job well you have to select your own tree — one with some character and lots of clefts and small branches to allow the easy location of plants. The branch should have a generous thickness of fresh sphagnum moss tied to it with plastic covered wire — by keeping the moss damp the plants on the tree will actually grow and be much more attractive (Fig. 5.8).

The more ambitious person may wish to tie carefully very thin plastic tubing along the branches of the tree before the moss is fixed in position. If the tubing is perforated in several places and the lower ends are secured into the end of a hosepipe, the other end of the pipe can go onto a small electric pump to push water through the tubing. The attraction of this feature when the tree is located with the branches overhanging a pool in the conservatory, is that there will be a continual and fascinating dripping of water into the pool below. There are few more attractive features connected with water when the tree has been carefully prepared.

The plants are fixed to the tree by first removing them from their pots and tying moss around the roots before securing them in position on the tree. Use the natural joints between the various branches of the tree to

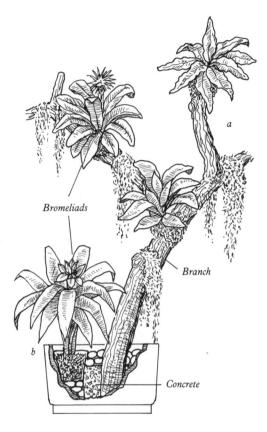

Fig. 5.8 Bromeliad tree. (a) A firm branch of pleasing shape is anchored in a pot filled with concrete before forms of bromeliad are secured to the branches. (b) While concrete is still wet a flower pot is embedded in the mixture so that it can be used to hold a decorative plant when the 'tree' is completed.

obtain good anchorage for the plants and to set them off more naturally. Choose plants which will provide a balanced effect when in place. There are many *Tillandsias*, *Cryptanthus*, as well as the smaller bromeliads such as *Guzmania* that will be ideally suited for this purpose. A few larger bromeliads can be placed around the base of the tree to camouflage the pot and offer a more natural look to the scene.

# CHAPTER 6

# *Climbing and Wall Plants*

In the conservatory climbers have a two-fold function that can make a world of difference to the overall display. Firstly, wall plants have the effect of a picture frame setting off other plants. Secondly, the more robust climbers can be trained to grow overhead to provide natural shade for the plants below. Some of the plants that are recommended for use as climbers are often over-rated in that they have a short flowering period with dull foliage for the rest of the year. If it is to be a choice between a climbing plant of this nature and a climbing plant that has attractive foliage but no flowers the latter is often the better option.

## Trellis framework

A light trellis framework is reasonably simple to fit and should be attached to the wall, but not tight up against it. The trellis should be erected so that there is a gap behind it (Fig. 6.1) to facilitate tying in of the plants as they grow.

Prior to introducing climbing plants, you must make proper provision for them — standing the pot close to the wall and tying the growth to a few nails hastily knocked into the wall might be inexpensive, but is not very secure. If nails are used, they should be nails that are specially manufactured for training vines. When knocked home much of the nail

**Fig. 6.1 Trellis frames.** The majority of climbing plants need some form of support, and one should shop around as there are numerous methods and materials, both cheap and expensive, that may be utilized for this purpose.

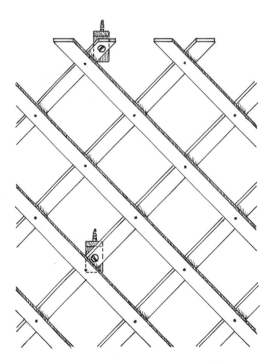

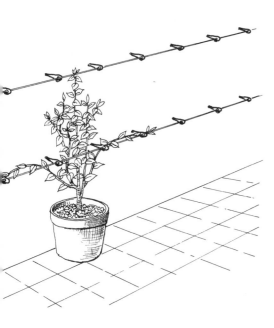

**Fig. 6.2 Vine eyes.** These are hammered into the wall like nails but have the advantage that when secured they stand proud of the wall for better air circulation when plants are attached. Holes or eyes in the flat side of the nails allow wires to be laced through them before the plants are secured to the wires.

stands proud; there is a hole through which wire can be fed in a much neater fashion than is possible with an ordinary nail. Wires can then be strained from one nail to the next so that the plants can be spaced out to best advantage (Fig. 6.2). This is a somewhat crude method, not at all attractive to begin with, but once the plants are well established, none of this primitive framework will be seen.

For overhead growth it is much the best either to have strained wires to support the plant growth, or nylon tubing, which is clear and less obvious. Plant growth very soon conceals any supports that are provided. Around

pillars in the larger conservatory it is much more attractive to use lightweight trellis for training plants.

If plants are to remain in containers then these ought to be well designed and suited to the plants. It will also be wise at the outset to put plants into containers of reasonable size as it will be difficult once they are established to pot them into larger containers. This will inevitably result in the plants being overpotted, which makes it important that they should be watered with great care, ensuring that the soil is very much on the dry side until plants are clearly growing well when normal watering and feeding can begin. Fig. 6.3 shows a variety of supports for container-grown climbing plants.

During the season you will find such plants as bougainvilleas, passiflora and stephanotis. At first glance many of these will not look in the least like climbing subjects as they are almost always wound around a hooped piece of wire that is secured in the pot. Much of the reason for this tortuous handling of the plants is to keep them under control at the nursery where they are grown and to make their transportation easier and perhaps less costly. Notwithstanding, these could be worthwhile purchases if you have time to unwind the growth. Care and patience are needed here.

## Passiflora

If the plant is on a single supporting cane when purchased, as most of them are, it should be carefully disentangled and then trained out on the supporting frame. However, a plant such as the passiflora is a very rampant plant and will grow through the roof if given such generous treatment in prepared soil. For the passiflora a small hole should be dug. This should be lined with slates or slabs before infilling with the same soil and planting (Fig. 6.4). This treatment will obviously restrict the roots of the plant, and such restriction will in turn curb the production of leaf growth. Even so, because of its vigour, you must make a firm decision as to whether or not there really is sufficient room in which to accommodate the plant — particularly important in a hot-box style of conservatory. When unwound the

**Fig. 6.3 Plant supports.** Most taller plants need to be supported and there is a wide choice of supports as shown by these five examples. Bougainvillea and passiflora are often sold on hoops, but it is usually necessary to carefully disentangle plants and to arrange them on taller trellis supports in the conservatory.

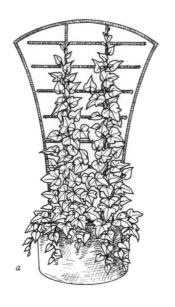

a

b

c

d

e

passiflora could well be 4.5 m (14 ft) or more in length. After planting it can be arranged on a supporting frame to give a full green background with colourful passion flowers to follow.

## Vines

Vines are probably even more vigorous than the passiflora, but they are much more attractive when in leaf and hanging bunches of grapes will be a real bonus, adding an exotic touch to the surroundings (Fig. 6.5). Plants will be quick to grow and provide almost perfect dappled shade for the plants that are growing underneath. When selecting a variety it is important to inform the supplier of the amount of space that is available so that a suitable variety is obtained.

## Jasminum

Wherever possible it is wise to see mature plants so that they can be assessed for value when growing at their full vigour. Enjoying the fragrance of jasmine during the winter months could well persuade you that this is the ideal plant for the conservatory, but it is worth remembering that this is a plant with a comparatively short flowering season. It is also a rampant grower that will be little more than a great mass of blackish green leaves for the greater part of the year. This disadvantage ought to be considered. It might be better to have a plant with more attractive foliage and to stand a few bowls of hyacinths around the conservatory in order to enjoy the fragrance!

## Bougainvillea

For sheer brilliance there are very few plants that can compare with the bougainvilleas, and they really are not nearly so difficult to manage as is sometimes imagined. It is important that they should have very good light in which to grow, that they be trained to a support, that they are not watered excessively, and that from the time they naturally shed their foliage in the autumn they should have no water whatsoever. In time, a plant may well grow to extend into the upper reaches of the conservatory so providing a modicum of shade for the plants below. In the winter they will be nothing more than a lot of twigs with many nasty barbs

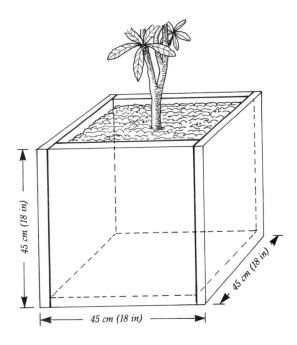

**Fig. 6.4** Vigorous subjects such as passiflora and jasminum need to have their roots restricted and one way of doing this is to dig a hole and to line the sides and bottom with large slates or slabs.

**Fig. 6.5 Vines for shade.** Trained on overhead wires grape vines offer the dual advantage of both shade and an exotic effect – you may also have grapes!

protruding from them; it is not until February when new growth is evident and watering begins that things begin to happen. Colourful bracts will appear outshining everything around for months on end.

They can be planted in the ground in prepared soil or they can remain in pots of good size. The latter is sometimes the best option as plants can then be moved out of doors in full sun during the summer. During the growing period, they need to be kept moist and fed, but they are not demanding plants. If plants can be moved out of doors, you should provide a growing framework that is anchored into the soil in the pot as opposed to being attached to the wall. In order to reduce weight and make the support less bulky it can be made with stout garden canes instead of heavier trellis work.

You may wish to plant directly into the soil; this will involve making proper preparations. Unless you are very fortunate, the soil that is already there is very unlikely to be suitable for potted plants. Plants may never look as sprightly as they might. Ideally, a fairly large hole should be dug to at least twice the dimension of the plant rootball and the soil that is removed should be distributed around the garden. The bottom of the hole should be forked up and a good layer of gravel should be placed in the bottom to assist drainage. The hole is then filled with a loam-based and properly prepared potting mixture. The plant should be potted firmly into this mixture and watered in when the operation is completed.

The plant that is most often offered for sale is *B. glabra*, but there are many others of brilliant colouring — orange, yellow, white, as well as double flowered forms. The less usual varieties are not readily available, so keep in touch with suppliers and look for new arrivals at the plant centre.

Once plants have been obtained it will not be difficult to increase stock by means of cuttings. These can be taken when plants are dormant by removing a firm branch and cutting it up into sections some 13 cm (5 in) in length. These should be inserted in sandy mixture in warm conditions; early February is the best time. Having obtained your supply of small plants, you can swap varieties with other inter-

ested owners. Many plant collections develop in this way and it is a good method of meeting others who are interested in less usual plants.

## Mandevilla

Another fine plant for rambling along against a wall, and sometimes into the upper reaches of the conservatory if conditions are to its liking, is the *Mandevilla*. In the plant shops many of these will more often than not be labelled as *Dipladenia*, but they are both one and the same. Growth is soft and green; the flowers are rose coloured in *M. rosea*, and salmon pink with a white throat in the variety, *M. sanderi* 'Rosea'. The nice thing about these plants is that the foliage is pretty all the year round and if cared for really well they could be producing flowers the year round. Growth should be trained to shape and any untidy pieces can be removed at any time.

## Allamanda

For the person who can provide the right conditions and the right sort of expertise, there are challenging climbers in the allamandas, with *A. cathartica* and its variety *A. cathartica grandiflora*. Both of these produce flowers that stop you in your tracks, being a lovely shade of yellow; in the cultivar, individual flowers can well be 13 cm (5 in) in diameter. In ideal conditions they will attain a height of 3 m (10 ft), and should be trained by first tying in branches to the wall support and eventually to overhead wires so that the plants are close to the glass. One of the first jobs of the year should be the pruning of the previous year's growth back to a few centimetres from the main stems of the plant. This all sounds easy, but the allamandas are difficult plants to manage and will need a minimum temperature of at least 16°C (61°F) and careful attention in respect of watering and feeding. When plants are being pruned, keep the prunings for cuttings: make these some 13 cm (5 in) in length and insert them in a sandy mixture in a heated propagator where regular syringing with tepid water will encourage rooting.

## Gloriosa

*Gloriosa* is another challenging plant that can be tied in and encouraged to cover wall space.

These can be purchased as growing plants during the summer months, or they can be bought as slender tubers earlier in the year.

The tubers should be started into growth in early spring in peaty house plant soil, in the hope that by summer they will produce their exciting lily-like flowers; these are ruby red and yellow in *G. superba* (syn. *G. rothschildiana*), which is the species that is most easily obtained. They will need a growing temperature that does not fall below 18°C (54°F) at any time while plants are in growth. Being deciduous they are dried off in the autumn and stored warm until the following season when they are replanted and brought into growth.

## Clerodendrum

Another challenge will be *Clerodendrum thomsoniae* which is generally available in garden shops as small plants during the summer months. They have rather coarse dull green leaves but attractive bract flowers that are produced in white and red clusters over a lengthy period. These should be cared for in much the same way as recommended for allamanda, with the difference that they require very little water from December until they show signs of growth in the early spring. Temperature should never fall below 16°C (61°F). Plant roots should not be kept too wet over long periods.

## Stephanotis

Any plant with attractive flowers that also offers fragrance will always be a blessing; stephanotis fits the bill nicely. The leathery green leaves are very ordinary but the clustered tube flowers have a fragrance that knocks almost all the others for six. Well managed plants will have flowers right through the summer once they have become well established. Planting them out in prepared soil in a border will give best results; they will make their own way up the supports that are provided, or they will simply twine around any anchorage that might be within range.

Plants are evergreen and should be fed during the spring and summer with a tomato fertilizer. One of the problems is that they are prone to mealy bug pests which get amongst the twining branches with the result that they are difficult to make contact with when treating plants with insecticide. It is best to be vigilant and to hand-clean any plants that have the bugs present. This is difficult as stephanotis plants grow away in the upper reaches of the conservatory. Flowers of the stephanotis can be cut and floated in a shallow dish of water to add their fragrance to other rooms in the house. During the summer when well grown the fragrance of this fine plant will seem to be all pervasive.

## Pelargonium

The foliage of stephanotis is not so pretty, and the flowers tend to be in the upper branches, with the result that the lower area of the plant is less appealing. An answer might be to give the stephanotis a growing companion that has more decorative foliage. The climbing pelargonium with yellow and green foliage, *P.* 'A Happy Thought', is a perfect choice for keeping the stephanotis company as they need similar conditions, and will offer a splendid picture when growing through one another. Actually, doubling up like this should be done more often to make the conservatory more attractive — something that is particularly important where the conservatory is small and one is anxious to increase the plant collection. There are lots of other pelargoniums that can be utilized as climbers if they have their shoots tied in as they develop. Even the plants that are designated as trailing, such as the splendid cascade varieties, can be tied in so that their bright clusters of flowers hang free from the background of foliage.

## Hedera

Another way of achieving dual effect when setting up the conservatory display in a conservatory that has a solid brick wall which can be kept moist, is to utilize natural clinging climbers such as ivies. There are many lovely small leaved ivies that will retain their brightly coloured foliage right through the year, *Hedera helix* ssp. *helix* 'Oro di Bogliasco' (syn. *H.h.h.* 'Goldheart') being an excellent example with gold and green foliage. These need only be planted at the base of the wall (in a pot with something else if need be) for young growth to develop adventitious roots that will tightly

## Ficus

Another humble plant that will be in its element when clinging naturally to a damp surface in a warm conservatory is the creeping fig, *Ficus pumila*, which has attractive pale green leaves, attached to wiry stems. The latter will produce natural clinging roots like the ivy in order to spread its greenery over the damp surface, and it will not mind if something else is planted in front of it so that it is simply providing a background of soft colour. However, with all plants that cling in this fashion by roots produced along their stems, it is essential that the wall surface is kept moist.

## Annual climbers

There are other cheap and cheerful plants that can be provided at little more cost than the price of the seed: annuals such as trumpet vine, morning glory and blackeyed Susan are well worth considering when the walls of the conservatory are being furnished.

### Eccremocarpus

In cool conditions that offer good light there can be few more rewarding plants than the trumpet vine, *Eccremocarpus scaber*, a half-hardy plant that will cover a wall in no time and throughout the summer will never be without its masses of orange and yellow flowers. It also obliges with masses of seed that can be saved to produce plants in the future. This is a plant that does not seem to have any enemies.

**Fig. 6.6 Framing the doorway.** A lightweight trellis framework around the doorway of the conservatory can be utilized for numerous climbing plants, in particular the ipomoea, or morning glory.

### Ipomoea

With startling blue flowers that last for but one day there is the vigorously climbing morning glory which has large, open trumpet flowers indicating that the plant is, in fact, a giant convolvulus. For pretty effect it can be trained around the doorway of the conservatory (Fig. 6.6) where it will not mind draughts and a bit of knocking about.

### Thunbergia and Rhodochiton

*Thunbergia alata*, blackeyed Susan, and *Rhodochiton atrosanguineus*, purple bellerine, can be put to use in much the same way, and will not be difficult to raise from seed down in warm conditions in early spring.

bond the plant to the wall with no need for further support. In the larger conservatory the bold leaves of *Hedera algeriensis* (syn. *H. canariensis*) could well be a useful plant, but this one will need to be tied in as it progresses. The leaves are very bright green and white in colour, but the plant has a nasty habit of attracting red spider mites which will be a disadvantage.

## Monstera

For clothing the walls of the conservatory there is much to be said for the use of bold green foliage as a background. Foliage will be really lush and glossy green if plants are free planted in a border or display bed of rich soil.

The very ordinary cheese plant *Monstera deliciosa*, becomes a totally different plant to those often offered for sale as house plants. When planted in warm and moist conditions the plant will soon show its gratitude by developing stiff glossy leaves that will at first be deeply cut along their margins, soon to be followed by natural perforations extending from the midrib (Fig. 6.7).

## Philodendron

There are also the many wonderful philodendrons with larger leaves, plants such as *P. hastatum* that will fill the upper reaches of the conservatory with its magnificent arrowheaded leaves that are soft green and attached to stout petioles. These will all need a solid framework to which growth can be attached as it progresses. The monstera and the philodendrons all belong to the family, Araceae, and are usually referred to as aroids. These are true jungle plants that will thrive in conditions that are warm, humid and shaded. They will also like lots of water and frequent feeding while in active growth. When these requirements are properly attended to the conservatory will have a really full, jungle feeling that will please every plantsman who visits.

## Pyrostegia

Finally, a climber that will clamber through the upper reaches of a high-ceilinged conservatory, producing clustered orange coloured flowers over a very long period of time is *Pyrostegia venusta*, flame vine. It will be difficult to acquire, but if you find one, plant it in a prepared bed in agreeable conditions and offer it supporting wires. It will then be on its way up into the light to become one of your prize plant possessions.

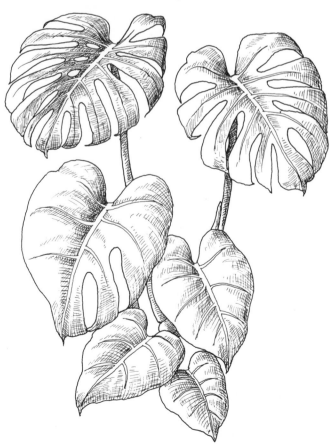

**Fig. 6.7** The cheese plant, *Monstera*, is an old favourite but still one of the most majestic of the larger plants when carefully grown.

## CHAPTER 7

# *Hanging and Trailing Plants*

When completed and standing empty the larger conservatory will seem a vast area, but it is surprising to see just how quickly the space is utilized as fresh plants are brought in. You come to the stage eventually whereby you are wondering where everything is going to find a home. Hanging them up is a good suggestion! Provided the ceiling is of adequate height, this space can be used for all sorts of plants. While climbing plants provide a frame for other plants in the conservatory, it could be said that the hanging plants become the top edge of the picture frame.

You can grow almost anything in baskets and containers if they are of sufficient size and they are properly cared for. If you feel the urge you can grow cabbages, rhubarb, even tomato plants in hanging containers, but something more decorative is obviously more interesting.

### Anchorage

An important requirement for suspended plants is a secure anchorage; a collection of baskets when filled with soil and wet from watering will be of considerable weight. Stringing a few wires from one side of the conservatory to the other will not be the answer as wire will sag with the weight of containers. Provision for hanging containers can be made at the building stage. This could, for example, consist of slim metal rods that are fitted north/south and east/west so that a squared pattern of supports is provided (Fig. 7.1). These can be painted to match the colour scheme of the interior. Many containers can then be hung and displayed at their best at almost any point within the building.

Hanging containers of all kinds are becoming increasingly popular for decorating walls and patios around the home, but most of these containers are very badly displayed. Often the brackets are fixed much too high, making proper maintenance in the way of watering, feeding and general cleaning almost impossible, or they are hung like soldiers on parade in uninteresting, straight lines.

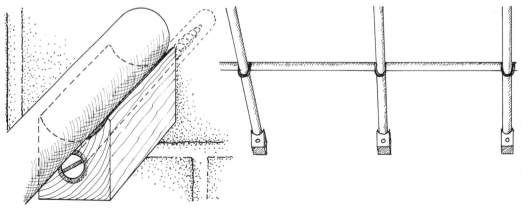

**Fig. 7.1** For climbers and in particular for decorative hanging baskets an overhead framework of thin metal rods attractively painted will prove to be a worthwhile consideration when building work is nearing completion.

If a secure overhead framework is fitted there will be no need in the conservatory to worry about the 'regimented' look, as it will be possible to hang containers just about anywhere. However, you will need to hang them out of the way of the general flow of people who are using the building. They do not all have to be hung at or above head level. Many of the semi-hanging plants, such as *Begonia* Tiger are very much more attractive when you look down on their leaves rather than look up at the bottom of the container that is holding the plant, so lower the plant to a level where it can be better appreciated. There is no reason why some should not be down almost to floor level if they are not interfering with other plants.

Fittings offered for suspending hanging plants are frequently large and consist of ugly white plastic chains. Fittings and fixtures for displaying suspended plants should be as un-obtrusive as possible — the plants ought to be the attraction. One of the least obtrusive of all is anglers' fishing line. Choose clear nylon with a high breaking strain and although it may stretch a little, it will be capable of anchoring baskets of almost any size. The nice thing about fishing line is that it is virtually invisible amongst the plants.

The alternative to festooning the centre area is to use wall space for displaying baskets. Do this by fixing wall brackets from which baskets can be suspended, but not in straight lines like soldiers. Brackets can be secured at various heights so that when the baskets are placed in position you have a virtual wall of colour. Baskets can be hung from top to bottom of the wall so that maximum use is made of the available space.

If you do not want to use the walls and ceiling but at the same time wish to enjoy the pleasures that a well filled and colourful hanging basket can bring, place the basket on a pedestal that has been specially made for this purpose. A benefit with this style of display is that it will be portable and easy to move around from one location to another. This is an important aspect of plants in conserv-atories — you can simply move them from the sun to shade if it is very hot, or they can be taken out altogether if the room is needed for some other purpose than the display of plants.

## Containers

Diehard gardeners will tell you that there is nothing to match a moss-lined wire hanging basket when it comes to growing trailing plants. This may well apply as far as plants growing out of doors are concerned, but they are a bit of a nuisance for conservatory interiors. One difficulty is that water runs straight through the moss and makes a mess everywhere, and another is that such baskets are much too heavy for internal use. Worst of all, until they are well furbished with growth, these mossed baskets can be very unattractive.

Plastic baskets in their many designs and colours are far more appealing when hanging in the conservatory, with the considerable advantage that they do not dry out nearly so quickly as mossed baskets. For those who cannot bring themselves to handle plastic containers, try putting the plastic container in a woven hanging basket (Fig. 7.2). These are reasonably priced, most coming from China, very attractive and more compatible with the plants. When seen from a sitting position these natural baskets have much to commend them. It is best to choose those that are already equipped with a plastic liner.

## Planting baskets

Planting up is best done in the greenhouse, garage or shed rather than in the conservatory. The first step is to choose a colour theme that will complement the surroundings. Most of the plastic containers will have some sort of drip tray attached and it is wise to remove these before any planting is attempted, otherwise the saucer fills with soil and becomes very messy. These saucers are there to collect surplus water draining through the holes in the bottom of the container, but it is important not to have sauc-ers permanently filled with water. The soil in the container can become waterlogged with the result that roots rot and die. The container should be allowed to drain for a time following watering but it is then essential to hold the bas-ket slightly to one side so that surplus water can be disposed of.

### Soil choice

Soil is almost the most important factor as far as the plants are concerned, and must be

**Fig. 7.2 Hanging baskets.** The need for careful preparation when preparing and planting baskets will prove to be time well spent when the season gets under way.

chosen with care if the plants are to prosper over the season — certain evergreen plants could be in the same hanging container for several years. Preparing your own potting mixture is really a task for the enthusiast. Most people can visit the garden shop and specify soil for hanging containers so that the right mixture is supplied. Soil manufacturers now produce a hanging basket soil mix that will contain slow-release fertilizer and possibly chemicals with water-absorbing qualities that will prevent the soil drying out too rapidly.

Plants that go into soil containing slow-release fertilizer will generally grow better than plants in a standard mixture. This type of fertilizer acts as a buffer and becomes available to the plants over a long period of time, but it does not mean that feeding with a conventional liquid fertilizer should be neglected. However, it must be said that many plants in baskets fail, not from lack of feed, but because they are given far too much. It pays to read the directions on the packet or bottle and to follow these rather than take chances with hit and miss doses.

**Planting up**

The best way to plant containers is to secure the container first in a larger pot and fill it with the chosen potting mixture — the soil should be moist but not too wet. The plants should all be watered before they are firmly planted in the

*a*  *b*

**Fig. 7.3 Potting plants on.** Avoid damage to plants such as saintpaulia by making a mould with the pot that the plant is being removed from – follow this by simply placing the rootball in the prepared hole.

mixture. Planting may be easier for the less experienced person by removing the growing pot from the plant and potting this. The pot is subsequently removed to leave a perfectly shaped hole into which the plant can be dropped and firmed into position (Fig. 7.3). This is a much simpler method when potting plants such as begonias which have lots of brittle leaves hanging over the sides of their containers.

**Watering**
The next step is to place the planted container still in its supporting pot, on the floor so that it can be thoroughly watered—this will mean using a fine rose to go over the top of the plants several times at intervals. One application of water from the rose will simply wet the leaves and the surface of the soil; it takes some time before water is absorbed by the soil. so that there is sufficient to penetrate through to soil at a lower level.

Ideally, following planting, the unit should stand in a greenhouse at floor level away from the sun for several days to settle down before being hung in its final position. During this interim stage one should go over the plant several times with a fine rose — this may be necessary several times during sunny days. When you are ready to position it in the conservatory, it is important to check that the linkage, chain or plastic, is in good order and properly fitted. It may be necessary to replace the plastic fitting with something that is more robust — plastic covered wire for example.

**Care of baskets**
Care of baskets in the conservatory will require an initial step of ensuring that plants are afforded adequate protection from the sun which can be very damaging to the plants that are closest to the glass. Where it is practical, the protection ought to be in the form of a screen that can be drawn back at times when the sun is not presenting a problem. Although hanging plants do not want to be scorched by the sun's rays, it is essential for the majority that they should have good light in which to

grow. The ideal is to provide dappled shade that will filter the rays of the sun but at the same time offer plants ample light.

Suitable plants for growing in hanging containers can be found in all temperature ranges, with the more delicate kinds in the warmer section — the older gardener will still refer to these as stove plants, plants for really warm and humid conditions. However, with the need to economize all round on heating many of the plants previously thought of as stove plants will, in fact, tolerate lower temperature levels provided it is not very cold.

Anyone who finds it difficult to water hanging plants can attach the containers to a spring pulley which allows the container to be lowered to more manageable level.

## Choosing plants

Hanging containers chosen for the interior of the conservatory should not be too large, putting everything out of balance. Baskets filled with hanging lobelia, *Helichrysum peltatum*, pelargonium, fuchsias etc., are fine for the outside of the house but they seem to have little place in a confined space. Often the best effects in the conservatory are achieved by simply planting the container with one plant variety in preference to a collection.

Shortage of suitable plants is not a problem. As mentioned earlier it is perfectly possible to grow marble-sized tomatoes, which are a lot of fun, but baskets with vegetables need to be large and they also require a lot of attention in respect of watering and feeding.

### Tradescantia

Avoid the more delicate plants until some experience has been gained. Some of the easiest and among the most satisfying trailing plants are the tradescantias — these can be both propagated and grown with little difficulty. Details are provided concerning their general care in the A–Z section, so here the only comments will relate to their conservatory treatment. Light is essential but not strong sun as the leaves of these plants are very thin and easily scorched. The most difficult time for them will be the winter months when growth will have slowed down considerably; this is an indication that watering should be much re-

duced and feeding should stop. In baskets these are generally plants that do well for one season only, so fresh plants should be made from cuttings taken at the turn of the year.

### Ivies

Ivies in the cold or cool conservatory will be fine for the winter months and are available in many attractive colours; in particular some of the variegated forms will give an excellent display throughout the year.

### Campanula

In the same cool and light conditions, *Campanula isophylla* in both blue and white colouring, will be a superb hanging plant, but it must have dead flowers regularly removed. With large plants this could well be a daily task, one that can be tedious but it will have its rewards.

### Begonia

In the middle range of temperature, there are many fine plants that can be planted as individuals in containers of modest size. A very attractive plant in this group is *Begonia sutherlandii* which must be one of the most accommodating of plants when it comes to propagation. If it is suspended over a tray of gravel or soil it will drop seed, pieces of stem, small corms and all of them will sprout into growth in the spring of the following year when potted up. The stems are not fully pendulous, but the plant produces a mass of pale green foliage, the weight of which will make the stems sag to give a pleasing effect in a basket. Keep them free of bright sun and there will be masses of lovely orange flowers right through the summer.

### Kalanchoë

For a small hanging container there is the succulent, *Kalanchoë pumila* which has silvered foliage all the year round and dusty pink flowers in the spring. Easy to propagate from cuttings, it will tolerate a wide variation of conditions, but for preference should be kept warm, in good light and never too wet at its roots. *K. blossfeldiana* 'Tessa' produces masses of small orange-coloured bell flowers during the summer months.

## Columnea

In very much the same category are the columneas, *C. × banksii* in particular, but these should not be dry at their roots other than in December and January when a slightly cooler temperature of around 10°C (55°F) and dryer soil conditions will encourage them to flower more freely. When this one flowers well it is one of the finest flowering subjects during the first months of the year.

## Fuchsias

Fuchsias must be among the best of all flowering plants for baskets, and they will tolerate varying conditions. Bright and prolonged sunlight will be a very definite discouragement in respect of flower production, so light shade must be provided. They should be well watered and fed with a tomato fertilizer through the summer; if the dead flowers are regularly removed they will go on flowering for very much longer. There are innumerable varieties, but one should specify that plants are wanted for hanging containers when purchases are being made.

## Episcia

There are lovely basket plants in the more delicate range for the conservatory with ample heating, adequate shading and knowledgeable care. One of the best in this respect is *Episcia cupreata* which has attractive green and silver mottled leaves trailing gracefully, augmented later by the presence of bright red flowers. It will need warm and shaded conditions with careful watering. There is a much easier species, *E. dianthiflora* (now reclassified as *Alsobia dianthiflora*) with the common name of snowflake plant, which relates to the unusual shape of the flower. This one can be grown by anyone and it propagates with ease.

## Chlorophytum

One of the most useful plants either for a wall unit or a hanging pot is the chlorophytum, the spider plant, with bright green and cream

**Fig. 7.4** The tried and trusted spider plant (*Chlorophytum*) is excellent value in many situations, particularly when specimens are seen growing in hanging containers.

variegated grass leaves and baby plants that will hang down to become very decorative (Fig. 7.4). Complaints are often made about these plants not developing their baby plants, but once they have been planted into a larger container with fresh soil from the small pot in which they were purchased they will very soon put on new growth and have their babies at the same time. The reason for non-production of the latter is nothing more than starvation—feed them well and the right result will be almost guaranteed.

# CHAPTER 8

# *Displaying Your Plants*

This aspect of conservatory gardening probably gives the owner more pleasure than any other, with the possible exception of having raised and maintained healthy plants in the first place, but it is not everyone who knows what is required when putting a few plants together in order to improve the appearance of the interior of the conservatory. There are many skills involved in the effective display of indoor plants.

The first of these is to understand that the plants need to be seen when placed on display. It is surprising the number of conservatories that will be arranged with the greatest care only to have the plants disappear from sight when the chairs and tables are returned to the scene. If space in the conservatory is limited it is only taller and more slender plants that will be effective when placed at floor level — very small plants will be totally inappropriate as they will never be seen.

Another aspect of display that is frequently ignored is that of change — in the department store window there is continual change in order to catch the eye of the would-be customer. The display person in the store is only too well aware that if the same old merchandise is left on view for months on end the window will die and no one will bother to look. It is not suggested that one should have a display window in the conservatory, but if the plants are periodically relocated they will create a great deal more interest. However, it is not wise to be continually moving plants around, as many of them will settle to particular locations where they seem ideally to fit. Very large and unwieldy plants and plants that are growing through a framework on the wall cannot be easily moved, but these will provide the background for any display that is considered and ought to remain in position. It is the smaller pots which will add variety.

## Balance

Getting the right balance with plants in larger displays is also important, with a need to gauge the height of taller plants so that they are in harmony with the smaller plants that are placed near the front of the finished array.

The chosen selection of plants will contribute almost more than anything to the display — you need rounded plants like the Boston fern, slender and colourful plants such as the many variegated dracaenas that are available, and bolder anchor plants that will set off the rear or centre of the display. The latter can be chosen from philodendrons, ficus, palms or heptapleurums which will offer either green or variegated foliage. The specimen, or mature plants are generally better if they are green in colour so helping to set off brighter plants that are placed in front of them.

One should try to avoid complicated displays as plants are simple things that do not require too much fussing over in order to be effective. When arranging plants you should not crowd them in too much — give them room to breathe and they will look and grow very much better. Any props that may be utilized to set off the plants should also be simple rather than complicated, and of natural material that will blend in more readily with the plant selection.

The display ought to be interesting enough for the visitor to ask questions about the various plants that are there. This will mean shopping around to locate different bromeliads, dracaenas, calatheas and such like, all of which will be found in a good garden shop.

## Colour

Colour is very much a personal aspect with plants of brighter colouring being chosen so that they blend in with the furnishings of the conservatory in many instances. Although it is pleasing to see colours being used that go well together this aspect is not desperately important if a reasonable number of foliage plants can be used to tone down the brighter colours of flowering plants. In fact, flowering plants can be very effectively used to create the changes that were mentioned earlier. Do this by arranging the flowering plants in groups, in a large bowl perhaps, so that the flowers that have passed their best can be removed and easily replaced by fresh flowers that can be of different species as well as being of different colouring.

## Overhead and wall space

The simple approach will be the best in small garden rooms, particularly where there is a solid floor. Simple in this context means utilizing a selection of containers that will be interspersed amongst the furniture that the plants will be expected to live with. In the smaller room it is almost essential that the overhead and the wall space should be put to use as this is where the greatest amount of available space will be. There is a wide selection of both easy and difficult plants available for this purpose as far as plant care goes. See the selection mentioned in Chapter 7.

When the conservatory is being constructed recesses could be built in any large area of brick wall that is part of the building. These recesses can be set at different levels and can be arranged so that there is a sill protruding from the wall in order to accommodate pots of reasonable size (Fig. 8.1). A varied selection of flowering and foliage plants can be used, and those that trail. Such an arrangement will be clean and effective, and a little different. In such a situation, decorative ceramic pots of varied design and colouring will come into their own.

## Floor space

In limited space some of the best plants for placing at floor level will be those that are growing in 8 cm (7 in) pots, most being a little over 1 m (3 ft) in height when seen at the plant

Fig. 8.1 For smaller decorative plants, wall shelves are ideal and should preferably be built in during construction rather than added on as an afterthought.

**Fig. 8.2 Decorative pedestals.** (*a*) Hanging containers can often be more effective when placed on a pedestal stand that is designed with baskets in mind. (*b*) A more conventional pedestal stand.

shop. The selection of plants in this particular size is very extensive, so there should be little problem when it comes to choice. The great favourites for providing the exotic touch are the palms, the kentia palm in particular. Be warned, however, this needs minimum temperature of at least 16°C (61°F), and it should be shaded from bright sun. Much less demanding and tolerating cool conditions if the soil in the pot is not too wet are the scheffleras, the parasol plant, available in both green and variegated forms. There are many attractive containers that will suit plants in this size of pot, many of them on stands which will provide a pedestal effect giving the plant a more important appearance when it is placed in position. Pedestals (Fig. 8.2) are also useful for hanging or trailing plants; they can be of various sizes, but do ensure that they stand firmly and, once planted up, are not top-heavy and liable to topple over when brushed against.

**Troughs and trays**

Larger troughs and trays are available in a wide range of colours and materials and these can be very effective when planted either with a selection of different sorts of plant or with plants of all one variety and colour such as begonias or chrysanthemums (Fig. 8.3).

Large, shallow trays can have gravel placed in the bottom before they are filled with saintpaulias, kalanchoes, impatiens or other small flowering plants. Grouped together in this manner plants will grow better if the gravel is kept moist and they will provide a bolder, more eye-catching display.

**Grouping**

In small or large rooms, an alternative to baskets on the wall could be shelves or windowboxes that are put to a different use. The windowbox can be planted with a selection of smaller plants with ivies spilling over the front and the shelf can simply accommodate plants in decorative pots. This sort of approach will increase the number of plants that one can have in the room but, importantly, it will not result in loss of valuable floor space. In similar fashion, any table can be used for standing plants on: at raised level, plants will be easier to care for, and will grow and also look better.

## The planted border

The planted border is perhaps an old-fashioned term in respect of the modern conservatory, as the border was generally associated with the greenhouse rather than the sort of leisure room that the conservatory has now become. It simply means that a border is left around the perimeter of the conservatory that can be planted up with decorative plants. If there are to be beds or borders accommodating plants that are taken out of their pots to be placed in the soil, then one should best think about this before the building is constructed. Otherwise it might be found that the builder has concreted over the entire floor area.

**Fig. 8.3** In numerous shapes and made from many different materials, troughs large and small will prove both decorative and useful for plant groupings.

The border could well be planned as an integral part of the conservatory design; it should be dug over during the building phase — a task that would be frowned upon once the building has been completed! The border can also be given a more finished look by constructing a

93

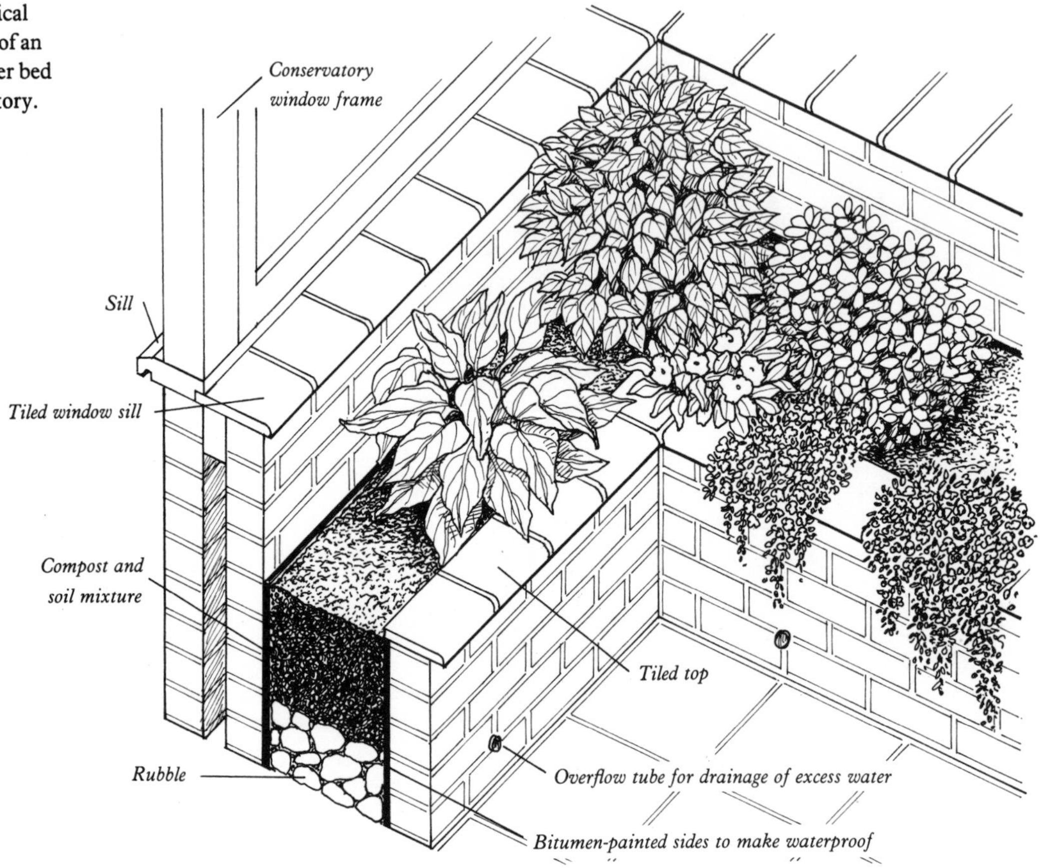

**Fig. 8.4** Typical construction of an integral border bed in a conservatory.

*Conservatory window frame*

*Sill*

*Tiled window sill*

*Compost and soil mixture*

*Rubble*

*Tiled top*

*Overflow tube for drainage of excess water*

*Bitumen-painted sides to make waterproof*

low retaining wall made from attractive stone or brick (Fig. 8.4).

## Corner beds

Should a border along the side of the room appear too formal there is the possibility of utilizing the dead corners, those that are away from the normal two doors that the conservatory will have fitted. The corner bed can be organized in very much the same way as the straight border with well prepared soil and a retaining wall along the front (Fig. 8.4). This arrangement will usually require one large plant at the back of the bed, two or three intermediate plants in the centre with a selection of

lower and trailing plants to the front.

An alternative to filling the beds and borders with prepared soil and removing the pots from the plants before planting is to dispense with the soil idea and to infill the space behind the retaining wall with gravel. A good depth of gravel provides an attractive surface and the bed will hold moisture which is important to the plants. The principal benefit is that the plants are not fixtures, with the result that they can be moved around to change the scene at any time. Also, the plants will grow more slowly which can be an advantage when there is not a lot of space available. In the gravel bed it will be inevitable that plants will root through the bottom of their pots and into the gravel, so it is necessary periodically to lift the pot from the gravel so that the roots can either be removed or drawn back into the pot. Loss of a small amount of root as a result of this exercise will not be harmful, but larger roots may well cause leaf drop if they are cut through. The answer to the latter problem is to make more frequent checks to ensure that roots of this kind are not developing. Many of the species of fig that one will use for display are very prone to producing an extensive root system through the bottom of the pot, *Ficus benjamina* and its numerous varieties in particular. These are all plants that will shed leaves, often alarmingly when their roots are cut. Growing in very poor light is a further reason for these plants shedding leaves — something they may also be inclined to do if they are moved around too much.

### Suitable plants

A border of this kind will be extremely valuable for growing all sorts of interesting and colourful plants. The plants selected can be a combination of permanent and temporary plants — the latter can be annuals raised in your own greenhouse, or flowering plants that are purchased from the plant retailer. The last option will be the more expensive, but will present a great deal less bother and the plants will probably be fuller and of better quality. In fact, some of the potted flowering plants can become permanent if one is prepared to see them without flowers for spells during the course of the year.

Kalanchoë in its numerous flower colours is such a plant — something that can be purchased at little cost in a small pot at almost any time throughout the year. If planted in good soil and placed in reasonable light the tiny plant will quite quickly produce stout stems and lots of new growth that in time will become a very fine flowering specimen that will be comparatively easy to care for.

You could purchase a poinsettia plant in its pot, bearing colourful bracts, and plant it in the border once the bracts have shattered and fallen. This is a plant that prefers to be warm and growing in good light; you might discover that it actually grows too well, as it is a very vigorous subject when given a free root run in a good growing medium. Encouraging the plant to produce its colourful bracts in the conservatory might also present difficulties, but worth trying if space permits.

Ivies and *Ficus pumila*, the creeping fig, can be used in the border to spill over the retaining wall and to fill in between other plants; they might in time reach the wall where they will climb by clinging on with their natural roots to form a nice background for other plants. These will need virtually no attention other than the removal of any growth that is appearing where it is not wanted.

Old-fashioned plants that will get on very well in the cool room offering good light are the scented-leaved pelargoniums, *P.* 'Lady Plymouth' in particular having scented variegated foliage that will grow with great freedom when planted out in good soil. Also for the border there are a great number of plants that come under the banner of houseplants. These are available in all garden shops, but one should ascertain their temperature requirements before purchasing just to ensure that they come within the minimum that one can reasonably expect to maintain.

## Water features

Whatever the size of your conservatory there is usually room for a small pool of some sort. It does not have to be a conventional pond. It can be any shape or size, integrated into a raised bed or a true 'feature' in the centre of a conservatory. The only hard and fast rule is that the water must be kept moving, thus aerated by means of a small pump to prevent excessive growth of algae. The pool must clearly be watertight, so whatever material you choose to form the pool, e.g. butyl liner or preformed plastic, do ensure it is of good quality that will not deteriorate or split with the passage of time. If space is limited you can use a larger watertight trough; the only critical measurement is its depth as the smallest pumps need 20 cm (8 in) of water to perform efficiently (Fig. 8.5). Other than depth, the only specific information you need is that the base of the container should rest on a stable material such as sand or gravel so that it does not shift.

Fountains and waterfalls are a personal matter but, in any event, this aspect should not be overdone. A still pool that reflects the foliage of the plants that surround it can be much more soothing and attractive than continual splashing water.

### Fountains

One of the simplest ways of putting water to use very easily and effectively is to include a free-standing fountain within the plant display, or in isolation if need be (Fig. 8.6). Such features ought to be of reasonable size and height to give them more importance. These come in sections that can be very easily assembled on site by willing hands. The best of these fountains will have a large lower dish that acts as a sump where water drains back into from the upper levels. A small electric pump is

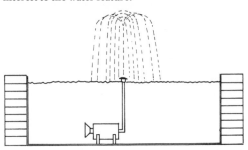

**Fig. 8.6** A free-standing fountain in the pool adds interest to the water feature.

**Fig. 8.5** Construction of a small pool feature for the conservatory. Such a pool will provide useful humidity for the plants.

96

A 'warm house' provides a secure environment
for many varieties which we regard as 'house'
plants. Correctly cared for they will seem to grow
before your eyes.

*Opposite:* Although the jasmine family do not flower over a sustained period many will feel their inclusion a necessity if only for the scent that they provide.

*Plumbago capensis* is not for the tidy minded, but if you are seeking flowers over a long season, this is the plant for you.

*Above:* Trailing fuchsia flowers for many months over spring and summer. Remove dead flowers regularly to encourage fresh blooms.

The beauty and permanence of plants grown purely for their foliage is often overlooked and ivies look good where ever they are planted.

*Tradescantia
fluminensis
variegata*. Ideal
hanging plants
with silvered
foliage throughout
the year – pinch
out leading shoots
to encourage
compact growth.

102

*Opposite: Columnea gloriosa* 'Purpurea'. Something of a challenge to grow, these are spectacular trailing plants for the heated and shaded conservatory.

A raised pool is an easier option than one made by digging into the floor; also it offers more interesting possibilities by way of shape.

Where space is available a pool of warm water with water and marginal plants is an instant attraction.

Plant display. Given adequate space there are many interesting and colourful options when one contemplates conservatory decoration with a varied plant selection.

located in the sump for recirculating the water which tumbles gently from one level to the next, almost soundlessly.

A feature such as a fountain can be decorated around the base with a selection of plants that will not be too demanding on available space. The area for the fountain should be chosen and a large sheet of strong polythene placed on the floor to extend well beyond the base area of the fountain. The fountain is then positioned (not forgetting supply of electricity) and a small tropical garden is created around it. Bricks or stone walling can be utilized as a retaining wall inside which prepared soil can be placed. At the front the soil should only be as deep as the depth of a 13 cm (5 in) pot. The importance of this is that when plants in their pots are set in position the pots will not be visible, thus giving the garden a natural appearance.

The planting around the fountain will be a matter of personal choice but try not to overdo it. Let all the plants have space in which to thrive.

### Decorating with plants

Once you have installed your water feature, you could really extend your plant range. In a really large heated pool you could grow the queen of tropical water plants, *Victoria amazonica* (syn. *A. regia*), which produces floating, circular leaves reaching up to 1.5 m (5 ft) in diameter. The plant flowers at night and over three nights the colouring changes from white through pink to red. Another surprising feature of the plant is that sown annually in late winter and given a high temperature, its spread of floating leaves may be as much as 10 m (32 ft) in one year. If this is too big for you, perhaps marginal planting around a 1.5 m (5 ft) diameter pool is more realistic!

Ferns of all sorts will love the moist warm atmosphere found beside such a pool, and the interesting *Cyperus* will grow well either in or out of the water.

### Growing cases

Plant growing cases will also add much interest, as these can be used for growing the sort of plants that might not take too readily to the large, and often cool conditions that prevail

**Fig. 8.7** A growing case with controlled separate temperature is useful for more tender plants in the conservatory that is otherwise inadequately heated.

through the night in the conservatory. The growing case is nothing more than a small heated greenhouse within the conservatory, the case being as decorative or as simple as you like (Fig. 8.7).

Some of these are very well designed and built, using aluminium and glass as their main constituents. Ideally, these cases should stand some 2 m (6 ft) tall with three shelves for plants. For added effect the rear of each shelf is fitted with a mirror that will reflect the plants to make it seem that there are twice as many. Each of the three shelves is closed in and has a strip light that is fitted to the underside of the upper shelf to provide sufficient light for plants to grow — in poorly lit locations, the light ought to be left on for at least 12 hours each day.

To maintain temperature it is also necessary to fit all units with a small electric heater, often to the undersides of the shelves on which the plants are standing so that they are not too obtrusive. This will also ensure that the plants placed on the shelf above will get maximum benefit from the heater. Shelves should ideally have a layer of gravel for plants to stand on so the gravel and the roots of the plants will also be kept warm.

Any of the smaller plants, such as fittonias, will benefit considerably from this sort of treatment, but the plant that will be sure to catch attention is the *Saintpaulia* (African violet). These are plants that adore warmth and light conditions. They will also flower very much better. With a growing case of this kind it will not be long before you are converted to becoming a *Saintpaulia* specialist. These are very bright and rewarding plants, but they do need careful watering — this means watering the soil well with tepid water and then waiting until the leaves feel just limp to the touch before repeating the exercise. Hygienic conditions will also be necessary, which will entail almost daily cleaning away of any dead flowers and leaves that may be present.

Cases of this kind can also be made of wood, and if this is given a bright coat of white paint it might well prove more satisfactory than a metal construction that will tend to be colder. Tiered shelves that are both warm and light will also provide an almost perfect propagator, which will allow you to indulge in a few experiments with snipped off cuttings. If these are firm and from healthy plants there should be no problem in getting them to root. Insert them in clean peat or in a houseplant soil if they are easily rooted subjects such as ivies or tradescantias.

# CHAPTER 9

# *Pests and Diseases*

Pests are more numerous during the spring and summer months of the year when there are fresh and tender shoots and leaves available for them to feed on. Over the winter months in the warm conservatory, pests such as aphids and whitefly will remain active, but in greatly reduced numbers, while others will hibernate in the soil or in other areas where they will obtain protection from the elements.

Where they come from is often asked by the conservatory owner. Many will be in the garden over the summer months and will transfer to the warmer conditions in the autumn to become troublesome pests when weather conditions improve from spring onwards. In the warm conservatory, pests such as red spider mites and whitefly can increase very rapidly at this time of the year if they are allowed to go unchecked.

Not all pests find their way in from the garden — many of them are bought-in with plants by the owner of the conservatory, or they are actually donated by a well meaning acquaintance. The ones that are actually purchased may come with the plant from the garden shop, but this is not now so common. With modern methods today's commercial grower has much better control over pests. There are stringent rules concerning pest control, in operation throughout the year. Plants leaving commercial premises will invariably be free of problems. Gifts of plants from friends will help fill the gaps in your plant collection, but it is better to refuse all gifts of this kind as any that are accepted will have to go on display to please the donor. Plants with serious pest problems will be very difficult to clean up. Adult bugs and offspring will be in various stages of development. It is best to dispose of sickly looking plants otherwise the pests will transfer their attentions to other plants in the conservatory.

**Fig. 9.1** Regular inspection for the presence of pests is most essential, paying particular attention to the undersides of leaves.

Any plant that is bought or donated should be carefully inspected for problems. Particular attention should be given to the undersides of leaves and to the softer growth at the growing points on the plant. It would not be too drastic for every new plant introduced to be treated carefully with a general fungicide and insecticide as a precautionary measure before it is placed anywhere near other plants in the conservatory.

Attention to general hygiene is one way of discouraging pests, and this means that the area around your plants must be regularly cleaned so that there are no convenient places for pests and diseases to thrive.

When dealing with pests it is of considerable importance to ensure that spraying of leaves, or any control measure, is done thoroughly. For example, when spraying plants with insecticide to discourage red spider mites and whitefly, it is extremely important to ensure that the undersides of the leaves of the plants are given the most attention as this is where almost all of those pests will be (Fig. 9.1). To spray a few misty droplets of insecticide on the upper surface of the foliage will do no good — you must make direct contact with the pests. Even then you may need second or third treatments.

## A-Z of pests

*Aphids* are among the most common of pests and are usually referred to as greenfly, but they may appear as black, orange or grey leaf-sucking pests. These can multiply alarmingly if left to their own devices, but it is fortunate that they are relatively easy to control, a wide range of insecticides being available for this purpose. Aphids are mostly to be found on the tips of new growth which are soft and easy for the greenfly to probe into.

*Caterpillars* are infrequent visitors to the conservatory but they can cause a lot of damage by eating leaves should they appear in numbers. There will generally be only the odd few about and these can be picked from the plant by hand.

*Eelworm* is a soil pest that the amateur grower is not often confronted with as the worms are so small they are very difficult to detect. Unexplained brown patches on the leaves of chrysanthemums, for example, could be an indication of their presence. If the roots of suspect plants are examined, the sign to look for is unnatural swelling of the roots. Immediate disposal of the affected plant is the best action, but this is not a very troublesome pest as far as plants in pots are concerned as they are all potted into clean soil that should be free of problems of this kind.

*Fungus gnats* or sciarid fly are very different from eelworms and do little or no damage. They are, however, an indication that the soil in the pots is sour and probably in need of replacement. The flies will be seen jumping around on the surface of the soil. Their maggots eat the softer roots. Thorough soaking of soil with a solution of Malathion insecticide should be sufficient but do this job out of doors as this insecticide has a very unpleasant odour.

*Leafminer* explains itself; it is a pest that burrows its way through the leaves of plants, leaving a cream-coloured pattern where the pest has been at work. They spoil the appearance of leaves but, unless present in large numbers, they are not too much of a problem. They have preference for particular plants, such as cinerarias and chrysanthemums.

*Mealy bug* is quite another matter as it is destructive and very messy when present in large numbers. The adult bugs have the appearance of woodlice that have acquired a white powdery coating as a result of strolling through a bowl of flour. Unlike woodlice which live on rotting matter, mealy bugs find their way into all sorts of nooks and crannies on all manner of plants in order to suck the life out of them. In the stephanotis, for example, they infest the areas where the twining stems encircle one another. These twining stems tend to be well above head level and out of sight with the result that the bugs often establish a very firm foothold before their presence is detected; this is a good reason for getting the steps out periodically to check that bugs are not present. A further indication of their presence is a black sooty deposit on the leaves underneath those where the pests are actually active. The sooty mould is a fungus that feeds on the excreta of the bugs and in itself is not damaging to the plant, but should be cleaned off with a damp cloth if only to improve the appearance of the plant. The eradication of the bugs is a very different matter as they seem able to find the most impenetrable areas of the plant with the result that contact with an insecticide becomes very difficult. Malathion is recommended for their control and although effective in a greenhouse situation where you can spray the plants then close the door and leave them to it, in the conservatory the smell of Malathion would seem to be a problem. The alternative solution is more laborious — use a cloth that has been soaked in methylated spirit or in derris solution, to wipe the leaves and stems of the plant clean. For the more difficult areas an old toothbrush soaked in one of these solutions can be used to get into the crevices to clean them out. The main difficulty is that the adults wrap their young in a waxy cotton wool-like substance that is almost impossible to penetrate with an insecticide.

*Red spider mites* are mostly flesh coloured when viewed under a magnifying glass, which immediately presents a touch of confusion. There is, however, no confusion regarding the amount of damage they inflict on a very wide range of plants both indoors and out. They favour hot and dry conditions and will multiply at a fast rate if left. Signs of their presence are brown discoloration of foliage and eventually webs appear across the area between the leaves and stems at the top of the plant. If you have waited this long before taking any action then it is too late because there is no way that you are going to control an infestation of red spider at that stage. Badly infested plants should be burnt. The professional grower can detect the signs of red spider almost before they have begun to nibble at his plants, but this is an inborn skill that the amateur could not be expected to have. The alternative is to examine plants very frequently by inverting the plant pot and checking with a magnifying glass that minute spiders are not on the move on the undersides of leaves. Detected at this early stage, these pests can be controlled by frequent spraying with several insecticides recommended. If it is possible, you could damp down the floor of the conservatory and mist the upper and lower sides of foliage, particularly when the atmosphere is hot and dry.

*Root mealy bugs* are not very common. They can be present on the roots of many plants without the owner being aware of the fact. They seem to have a liking for cacti among other plants and their presence can be detected when plants are removed from their pots and a white, snowy deposit is seen on the inside of the pot. Closer inspection of the plant roots will show the bugs in the soil around the roots of the plant. The root bug is much smaller than its aerial counterpart and can be controlled by thoroughly soaking the soil with Malathion solution. The best way of doing this is to prepare the solution in a bucket and to wear rubber gloves when holding the pot submerged to ensure that every particle of the soil is wetted and that the bugs have their fill of Malathion. Cacti, incidentally, are also high on the list of plants favoured by the aerial types.

*Scale insects* are also dirty and unpleasant pests to have on the premises, and are found on the undersides of leaves and on the stems of numerous plants. The plant on which they will be seen most clearly is the bird's nest fern, *Asplenium nidus*, which has pale, glossy green leaves formed in the shape of a shuttlecock — the dark coloured scales will be evident near the midrib on both sides of the leaves. The adult scales are dark brown in colour and their young are paler, flesh-coloured. The scales can be wiped off the leaves using a cloth or sponge that has been soaked in one of the numerous insecticides recommended for dealing with these pests — it is advisable to wear rubber gloves when doing any job of this kind. These are insects that will also cause sooty mould to form on plant leaves and it is advisable to clean away the black deposit from the leaves of all plants as soon as it is seen. Scale insects are difficult to eradicate simply by spraying insecticide on to the leaves of infected plants, as the hard scale forms an almost impenetrable protective covering. In the early stages of their development the young scales are protected beneath the parent scale.

*Slugs* are not much of a problem and can easily be dealt with by hand. They thrive on dead vegetable matter so good hygiene is essential.

*Thrips* are becoming an increasing problem and are said to be one of the worst flower crop pests in North America where they are referred to as the Western flower thrip. These are very small creatures not unlike thunder flies in appearance, but they do extensive damage to many plants, including fuchsias and begonias. Thrips cause silver streaks to appear on the leaves of plants, but will mostly be found in the blooms. They are black in colour and their presence can be checked for by removing a flower and tapping it over the palm of the hand. If thrips are present they will drop readily onto your palm. Suspect plants should be removed from one's general collection and all the flowers should be taken from the plant and burnt. If insecticides are being used a check should be made to ensure that the product is claimed to be effective against these pests.

*Vine weevils* have become an increasing problem in recent years, for which there does not seem to be an easy solution. There are only female weevils and she makes her appearance from about early spring through to early summer when she is busily laying her eggs in pots or garden soil. The eggs hatch into grubs that are the principal problem, as they eat the roots of plants to such an extent that the plant will collapse and die. The plant beginning to wilt is the first indication of their presence, and if one removes the plant from its pot it will be found that there are a number of white grubs with brown heads curled up in the soil. You could be very unlucky and have as many as thirty of these in one pot of tuberous begonia, and you may find that they have not only eaten the roots but also the corm. The adults move only at night, and can be anywhere in the garden and surrounding buildings which makes control with insecticides impossible, the grubs being almost impossible to kill with available insecticides. Mixing recommended insecticide powder into the soil when potting will deter them, but the only sure way of disposing of grubs once you know they are present is to remove plants from their pots and to check meticulously through the soil to weed out and kill every grub. Repot the plant in fresh mixture. To be absolutely sure that all the grubs have been eradicated the roots of the plant should be washed free of every vestige of soil before repotting. To go out with a torch at night and catch the blackish-grey coloured adult when she is active is an exercise that is often recommended, but this will be a futile waste of time.

*Whitefly* is another very persistent pest. They increase at an alarming rate if efforts are not made to keep them under control. Fuchsias, for example, can be reduced to a black mess of leaves, almost sagging from the weight if nothing is done to control the fly. Hanging bright yellow stick cards around plants will reduce the numbers of whitefly by an estimated 30%, and will catch a wide assortment of beneficial and other insects at the same time. The best initial precaution is to inspect plants when acquiring and to reject any that show signs of either flies or their eggs on the undersides of leaves. New plants ought to be thoroughly sprayed on both sides of their leaves as an elementary precaution before placing them with other plants. In the spring you can invert pots of fuchsias and other easily handled plants to check for whitefly on the undersides of leaves. Squeezing any that are seen between a finger and thumb is a very effective way of killing these marauders. Every one that is killed in the spring will mean that there are several hundreds less later in the year — nip them in the bud should be the maxim! Regardless of your most assiduous attention there will still be whitefly, so it is necessary to treat your plants very frequently. Damping down and misting may help.

## Diseases

Diseases are not such a big problem with plants in the conservatory, but should be attended to when noticed.

*Powdery mildew* has the appearance of a filmy covering of snow on the leaves as the name suggests. Avoid buying plants that are seen to have this condition, and treat any mildew that may appear with a fungicide.

*Botrytis* is a mould that can affect many plants and is not unusual among the leaf stalks of cyclamen that have been growing in wet and airless conditions. Badly affected parts of plants should be removed and burnt and the remainder of the plants treated with a fungicide. Plants that are really bad should be carefully disposed of so that spores are not allowed to get into the atmosphere and infect other plants.

*Rust* on the undersides of fuchsia leaves could be a more serious problem that will quickly spread through plants and in time cause them to be defoliated. It forms in brown patches on the undersides of leaves, and when detected the best action is to remove all infected leaves and to burn them. Treat the remaining plant with fungicide. Fuchsias have wonderful powers of recovery and will soon refurbish themselves with clean leaves and a much better chance of surviving. Where rust, pests or whatever have been detected on plants it is wise to treat all the plants in the conservatory with the appropriate cure as a precautionary measure.

# CHAPTER 10
# *The Feeder Greenhouse*

The feeder greenhouse was the mainstay of the prestigous plant displays that were created in the Victorian conservatories where plants were much more important than the leisure aspect of these buildings. The Victorian conservatory was a show piece for plants, many of them gathered during sponsored plant hunting expeditions throughout the tropical world. Such plants were brought home by the plant-

hunting adventurers of the time and had to be jealously guarded and grown with meticulous care.

The same principle should apply today if one wishes to have attractive, on-going displays in the conservatory. When properly set up and maintained the greenhouse should be one of the most interesting features in the garden.

**Fig. 10.1 The feeder greenhouse.** There are many designs that one may choose from, but it is important to consider that adequate space is provided as there are often many plants to accommodate.

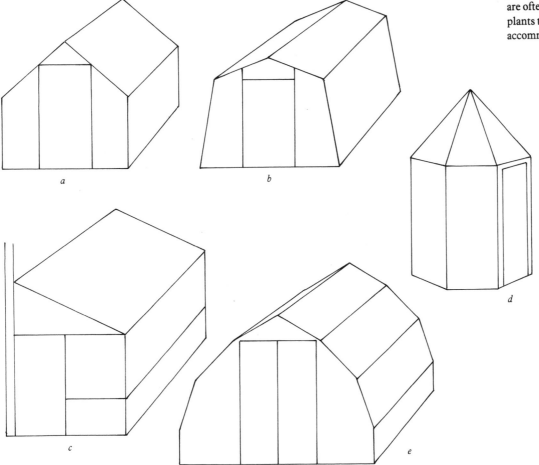

## Siting the greenhouse

The greenhouse should be close to the house so that water and electricity can be easily laid on, and essential jobs can be seen to. The house should be of good size and of good height to allow for hanging plants, and with capacity for

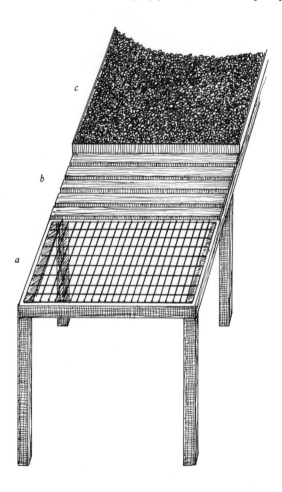

**Fig. 10.2 Greenhouse staging.** In the feeder greenhouse some form of staging is essential and staging ought to be selected with care to ensure that it is strong enough for the job and that it offers ample space for plants.
(a) Stout wire mesh. (b) Slats – usually timber.
(c) Shallow tray strewn with moisture-retaining material.

staging on both sides to ensure that one can accommodate a good number of plants (Fig. 10.1). Ensure that there are sound foundations. Placing the house under trees should be avoided, but the greenhouse can be set at any angle as it is going to be shaded from the sun for most of the year.

Once the greenhouse is erected, landscape the surrounding area by laying a few paving slabs all the way round, if possible. The slabs can then accommodate attractive pots of plants right through the year — colourful fuchsias and geraniums in the summer and hardier hebes and heathers in the winter.

The greenhouse should have ample ventilation from roof windows and side windows, and from double doors that can stand open in the summer. Double doors of this kind will afford visitors an immediate feeling of lushness when you show off your growing expertise, and double doors will make the movement of plants very much easier.

## Uses for the greenhouse

One thing that the greenhouse should not become is a dumping ground for near dead plants from the conservatory. These plants should be thrown away. Reviving sickly plants is not the easiest of tasks, and pests can be brought into the greenhouse thus totally undermining the concept behind the feeder greenhouse.

It is very much better to rotate plants on a more regular basis (obviously not the very large plants) so that plants do not lose their sparkle.

The greenhouse should be the workhouse for the conservatory — the place where all the messier work is done. Plants that are in need of potting into larger containers can be handled much more satisfactorily in the greenhouse where facilities for such tasks can be better organized. It may well be found in time that a potting shed will be necessary. The greenhouse really ought to be a place for the growing and the bringing on of plants, as opposed to an untidy work area. The greenhouse should be very clean with the benches (Fig. 10.2) on either side well filled with attractive plants.

The area underneath the benches ought to be free of clutter. The latter area can have a covering of gravel for plants suited to shady conditions. There are lots of plants that will revel in such places where they can have a reasonable amount of light and regular watering and feeding. Many of the ferns will do very well under the staging while awaiting their turn for doing duty in the conservatory. In particular *Asparagus densiflorus* 'Sprengeri' (the asparagus fern) with its bright green needle leaves will usually grow with abandon. Not the most wildly beautiful plant, but one that can be relied upon to do good service in the darker, floor level areas of the conservatory. This is a ground cover plant that will clamber everywhere, and will also demonstrate its versatility by climbing the walls if there is some form of support.

The greenhouse is not the easiest of options — plants have to be watered and kept warm during the winter months. The hobby of growing plants is time-demanding and there is no easy way out. Watering devices and mechanical aids for opening and closing ventilators will help, but personal attention is generally the most pressing need. There are all sorts of heaters for greenhouses and one should examine a good selection before deciding; electric heaters will usually be more efficient and less demanding than other types of heating.

## Propagation in the greenhouse

One of the most interesting aspects of growing plants in a greenhouse is that of propagation, making new plants from seeds, cuttings, division or whatever method is required to increase plant numbers. Increasing your own plants ensures there is always something there for filling any gaps that appear in the conservatory. By having lots of spare plants it is easier to decide on disposal as opposed to resuscitation when ailing plants are brought out of the conservatory.

For the slightly more difficult plants, the chances of success will be much improved if there is a heated propagating case available. The size ought to be generous and with good height. The height may be important if there are more tender taller plants that need that extra bit of care to bring them along. With a heated propagator one will be able to choose a

more adventurous selection of seed from the catalogue. There is no limit to the interesting seed offered by the seedsman specializing in more unusual subjects. For the novice select the easier subjects and get these to grow before progressing to the more difficult varieties.

### Plantlets from parent plant

The easiest plants to propagate will be the ones that already have roots formed as in the case of the spider plant, *Chlorophytum*. This is a very common plant and is invariably at its best when seen growing in a hanging container. If the container is reasonably large and the plant is getting ample nourishment it will produce lots of plantlets on the ends of long stalks. There will be none on a plant suffering from starvation. The young plants when first developing will be sprayed out most attractively around the parent plant, but as these age the weight of young plants will pull the branches well down so that they are much more clumsy in appearance. Such plants ought to be propagated before the older plant is disposed of. The cuttings need no particular attention and should be removed from the plant by holding the stalk that attaches the baby to the parent and giving it a gentle tug. The babies can then be pressed firmly into peaty soil in 8 cm (3 in) pots, watered in and simply placed on the bench to develop roots.

### Cuttings

*Impatiens*
The colourful busy lizzies will produce lots of flowers over a very extensive period if well cared for and they will also produce roots from cuttings with little difficulty. There are numerous varieties, and one should choose only the best as there is little to be gained from filling the greenhouse with plants just for the sake of it. They can be propagated at almost any time other than mid winter unless conditions are agreeable and cuttings are available. Take cuttings from the top of the growing stems, removing any flowers that may be present. Never allow either cuttings or the plants from which they have been removed to dry out, and keep them moist by frequently watering with a fine rose. Peat and sand is normally

**Fig. 10.3** *Begonia rex* **propagation – Method 1.**
In this method, a sharp knife is used to make
numerous cuts through the prominent veins in a
leaf, which is then placed on the surface of a
peat/sand mixture. In due course young plantlets
should sprout from around the cuts.

recommended as a propagating medium, but
for cuttings that are very easy to root it is better
to use a houseplant potting soil as plants will
root into this and begin to grow with no check.
Thorough preparation is not necessary for all
cuttings. They can be inserted single into 8 cm
(3 in) pots and placed as a group with their pots
touching on the greenhouse bench where they
will be protected from direct sunlight — small
groups of cuttings will invariably do better
than isolated individual pots. Once inserted,
watered and placed together, the cuttings can
then be completely covered with a sheet of
clear polythene that is tucked under the outer-
most pots so that there is a complete seal. The
cuttings in this sort of situation will be permanently moist and can be left until they have
rooted before the polythene is removed. It is
only necessary to remove the polythene prior
to rooting if it can be seen that there are problems with rotting developing, in which case the
cover is removed and the plants cleaned before
it is replaced. It is important that young cuttings get some protection from the sun, and in

an emergency this can be simply done by
covering them with a sheet of newspaper.

*Begonia*
Rex begonias are grown almost entirely for the
decorative leaves that are multicoloured. Not
the easiest of plants to care for, they need a
minimum temperature of around 16°C (61°F)
and careful attention in respect of light, shading, watering and feeding. They can be grown
to a remarkable size when enjoying the care
and attention of a skilled grower. Their propagation is made from mature leaves. There are
two methods. The first and least interesting is
to remove leaves and to cut away the leaf stalk
before placing the leaf coloured side down on a
flat surface and using a sharp knife to make
numerous cuts through the prominent veins
(Fig. 10.3). A seed tray filled with peat and
sand mixture is prepared and the leaf is placed
on the surface of the sand with the coloured
side uppermost. A few small pebbles can be
placed on the leaf to prevent it curling up and
the edges and the box can be watered before it
is placed in the propagator at a temperature of
not less than 18°C (64°F). Given steady
temperature, light shade and a little luck young
plants should sprout from around the cuts
made through the leaf. Allow them to become
well rooted before digging them up, separating
and potting in houseplant mixture.

The other method will produce many more
cuttings from the leaf and will bring a look of
disbelief to visitors. The leaf is laid down in the
same way and the knife is used to cut it into
strips and subsequently into squares a little
larger than a postage stamp. The postage
stamps are placed coloured side up on moist
peat and sand and are kept moist all the time
that the cuttings are in the propagator. You
need to be a trifle lucky, but if the conditions
have been satisfactory the postage stamps will
begin to produce tiny leaves in about six weeks
(Fig. 10.4).

*Sansevieria*
There are many other plants, particularly foliage, that can be increased by means of removing and cutting their leaves into sections. One
of the best known of these is mother-in-law's
tongue, *Sansevieria*; the upright leaves are a

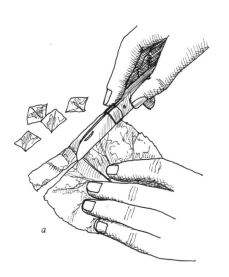

dull yellow and green in colour with a decorative yellow band along the leaf margin. Individual leaves can be removed and cut into sections about 8 cm (3 in) in length and put into a peaty mixture in a temperature of not less than 18°C (64°F) where they will not be too difficult to root. As with all aspects of sansevieria care it is important not to have the cuttings too wet while they are in the propagating case. The fascinating part of this way of preparing the cuttings is that the resultant plants when they begin to grow will have lost their decorative yellow margin, so that green mottled leaves are the result, a deal less attractive.

To obtain plants with the attractive margin it is necessary to have mature parent plants that have begun to develop young plants around the base of the older plant (Fig. 10.5). These ought to be allowed to develop to a height of some 20 cm (8 in) before a sharp knife is used to slice down between the parent root and the root of the young plant so that the latter is cleanly severed. It might be easier to remove the plant from its pot so that there is a reasonable amount of soil around the young shoot when it is detached. Once severed in this way, the young plant can be potted into a loam-based potting mixture and kept very much on the dry side. It is advisable to always have these plants in this condition. The plant that grows from this method of propagation will have the yellow margin to its leaves.

**Fig. 10.4 *Begonia rex* propagation – Method 2.** Here the leaf is cut into postage stamp-sized pieces, each of which should produce tiny leaves in about 6 weeks' time.

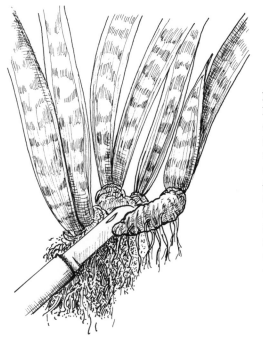

**Fig. 10.5 Propagation by division.** The sansevieria is a good example of this way of increasing plants, which should be done by removing the mature plant from its pot and using a strong knife to sever the outside growths from the parent before planting individually.

## Dieffenbachia

The dieffenbachias are also very decorative conservatory plants that can be propagated reasonably easily if there is adequate temperature, not less than 18°C (64°F). It is wise to wear rubber gloves when handling this plant, particularly when the stems have to be cut in order to propagate, as contact with the sap may cause a skin rash. The sap smells very unpleasantly when the stem is cut, so there is little likelihood that anyone would wish to eat the plant, but take note that the sap can cause toxic problems, although these plants are handled in their millions annually with no apparent problem.

**Fig. 10.6 Propagating dieffenbachia.** Use mature stems and cut them into sections ensuring that each small section has a bulging growing eye from which new growth will develop. Provide warm conditions and thoroughly wash hands when the task is completed.

The dieffenbachias are increased by cutting a mature stem from the plant. Use a sharp knife to cut the stem into sections, each section having a bulbous nodal part of the stem. The section of stem is then buried to about two thirds of its diameter in peaty compost with the nodal part uppermost (Fig. 10.6). In time roots will develop and grow into the soil and some while later the node will be seen to swell and from the node new growth will eventually appear. When two or three small leaves have formed the young plant can be potted into a pot that is appropriate to its size, again using a peaty mixture.

## Monstera

In the well managed conservatory the majority of plants will grow with little difficulty, and some of them may well grow too vigorously for their allotted space. The cheese plant *Monstera*, falls into this category, and as it increases in height it may well shed some of its lower leaves with the result that the plant becomes less attractive. (Monstera plants are

normally begun from seed by the commercial grower with the result that several plants are potted into 13 cm (5 in) pots so that they may become saleable in less time than would be possible with a single plant.) To remedy the problem use a sharp knife to remove two or three stems with two leaves attached, from the top of the plant and replant them around the older stems. Cuttings of this kind should not be taken from plants with soft new leaves as these will almost inevitably be damaged when handling. A dibber hole should be made in the soil and the cutting firmly inserted so that the lower leaf joint is well buried. It will not be long before the somewhat odd cuttings begin to root and grow to cover the lower part of the plant with new foliage. The stems from which the cuttings were removed will also begin to re-grow in time. If desired they can be cut back further at this stage to keep the plant within bounds. Any stems that still have their top sections intact can be left until the others begin to grow, when they too can have the same pruning treatment. Older plants will also tend to produce lots of aerial roots. These are roots that draw up nourishment for the plant when they reach ground level, and should be directed into the soil in the pot when they are long enough. In order to keep them tidy the roots at higher level can be tied neatly in to the main stem of the plant.

## Fuchsias

Fuchsias are probably the most popular of all potted flowering plants and can be used for a variety of purposes; there are many thousands of both hardy and tender varieties offered for sale annually. For propagating cut the current season's growth hard some time in July to the point whereby there does not seem to be much more than twigs left on the plants. This action will get rid of the majority of pests that will have been on the foliage and will also make subsequent spraying with insecticides much more effective as bugs will be fully exposed to the treatment. Some plants may be potted on at this stage and all of them will be watered and encouraged to grow, so that by October/November there will be lush green cuttings that are almost free of pests and ready for snipping from the plants for propagating.

There are many different methods of proceeding. One very simple method is to take the smallest possible cuttings from the very tip of the plant, normally nothing more than a pair of very tiny leaves. These should then be laid out on paper and dampened with a fine rose before they are inserted in the smallest pots that can be found — little larger than timbles. Carefully insert them in fine peat and sand mixture and cover with milky white polythene turned under the pots at the edges to make a perfect seal. In this way the strike rate could well be 100%. The cuttings should be shaded from the sun and the polythene can remain over the plants until they have rooted in about three or four weeks. Such tiny pieces of plant will have virtually no pests or diseases and this ensures that your plants are off to a perfect start when they are potted on. Keep them warm, moist and in good light once they have settled and are adding new growth — you could well become a fuchsia addict!

The thing to remember when growing fuchsias is that they like a good potting mixture and should be fed once they have become well rooted. Avoid long periods of total saturation but never allow them to dry out. For lots of flowers grow them in lightly shaded conditions. Once growth is well under way they should be fed with a high potash fertilizer such as a tomato fertilizer. For hanging containers in a cool and airy conservatory, they will be in flower for almost all the summer and early autumn when the procedure starts again.

## Ivies

Trailing plants are among the most useful of all plants for decorating the conservatory and for maintaining an attractive appearance in the feeder greenhouse, so it is always wise to have a good selection of these around. Such plants can be used for hanging containers, for adding the finishing touch around the edge of larger plant arrangements, for windowboxes, for edging planted bed arrangements and for trailing over the greenhouse bench or the edge of table displays in the conservatory.

Among the best of trailing plants for almost all the purposes mentioned above are the ivies, often disparagingly referred to as the common ivy which is a reference to the garden form that grows virtually everywhere. There are now some very fine variegated forms in both yellow and white, many of them also having interesting leaf shapes. There are skills to ensure that attractive plants result when cuttings are propagated.

Ivies grow very little in the winter so it is not a good time for taking cuttings; it is much better to wait until spring when strands of firm growth should be removed and cut into sections with two firm leaves attached. The very top section of the plant is generally very soft and should be discarded. Pots 9 cm (3 in) in diameter should be filled with peaty potting mixture that is well firmed before cuttings are inserted. Depending on the size of the leaves, five to seven cuttings should be pressed firmly into the potting mixture so that there is little to be seen of the soil — in this way you get a very full and attractive plant display. The cuttings are watered with a fine rose before being covered with thin gauge polythene that is carefully tucked under the outside pots in the group. Individual pots of cuttings can be placed in polythene bags, but it is generally more successful to prepare a small batch of cuttings rather than individual pots. These are plants that are useful in all sorts of areas so it pays to have a reasonable number at your disposal.

*Wandering Jew*

The above is the common name for the many tradescantias that one is likely to come across and, like the ivies, these too are excellent and easy plants for all sorts of purposes. If anything they are even more accommodating than almost any other potted plant when it comes to ease of propagation. They can be treated in very much the same way as the ivies, with the exceptions that the cuttings are prepared from tip shoots with some three or four leaves attached (Fig. 10.7), and they prefer to be reasonably warm during the rooting process. The zebrinas are close relatives of the tradescantias and can be more attractively coloured with lots of pink and silver stripes in their leaves. When properly grown there are few foliage plants that are prettier when grown in hanging containers. Cuttings should be taken during the summer months when they

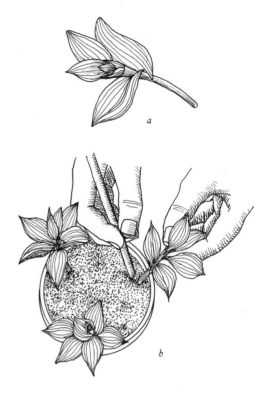

**Fig. 10.7 Increasing tradescantias.** Choose the brightest coloured pieces and insert at least five cuttings from the top section of the plant into a small pot filled with peaty mixture. Keep warm and out of direct sunlight and they will root in no time.

are both more plentiful and easier to root. With a batch of these rooted it will not be so painful to throw away the old parent plants at the end of the season, knowing that fresh stock is available for the future.

*African violets*

The African violet, *Saintpaulia*, is probably the most popular of all flowering plants — they can be seen on sale in every country of the world on almost every day of the year. Unlike the majority of flowering plants the saintpaulia is not seasonal and can be encouraged to flower right through the year if the growing condit-

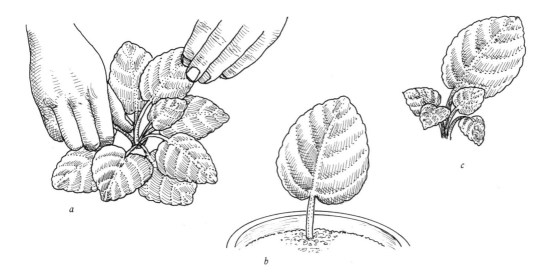

ions are suitable. There are literally thousands of varieties in an amazing range of colours and all of them can be propagated from mature leaves with reasonable ease.

Essential ingredients for success are firm and unblemished leaves with the leafstalk trimmed to a little under 5 cm (2 in) in length, and a heated propagator. Leaves are inserted in fresh peat far enough for them to remain erect, and can go into either small seed trays or small pots. Rooting powder will assist the rooting process, as will slightly damp and lightly shaded conditions (Fig. 10.8).

Much of the success with more attractive mature appearance of these plants lies in their care once they have produced the typical clump of young leaves at the base of the stalk of the parent leaf. Allow the clump to develop to a reasonable size, then carefully separate and pot individually what will be a collection of small plants that in time will produce perfect rosettes of leaves and attractive flowers.

## Air-layering

The rubber plant has lost much of its earlier popularity, but it is still sold in large numbers, both in the traditional green form and in numerous attractive variegated colours. These too are plants that in time can outgrow their

**Fig. 10.8 Saintpaulia propagation.** Remove a strong leaf with the complete stem (a) then trim the stem to about 4 cm (1½ in) before inserting four or five leaves around the edge of a small pot filled with moist peat (b). Once well rooted the small clump of developing leaves (c) can be teased apart to provide numerous tiny plants that can be carefully potted individually into pots containing a peaty houseplant mixture.

available space. The simple answer for plants that have become too tall is to reduce the plant with a pair of strong and sharp secateurs to a more satisfactory height. There will be an inevitable flow of sap when the stem is severed but this can be checked by putting a little wet soil over the wound. An alternative is to use a sharp knife and to cut half way through the stem, then turning the knife in an upward direction so that the blade can be run through the centre of the node. It is advisable to have someone holding the plant steady during the entire operation, or at least until a cane in the form of a splint has been securely attached to the stem above and below the cut mark. The incision can be held open by inserting a match; sphagnum moss enclosed in clear polythene

119

**Fig. 10.9 Air-layering *Ficus robusta*.** Do this at any time by using a sharp knife to cut upwards through a node – hold the gap open with a match-stick before wrapping wet sphagnum moss around the open wound. Wrap the moss inside a square of polythene (*a*) that is tied in position and use a cane as a splint to prevent the weakened stem from breaking. When ample roots are visible (*b*) remove the polythene and cut the stem below the moss before potting the new plant individually in peaty potting mixture (*c*).

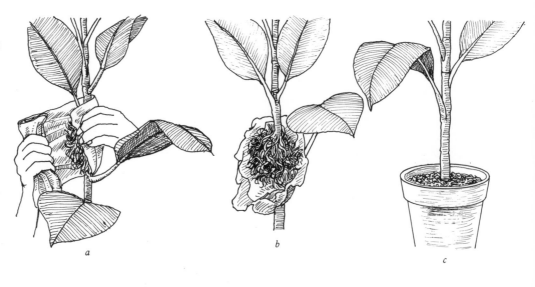

**Fig. 10.9 Air-layering *Ficus robusta*.** Do this at any time by using a sharp knife to cut upwards through a node – hold the gap open with a match-stick before wrapping wet sphagnum moss around the open wound. Wrap the moss inside a square of polythene (*a*) that is tied in position and use a cane as a splint to prevent the weakened stem from breaking. When ample roots are visible (*b*) remove the polythene and cut the stem below the moss before potting the new plant individually in peaty potting mixture (*c*).

can be put around the cut, the polythene tied firmly in position (Fig. 10.9). In about eight weeks lovely white roots should be showing through and one month or so later the top section can be severed below where the plant has rooted so that it can be potted into a pot of suitable size after the polythene has been removed. The large stump that is left will look a bit out of place initially, but should soon develop several new shoots from the nodes in the area around the top of the plant. This way you get two plants for one and will have the satisfaction of knowing that you have performed successfully a very interesting exercise in plant propagation.

### Rooting rosettes
Bromeliads are also very exotic and interesting plants for propagation. The majority take several years to produce their flowers, and having flowered from the principal rosette of leaves most will seem to die. However, as the rosette that produced the bract and flower begins to fade, the rosette will begin to develop young plants around the base of its short trunk. The plant that most people will know is *Aechmea fasciata* (syn. *A. rhodocyiana*) which has the common name of urn plant. The re-

curving leaves are an attractive silver grey in colour and the magnificent bract when it appears like a giant drumstick is soft pink with flowers of intense blue colouring nestling in the bract. The flower/bract will last for up-wards of six months before it begins to fade and die. Some time before this happens the plant will develop two or more young plants at the base — these should be left intact until they have attained reasonable size when a sharp knife can be used to cut them away cleanly from where they are attached. The young plants are then firmly secured in a pot that is filled with orchid potting mixture, which approximates the needs of bromeliads in order to succeed. To secure the young plant in the pot it may be necessary to wedge it in position. The small rosette of leaves will root and grow and will need potting on in stages to larger containers that will be in keeping with the size of the plant at the time of potting. From the point of potting it will take the young rosette three to four years before a fresh bract develops — it is a long job and one of the reasons the aechmea is an expensive plant to buy.

An alternative to the procedure described above is to leave all the small plants attached to the stump of the parent plant (the old rosette

should be cut away when it is no longer attractive). It will flower in appreciably less time than
with the former method. There could well be
five young plants at the base of the parent, and
when this number come into flower you have a
plant on your hands that is worthy of admir-
ation. There are many other bromeliads, large
and small, that can be treated in the same way,
all of them relatively easy to grow and to
propagate.

## Division

### Spathiphyllum

Division of plant roots must surely be the
method of propagation that no-one can fail to
succeed with, but there are not many of our
conservatory plants that can be increased in
this way. One of the most obvious is the peace
lily, *Spathiphyllum*, which can be separated to
make fresh plants at virtually any time of the
year (Fig. 10.10). There are two varieties that
are generally available, *S. wallasii* which is the
smaller and the more compact, and *S.* 'Mauna
Loa' with very much larger leaves and splendid white spathe flowers on long stems. It is
often said that plants that are in flower should
not be divided, but if one were to wait for this
plant to finish flowering it could be forever, as
white flowers seem to be in evidence throughout the year. You can cut the flowers, but it
really is not necessary as the plants immediately settle down after being divided. Plants
ought to be watered before they are removed
from their pots and a sharp knife used to separate the roots that are then potted individually
in a good houseplant mixture.

### Aspidistra

The aspidistra or cast-iron plant may be done
in much the same way, but the root system is
very much tougher; in older plants a saw may
be required to divide the root system into sections. Following division the aspidistra should
be potted into a soil that contains a proportion
of loam to sustain the plants over the period of
years that will elapse before any further treatment of this kind will be called for.

**Fig. 10.10 Dividing *Spathiphyllum*.** The roots
of the peace lily should be watered before they are
removed from their pot and divided into separate
clumps prior to potting into peaty potting mixture.

### Aglaonema

Aglaonemas are among the most durable of
indoor and conservatory plants provided they
are kept reasonably warm and moist. Their
greatest virtue is an ability to grow apparently
unconcerned in poor light, a quality not shared
by many plants. The leaves sprout from soil
level and develop in tight clusters of growth,
either green or in mottled shades of silvery
grey and green. The procedure for potting is
the same as recommended for the peace lily
and can be undertaken at any time of the year,
with spring being best as plants are then
putting on fresh growth for the new season.

# PART III

## A–Z OF CONSERVATORY PLANTS

**ABUTILON** (*Malvaceae*) Chinese lantern

Indigenous to tropical America these are almost ideal conservatory plants where there is sufficient space to accommodate vigorous growth. Some form shrubby growth while others may very effectively be used as climbing plants trained to a framework against a solid, as opposed to a glass wall. Cool conditions will suit them well and they may be stood on the patio out of doors during the summer months, or planted amongst other subjects where they will offer that interesting exotic touch to formal planting schemes.

During spring and summer, plants must be kept well watered and fed, and any that have been saved from the previous year should be repotted into fresh compost in the spring. Pruning of unwanted growth can also be attended to in the early spring, quite hard pruning suiting the more vigorous varieties.

**Abutilon**
Pendulous flowers are produced even on small plants and the delicate maple-like foliage provides attractive room plants.

Where seed is available this can be sown in cool conditions in a sandy mixture in spring, or cuttings can be taken at the same time of year; the latter will require a temperature of not less than 18 °C (65 °F) in order to succeed.

***Abutilon × hybridum*** (flowering maple) has given rise to numerous cultivars that are variously referred to as flowering maple, Chinese lantern or parlour maple. An interesting aspect of these plants are the flowers that range in colour from yellow to deep red with many attractive hues in between. Besides colourful flowers many of the abutilons are also blessed with decorative leaves, and in *A. × hybridum* 'Savitzii' the foliage is almost white with minimal pale green colouring. As conservatories become more popular so suitable plants for their decoration become more freely available and it is not unusual today to find such plants as *A. × hybridum* 'Savitzii' being offered by better plant retailers. However, a word of warning – this is a very vigorous plant in agreeable conditions and will quickly attain a height of 3 m (10 ft). As new leaves are produced many of the lower ones will wither and die, but this is a common pattern in abutilons.

***Abutilon pictum* 'Thompsonii'** is a well established favourite among plantsmen, principally grown for its decorative foliage. Smooth, glossy leaves are multi-coloured in many shades of orange, brown and green. Like most abutilons it needs good light with some protection from strong sunlight.

**ACALYPHA** (*Euphorbiaceae*) copper leaf

The majority of these are varieties of ***A. wilkesiana***, their principal feature being spectacular leaf colouring matched by few plants. Needing warm conditions, not less than 16 °C (61 °F), they will grow freely during the warmer months of the year. Colder months will be the difficult time when plants should be kept as warm as possible using great care to ensure that watering is not overdone. Plants will do best when grown in pots as they can then be moved out of doors in warmer climates for at least part of the summer. Potting on is best done in the spring, a rich mixture being essential. Established plants will also need to be fed regularly while in active growth.

A lightly shaded location will suit them better than full sun or overshaded locations. In larger conservatories where the creation of formal beds of plants is possible the acalypha is an excellent choice of plant for a central, important spot within the bedding arrangement. New plants may be propagated from cuttings at almost any time while material is avaliable and good temperature can be provided to be reasonably sure of success. Cuttings should be prepared from top sections of the stem with two or three leaves attached, the lower and larger leaf being removed before the cutting is inserted in a peaty propagating mixture.

Red spider mites can be a problem in warmer conditions when growing these plants, so it is wise to keep a watchful eye for them and to maintain a moist, humid atmosphere wherever possible. Acalyphas are something of a challenge to grow, but most rewarding when done well.

## ACHIMENES (*Gesneriaceae*) hot water plant

Deciduous plants grown from small tubers and in flower for much of late spring and summer, these are neat windowsill plants available in numerous varieties which may be purchased by name from specialist growers. They can also be raised from seed sown in warm conditions in early spring so that a reasonably wide range of coloured flowers may be the reward. New plants may also be grown from cuttings taken in spring or, very easily, by removing plants from their pots when growth is about to begin in early spring and peeling off the scaley rhizomes that can be planted in seed boxes of peaty soil; these are later potted into small pots of houseplant soil once the young plants have got under way.

Offer good light but not bright sun and feed and water well while plants are active. Towards the end of their season plants will naturally begin to die back and this is a signal that watering should first be reduced and eventually stopped so that plants may be stored warm and dry until the following early spring when watering will again bring them back into leaf.

Not particularly exciting plants when displayed as individuals, they can have an added interest when a collection is grouped in a large, shallow container. In larger containers the plants should be left in their pots so that individual plant watering can be practised; it will also be a simple task to remove plants that have lost their vitality so that fresh plants can be introduced to improve the arrangement. The common name of hot water plant relates to the practice of plunging the potful of deciduous rhizomes into hot water to stimulate new growth at the start of the season.

## ACORUS (*Araceae*) sweet flag

Often sold as houseplants these are fine plants for the conservatory with a pool feature. They can edge the pool in the same way as one would use them out of doors.

They are easy to care for; their most important requirement is that they should never dry out. New plants can be made by dividing older clumps so that individual plant sections can be potted separately. Growth is grasslike and upright with colouring that is dull cream and green.

## ADIANTUM (*Adiantaceae*) maidenhair fern

One of the most delicate and beautiful of all foliage plants, these are available in numerous varieties, some more delicate than others. The lush pale green colouring makes this an indispensible plant when it comes to arranging groups of different varieties and colours together. The maidenhair fern is also the perfect plant for placing at the front of grouped planted areas within the conservatory.

It is not the easiest of plants to care for. One of the main reasons for failure is that plants are grown by the nurseryman in relatively small pots in order to conserve valuable space in the commercial greenhouse, with the result that when the plant is introduced to conservatory conditions there is not sufficient soil in the pot to sustain the plant. The answer to this problem is to water the plant on getting it home and to pot it into a slightly larger pot in a peaty mixture.

The most important requirements are: temperature above 16 °C (61 °F) never letting the soil become excessively dry and shaded conditions. In a sunny location the adiantum would indeed have a very short life. Older plants become coarse and less attractive if nothing is done with them: cut away all the older top fronds and by so doing allow younger fronds lower down on the plant to develop.

Propagation is best left to the commercial grower who will offer for sale plants of every size, even very tiny ones that can be treated as freshly propagated material to be nursed until they have established. The maidenhairs may well present cultural difficulties, but they are among the most beautiful of our plants when properly cared for.

## AECHMEA (*Bromeliaceae*) urn plant

All from tropical South America, there are many varieties of this particular plant that could well grace the conservatory of the owner seeking something that is different to show his visitors. Most have interesting foliage that is formed in the shape of an urn with tightly over-lapping basal leaves, providing a perfectly watertight urn that gives the plant its common name of urn plant. The latter applies in the main to **A. fasciata** (also offered as *A. rhodocyiana*), which is by far the most popular of all those that might be available. In the tropical forest smaller animals find that the vase of the aechmea and other similar bromeliads provides an ideal drinking vessel.

Whatever else may be said of the bromeliads in general there is little doubt that they are amongst the most durable of all potted plants – almost indestructable if their modest watering and temperature requirements are attended to. Temperature should preferably not drop below 10 °C (50 °F), and watering is a simple matter of giving a minimal amount to the mixture in which the plant is growing and to ensure that the urn part of the plant is never allowed to dry out. Neither feeding or potting

on is generally necessary as the main rosette of the plant will die off anyway once it has flowered and the flowers have died off.

Many of the flowers of the aechmeas are quite spectacular with often brilliant colour combinations. In *A. fasciata*, the plant at three to four years old produces the most wonderful bract from out of the urn, a bright pink with small intensely blue flowers nestling in the brush-like bract. This is the most freely available of the aechmeas although there are many others that one might chance to come across. As mentioned, all produce bracts of varying colour and shape, and all have the strange characteristic that results in the rosette dying off some time after the plant has developed its bract. The bract, in fact, lasts for some six months from the time it first appears and once it has lost its attraction it should be cut away from the plant. The parent rosette can remain until it is no longer attractive when it too can be cut down to the base. Care should be taken to avoid damaging the new young rosette(s) that should by then be making their presence known. The young plants can remain attached to the stump of the parent plant where

**Aechmea**
Showing the developing young shoots around the base of the parent stem – can be removed and propagated when large enough.

they will flower in about two years. Alternatively they can be left until they have made a half dozen leaves of their own, by which time they will be fit to come off and be potted individually to make their own way in life. An open, free-draining potting mixture is essential.

The aechmeas are in the same family as the pineapple, *Ananas*, which is the only member having commercial value other than decorative. In spite of their tough qualities and unusual appearance the bromeliads are not particularly popular plants among the buying public. This may be due to a fear that they are more tender than they appear to be. For the plant decorator, and this could well apply to the more adventurous conservatory owner, the bromeliads offer many possibilities in respect of exotic display on account of their general interest and often amazing shapes and colouring.

## AEONIUM (*Crassulaceae*)

*A. arboreum* and its cultivars is a common plant in Mediterranean regions, but can also be purchased now through cactus and other nurseries as it is a useful plant for conservatory and patio decoration. Tight rosettes of green or reddish brown colouring are borne atop stout stems. It is very easy to care for if given good light and modest watering with very little of the latter in winter.

*A. tabulaeforme* also produces a tight rosette on a short trunk of stem, but it is an altogether more eye-catching plant with green overlapping leaves which are almost perfectly flat on top and attaining the size of a large dinner plate when roots are confined to pots. This is one of the interest type plants that one can include in the conservatory collection as it is so different that virtually every visitor will be fascinated and want to know where it has come from. Cool, lightly shaded conditions that are not too wet will suit this one best.

*A. ×domesticum* and in particular its variegated form is a plant that deserves to be better known. It also forms rosettes, but these are loose and lax in habit and produced in great number on small plants. Excellent shelf or

table plants in the conservatory, they prefer lightly shaded conditions and although needing a reasonable amount of water during the summer months, they must at no time become excessively wet.

Making new plants is a simple matter – the already formed rosettes of leaves are removed with a reasonable length of stem and put into a sandy mixture in a warm, lightly shaded spot to be potted on once roots have got through to the sides of the original small propagating pot.

## AESCHYNANTHUS (*Gesneraceae*)
lipstick plant

In almost any conservatory situation the most free space that will be available for plants is usually above ones head – the ideal location for hanging baskets. The *Aeschynanthus* makes an

**Aeschynanthus**
Fine trailing plants for the warm room, having glossy evergreen foliage and attractive flowers over a long period of time.

127

ideal basket plant for the room offering a minimum temperature of not less that 16 °C (61 °F). Perhaps for the very reason that they occupy little space and are ideal for hanging containers, these are plants that have become increasingly popular in recent years.

*A. parvifolius* (syn. *A. lobbianus*) is by far the most popular, having glossy green leaves on pendulous stems and bright red flowers that emerge from a dark, reddish green tube. This is another plant both interesting as well as decorative with ability to flower over a very long period. Minimum temperature of around 16 °C (61 °F) is important and plants should enjoy a lightly shaded location. Water can be given reasonably freely during the summer months with appreciably less in winter. Feed plants while they are in active growth, and when potting them on use a peaty houseplant mixture. Cuttings of non-flowering sections of tip growth will not be difficult to root, but they will need to be warm and will fare better if a propagator can be provided.

## AGAPANTHUS (*Liliaceae/Alliaceae*)

Excellent tub plants for the larger cool conservatory, they are probably too space-demanding for the smaller room. In milder climates these plants are hardy out of doors and are fine in tubs for patio decoration. There is a white form, *A. praecox orientalis albiflorus*, but it is mostly plants with blue flowers that are available. Strap-like, evergreen leaves overhang the container in which they are growing but are not particularly attractive. Nevertheless, they are splendid plants, which may be brought into the larger conservatory while in flower and tucked away in a corner outside at other times. New plants can be made by dividing mature clumps in the early part of the year.

## AGAVE (*Agavaceae*)

On the whole, the *Agave* are not very suitable for the conservatory on account of their spined leaves and must remain at a distance from passing bodies, but for the larger conservatory

which can feature a cactus garden where plants can be placed out of harm's way, these are plants which will offer a new and interesting dimension to the scene. Planting these subjects freely in a cactus bed would, however, not be wise as they may well take over and be difficult to remove when a change of scene is contemplated. Plants with this tendency are invariably better with their roots confined to a pot that will restrict their growth and make any reshuffling very much easier.

As with the majority of cacti and succulents, these are easy care plants that will tolerate varied conditions provided they have sufficient light in which to grow and a watering programme that offers a reasonable amount during the spring and summer and very little at other times. Should potting become necessary, use a heavy, well drained mixture.

## AGLAONEMA (*Araceae*) Chinese evergreen

Finding plants for darker indoor locations presents many problems; the aglaonemas can very often be called upon to fill these areas. They are compact plants with spear-shaped leaves forming tight rosettes of growth with actual leaves sprouting almost stemless from ground level. There are several varieties ranging from dark mottled green to a mottled silver in *A.* 'Silver Queen'. Slow to grow, these are plants that abhor direct sunlight, but they will respond to conditions that offer humidity and temperature not falling below 16 °C (61 °F). When part of a mixed planting of foliage in large containers, they are excellent plants for placing at the base of larger specimens. For the conservatory garden that has a protected corner away from bright sunlight they will also provide what in the modern term is referred to as ground cover. The latter is an important requirement when arranging plants to give real impact.

New plants are made by dividing mature clumps at almost any time of the year. The parent plant should be watered and removed from its pot so that the clump of roots can be pulled apart – it may be even necessary to use a large, sharp knife to complete the surgery as clumps can be very tough. Plants should be watered and allowed to dry reasonably before the watering exercise is repeated. With feeding, do this at weekly intervals while plants are developing fresh growth, with no feeding whatsoever during the colder months of the year. Avoid too free a use of leaf-cleaning chemicals.

## ALLAMANDA (*Apocynaceae*)
golden trumpet

The older garden books refer to these plants as stove evergreen climbers. Stove is the old term for plants that needed very high temperature in order to succeed. Plants could possibly survive at less temperature, but for better results they should enjoy a minimum winter temperature of not less than 16 °C (61 °F) (higher where possible) and 22 °C (72 °F) while they are in active growth. They are exotic climbing plants originating from tropical South America.

*A. cathartica* is perhaps the most spectacular of those available and in agreeable conditions will be a summer spectacle. It must be stressed that this is not an easy plant, but when growing well it can be trained to a framework against a wall and, given ideal conditions, could well be trained on wires above head level to add the finishing touch.

A more freely available allamanda is *A. neriifolia* which also has large clear yellow flowers but is more of a shrub than a climber. It is a worthwhile plant nevertheless as it can be trained to a framework to give a pleasing show of colour at lower level. Good loam, leafmould and sand will be a better potting mixture than something that is too peaty – it will also be of benefit to incorporate a little charcoal in the mixture when potting plants on in the very early part of the year.

## ALOCASIA (*Araceae*)

For the connoisseur who can afford the heating bills for high temperature and has a degree of skill in the care of truly exotic plants this could well be an excellent choice. Decorative foliage colouring and leaf shape of dramatic appearance are the principal attractions. With the

proper conditions and care, some of these will develop into superb plants with *A. macrorrhiza* and its more colourful variegated form being particularly fine. Both these plants will require height and spread to accommodate the splendid leaves as they develop – the centre piece in a bed of mixed tropical foliage would be the perfect setting. Where space is more limited, there is also the choice of the old favourite of *A. lowii*. The form *A. lowii* Grandis is somewhat larger but, nevertheless manageable. There are several others but it must be said that all of them will be difficult to obtain, although there are now specialist nurserymen taking more interest in these fine plants.

Growing conditions and general care will be quite demanding with a temperature of not less than 18 °C (64 °F) should be the aim and high humidity involving frequent damping of the area around the plants will be essential. Plants can be grown in pots or borders but, in any event, it is important that they should have a peaty mixture in which to grow. As mentioned, moisture is important but one should avoid the temptation of forever filling the pots with water – better to damp the surrounding area. Feeding with a liquid fertilizer is needed during the time that plants are seen to be actively growing. *A. lowii* has particularly fine leaf markings that are a dark metallic green with prominent veins radiating from the central rib of the leaf, the raised area of the veins being silver to contrast with the darker background colouring. It is, however, considered to be quite a horticultural feat to grow this particular plant with completely unblemished leaves, but a successful challenge can be very rewarding! Place them in shade and with the humidity factor, this should give the conservatory a mini-jungle feeling.

## ALOE (*Liliaceae/Aloeaceae*)

For the light, airy and dry atmosphere conservatory this could be one of the plants to choose. Indigenous for the most part to southern Africa, they survive in the most spartan conditions in their native habitat. Care is needed when locating plants as most have vicious spines or sharp points to the ends of their leaves. The variety **A. brevifolia** has the common name crocodile plant, which ought to be sufficient warning to take extra care when handling. At the other end of the scale there is **A. vera** with the common name of medicine plant relating to the healing qualities of the pulped leaves when applied to burns and bruises, a quality that has given this plant considerable popularity in recent years.

The plants can survive for long periods without water and are not too particular when it comes to feeding. When potting on, place them in a fairly heavy mixture containing loam and grit as opposed to lots of peat. The heavier mix will also assist the plant in maintaining its equilibrium when growing in a pot. In respect of pots, these are plants that look very out of place when growing in modern plastic containers, so terracotta should be chosen. The actual potting exercise can be quite traumatic on account of the leaf spines. The suggested method of getting around this difficulty is to select a larger container and to remove the growing pot from around the roots of the plant and to pot the empty container into the new pot while the plant sits to one side out of harms way. Once the soil has been firmed around the empty pot in the centre of the new one, the empty pot can be removed and the rootball of the plant can then be simply dropped into the perfectly shaped mould. Because of their spiteful nature it is wise to make the potting operation a two-handed task and for both operators to wear gloves.

## ALPINIA (*Zingiberaceae*) Indian ginger

Attractive and to some degree different foliage plants for the warm conservatory where the temperature does not fall below 16 °C (61 °F), these plants may be grown in pots, tubs, or planted in prepared beds. There are numerous varieties (all in short supply) with **A. vittata** (syn. *A. sanderae*) being the plant generally available – it is also more compact and better suited to conservatories of more modest size. Lanceolate leaves are carried on stiff, upright stems that sprout from spreading rhizomes; the latter can be divided in the spring of the year in

**Alpinia**
Graceful foliage plants for the warmer conservatory where reasonable space is available. Alas, in short supply.

order to propagate new plants. The conservatory should be lightly shaded when managing these plants and when potting them on or preparing a planting bed they should have a soil mix of equal parts leafmould, peat and good loam, or as near that mix as one can achieve. Keep well watered while in active growth, also fed with a liquid fertilizer, giving no feed while growth is inactive.

## ANANAS (*Bromeliaceae*) pineapple

Of the numerous bromeliads that one may encounter while gathering the conservatory collection of plants, this is the only one that has a commercial value – all the others are grown for their ornamental qualities. The edible pineapple, *A. comosus*, develops a large rosette of green leaves from the centre of which the pineapple emerges, but in a decorative sense it is not a particularly appealing plant. Strangely enough its variegated form, *A. comosus* 'Bont Variegatus' is a highly colourful, even spectacular plant. The latter is a freely available plant that may be purchased as small plants for growing on or as plants that are actually bearing fruit. The latter are forced in greenhouses and do not attain the true magnificence of plants that are allowed to mature gradually over a greater number of months, perhaps years. Leaves are viciously spined along their margins so need careful handling and a location out of the way of passers by.

The interesting aspect of this particular plant is that as it is about to produce its pineapple fruit, the base of the leaves change colour to a bright shade of reddish pink which, combined with the developing fruit, presents a truly wonderful picture. Reasonably easy to care for, though taking several years to produce fruit, the pineapple needs good light and a temperature of not less than 12 °C (54 °F). At lower temperature the soil in the pot should be kept on the dry side. Feeding is not important but a little given occasionally will do no harm. Mature plants become top heavy so clay pots should be used when potting on. A rich, open potting mix will suit them best.

## ANTHURIUM (*Araceae*)
flamingo flower, piggy tail plant

The plant most freely available is *A. scherzerianum*, both its common names relating to the peculiarly twisting spadix of the flower. This is a compact and reasonably easy plant to care for if it can enjoy warm, moist conditions and light shade.

Its relative, *A. andreanum*, is a much different proposition, being a plant that must have a high temperature, never less than 18 °C (64 °F), high humidity and a shaded location. It will also require rich compost, and is often better in respect of performance when growing in a rich bed of soil as opposed to having its roots confined to a pot. The arrow-shaped leaves are carried on long petioles but are not

especially attractive – they are also demanding in respect of space. The principal attraction of the plant is the splendid flower that tops stems a metre or more in length, the flower colouring ranging from white to deepest red with many shades of pink in between. A further blessing is that the flowers when cut will last for many weeks in water, being almost the ultimate in respect of the flower arrangers requirements. New plants can be raised from seed sown in high temperature, but be warned it is a long, slow business.

In contrast, *A. crystallinum* is a plant that can be raised from seed sown in warm, moist conditions whenever ripened seed is available. Its principal feature is a foliage colouring of metallic green with superb veined patterns running through the broadly heart-shaped leaf. Given warm and moist conditions it is not an especially difficult plant to care for. They can be very effective when growing on an old-fashioned piece of horticultural apparatus known as a raft, which is virtually a hanging container made from slatted pieces of lathing. A rich mixture incorporating fresh sphagnum moss is simply packed around the roots and the container hung in a shaded part of the conservatory to add yet another small dimension to the scene. Mature and unblemished leaves of *A. crystallinum* really are very exciting for anyone who enjoys exotic plants.

## APHELANDRA (*Acanthaceae*) zebra plant

There was a time when the aphelandra was one of our more popular flowering plants for sale in pots of 13 cm (5 in) diameter, but over the years its popularity has declined dramatically. Occupying less greenhouse space the smaller *A.* 'Dania' came into favour with the commercial grower at the expense of the much superior *A. squarrosa louisae*. The latter is seldom seen being offered today, but if available it is by far the best choice. The leaves are splendidly marked green and silver to be eventually topped by beautiful golden yellow bracts. The bracts are long lasting, and the plant will also last longer if it can enjoy light shade, copious watering and feeding with a weak liquid fertilizer at frequent intervals.

When bracts have lost their appearance the plant should be cut back to a sound pair of leaves from the axils of which new shoots will eventually appear – these can be left on the plant to flower later, or they can be removed and used as cuttings when two pairs of leaves have been produced. There are numerous other aphelandras, all needing the same conditions but, alas invariably in short supply.

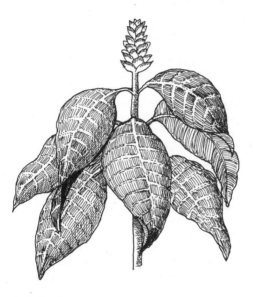

**Aphelandra**
Warm and shaded conditions necessary, likewise a need for ample moisture at their roots and frequent feeding.

## APOROCACTUS (*Cactaceae*)
rat's-tail cactus

Aporocactus is another fun plant that looks at its best when growing in a hanging container of some kind and adding further interest, even amusement, to the conservatory scene. In a planted bed the spined, cylindrical growths will creep along the ground, but in a hanger they will trail and be much more fun. Small, reddish flowers will in time add further interest. Offer good light, reasonable temperature and never have them too wet in order to produce ever longer rat's tails.

## ARALIA (*Araliaceae*) false castor oil plant

This is a plant that may also be seen labelled as *Fatsia japonica* (c.f. **A. sieboldii**), but aralia is the name that seems to be favoured by the commercial growers. With large green palmate leaves emanating from a stout central trunk, these are fine plants for large pots in the conservatory, but, being hardy in milder areas, they can also be planted out of doors, or can stand in containers on the patio for much of the year. They are not in any way difficult to care for provided they are grown in light shade and have regular watering and feeding.

When potting on use slightly heavier soil in order to keep growth compact and more attractive; in a loose peaty mixture they do less well. A careful eye should be kept for red spider mites on the undersides of leaves: it is a wise policy to give plants a protective insecticide treatment as a precaution rather than wait for the mites to appear and then take remedial action.

There is also a variegated form (**A. sieboldii 'Variegata'**) that will be more expensive to purchase and will also be more difficult to care for. Watering is more critical and must at no time be overdone – the best policy is to thoroughly water the soil and allow it to dry reasonably before repeating, bearing in mind that much less water is needed in winter than while plants are growing more actively in the summer. Again, watch for spider mites.

## ARAUCARIA HETEROPHYLLA
(*Araucariaceae*) Norfolk Island pine

More frequently offered by the commercial nurserymen as *A. excelsa*, this is a very fine plant with typical pine appearance, but looking very grand with tiered, pale green foliage standing proudly away from stout central stems. Although not a difficult plant to care for, one of the problems could be the fact that it will outgrow its allotted space just as the plant's appearance is becoming really spectacular. In the conservatory it will require light shade and ample watering and feeding while in active growth, with a little less water and no feeding in winter. In its natural habitat and throughout the tropics this is a plant that will have its head growing in the clouds, but while roots are confined to pots the amount of top growth will become very restricted to give several years of pleasure before they outgrow their surroundings.

## ARDISIA CRENATA (*Myrsinaceae*)
coral berry

Where the araucaria might well outgrow its allotted space, the coral berry is never likely to, being one of the slowest growing plants that could ever be imagined. The evergreen leaves are leathery to the touch and crenulated at their margins, the plant growing to about 1 m (3 ft) tall. The main attraction of the plant is the bright red berries that seem to be there throughout the year. Grow them in light shade with the usual requirement of dryish winter conditions and no feed, with more frequent watering and a little feeding at other times. Temperature can be very varied with a suggested minimum of 12 °C (54 °F) in winter.

**Ardisia**
Slow growing plants with evergreen leaves and red berries that seem to be ever present in bright clusters.

Not easy, but new plants can be raised from either seed or cuttings made in the spring in high temperature.

## ASPARAGUS (*Lilaceae/Asparagaceae*)
(asparagus fern)

The most popular decorative plants of the *Asparagus* genus is **A. densiflorus 'Sprengeri'** which is usually referred to as the asparagus fern on account of the needle foliage that resembles a fern. Less popular but an equally easy and pleasing plant is **A. plumosus**, a plant with delicate green foliage that does well indoors or in the conservatory provided it is reasonably warm and shaded from the sun.

*A.d.* 'Sprengeri' is a very accommodating plant that may be grown conventionally in a pot, in a hanging container to provide a wealth of greenery, or trained to a framework to clothe a wall and provide a background for other plants. Other than regular watering, feeding and potting on when necessary, they are very undemanding. Check regularly for repotting as they soon fill their containers with roots.

Needing similar requirements is the florist's greenery plant, **A. asparagoïdes** with its lovely trails of growth that will also make a fine wall plant if trained into the desired position.

## ASPIDISTRA LURIDA (*Lilaceae/ Convallariaceae*) cast iron plant

The true stalwart of the Victorian era on account of its durability, toleration of dark and generally inhospitable conditions, this is now perhaps a touch dull for the conservatory collection of plants, but when seen growing on a traditional Victorian pedestal, it does have a certain charm allied to a touch of nostalgia. One of the don'ts with these plants is that you should not treat the leaves with any of the many chemical concoctions that are available and sold as leaf cleaners – wiping leaves with a soft, damp cloth will be much more satisfactory. Peculiar mauve coloured flowers are produced at soil level, but don't offer much in the way of attraction. Avoid strong sunlight – otherwise very little bother.

**Aspidistra**
Choose compact plants when buying and provide warm and agreeable conditions to get lush green foliage.

**ASPLENIUM NIDUS** (*Aspleniaceae*)
bird's nest fern

With pale green leaves forming into the shape of a giant shuttlecock, this must be rated as one of the finest foliage plants of them all, although you may have difficulty in avoiding leaf blemishes. Overwatering and subjection to direct sunlight will cause leaf margins to turn brown, as will excessive feeding, or feeding with a fertilizer above the manufacturer's recommended dosage.

Small plants are readily available and these should be grown in moist, shaded and warm

surroundings. Inspect root development on purchase and pot plants on into peaty mixture without delay if they are well rooted – in agreeable conditions the time of year will not be important. Guard against slugs which will damage leaves and, in particular, keep a watchful eye for brown scale insects clinging to the undersides of leaves. These can be treated with an insecticide, but a surer way to dispose of them is to use a firm sponge or soft cloth to wipe them physically from their anchorages.

When planning and planting the conservatory one should never underestimate the value of contrasting and interesting foliage. In the bird's nest fern you have a plant with many qualities, qualities that may well appeal to you more as time goes on than the more exotic flowers in bloom.

**AUCUBA JAPONICA** (*Cornaceae*)
gold leaf bush, spotted laurel

We almost invariably think of the exotic when the conservatory is mentioned but, often enough, the conservatory can be a cold and miserable place for more tender exotic plants when the winter months begin to bite. So you also need more mundane plants for cooler conditions, and the 'spotted laurel' is such a plant. It does not object to low temperatures and gives a reasonable show in respect of leaf colouring with the added bonus of red berries. Very easy to care for, they will need good light in winter and can stand out of doors during the summer when the conservatory is filled with more colourful flowering plants. Keep fed, watered and potted as necessary.

New plants can be propagated from cuttings rooted in cool conditions in the autumn or from seed sown at the same time of year.

**AZALEA INDICA** florist's azalea, see
RHODODENDRON INDICUM

**BEAUCARNIA RECURVATA** (*Agavaceae*)
pony tail plant

Another fun plant, this develops an enormous ground level trunk as it ages, giving the plant the appearance of a bonsai plant that has lost its way. Young plants soon develop the bulbous base but take many years to really mature. The narrow recurving leaves are evergreen and glossy, but there is not much else that can be said for the plant at this stage other than that it is easy to care for and will tolerate a wide range of growing conditions if it is watered, fed and located in a lightly shaded location. Propagate from seed in spring, if obtainable.

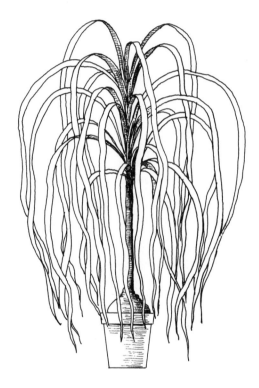

**Beaucarnia**
Older plants develop grotesque bulbous bases to their stems which, if anything, enhance the appearance of this unusual plant.

## BEGONIA (*Begoniaceae*)

The begonias range from fibrous to tuberous rooted, flowering to foliage, upright to pendulous plants – in fact, something for everyone. Surprisingly enough, one of the most remarkable of these plants is also one of the most humble – remarkable in that it will produce flowers virtually throughout the year and humble in that it is the common bedding plant, *B* × *carrierei* (syn. *B. semperflorens*). Towards the end of the flowering season outside and before frosts arrive, one should lift a few of the more attractive plants and pot them individually or in groups in a dish-type container. Given a modicum of care these lifted plants will virtually go the year round and still be in flower the following autumn, wonderful value from a packet of seed!

With a little more class, there has been remarkable improvements in the pot begonia, *B*. × *hiemalis* **'Elatior'**, which is now available in a very wide range of colours, the paler shades being especially fine. Normally growing in relatively small pots when purchased, these should be potted on without delay to ensure large plants and plants that will go on flowering in cool, light conditions for a greatly extended period.

To name all the many splendid begonias would be impossible here, but the named varieties of tuberous begonias should have a place. Unblemished flowers of every conceivable shade are grown by dedicated begonia specialists. Emulating the specialist in the conservatory is difficult, but you can get surprisingly good results by purchasing quality, named varieties at the outset. Start these in warm conditions in the early part of the season and grow them in lightly shaded conditions, paying particular attention to airing, an even temperature and carefully controlled watering.

Another class of begonia that is perhaps better suited to the less dedicated grower is the fibrous rooted cane type that can be either tall or spreading depending on the habit. Some, such as *B. sutherlandii* with its pale green leaves and bright orange flowers, present a splendid picture when suspended in a hanging container. These have the rewarding habit of dropping seed, small bulbils and assorted bits of growth onto the floor below. If the area below is gravel, peat or a planted bed, then there will be no shortage of this very agreeable plant as the 'droppings' root everywhere!

There are numerous taller growing cane begonias that are also reasonably easy to care for if given light shade, regular watering and feeding while in active growth, and a

135

temperature minimum of 12 °C (54 °F). Most will produce colourful flowers and many have the added attraction of colourful foliage often with an interesting shape.

The conservatory could well become the home for a begonia collection with colour and interest the year round, as opposed to a general mixture of plants.

## BELOPERONE GUTTATA
*see* JUSTICIA BRANDEGEEANA

## BILLBERGIA (*Bromeliaceae*)
queen's tears, summer torch

There are numerous splendid plants among the billbergias; probably the best known is the very ordinary *B. nutans* which produces cylinders of growth tightly clustered together. The habit of growth is better described as tubular but the tubes have splayed tops which are capable of holding a small amount of water;

**Billbergia**
Much underrated members of the bromeliad family, they are especially fine as hanging plants when pendulous flowers appear.

these should be kept topped up as far as possible. This is surely one of the toughest of all potted plants, and one that with a little care will oblige with its fascinating pendulous flowers at various intervals throughout the year. On account of its drooping flowers, the plants are best grown in a container of some kind and suspended at about head level in the conservatory.

Plants will go on for a long period without need for potting on once they are in containers of a reasonable size; they can be propagated with the greatest of ease by pulling clumps apart and potting individual pieces separately in pots filled with good compost, or several pieces could go direct into hanging containers.

There are also some particularly fine plants including **B. pyramidalis concolor** enjoying the common name of summer torch, which reflects the brilliantly coloured bracts which are short lived but vividly coloured. There are numerous others with similarly exotic colouring, but almost all of them are in short supply.

Plants prefer lightly shaded conditions and those other than the tough *B. nutans* will need reasonable temperature, minimum 16 °C (61 °F), for preference. Feeding is not important and one should avoid getting the soil too wet for prolonged periods, particularly over the winter months.

## BOUGAINVILLEA (*Nyctaginaceae*)
paper flower

Anyone holidaying in milder regions of the world must often sit and gaze at the magic of the bougainvilleas, scrambling like uncontrolled elevated weeds over any sort of support that may be available, and wonder how these plants could be adapted to grow in their own less tolerant climate. For such dreams to become a reality, it is necessary to have a glassed-in area so that plants can have some protection over the colder months of the year. During the summer months it is quite possible to grow bougainvilleas on a warm and sheltered patio.

In a conservatory, you could well consider growing these fine plants as a permanent feature within the protection of the glassed-in area. The variety that is most used by commercial producers is the tough and floriferous **B. glabra** which produces masses of reddish pink bracts giving the plant its common name of paper flower. However, seek out the more unusual and you will find many other bougainvilleas with flower colouring ranging from white through orange and pink to red, some with variegated foliage.

New plants are raised from cuttings of mature wood; in modest heat they are not difficult to propagate. The potting compost should contain a reasonable amount of loam and grit or sand to facilitate drainage. Keep the soil moist and fed while the plant is in active growth, and allow the soil to gradually dry out in the autumn until such time as it is bone dry; by late winter, fresh growth becomes evident. Plants can be pruned should they become untidy, but in the early stages of development it should be the aim to encourage all possible growth so that it can be trained to a framework within the conservatory. Growth of these plants can be very vigorous and strong once they settle and some of the stems should be encouraged to grow overhead on a framework, or strained wires in the conservatory; growth will then provide some shade as well as colour. The flowers of this plant are comparatively insignificant – it is the brilliant bract colouring that is the attraction.

Many of the plants offered for sale will be growing on a wire hoop secured in the pot: plants are trained in this way so that they can be easily managed at the nursery and so that they are less of a problem when it comes to packing and transporting. Unwind them and attach the growth initially to upright bamboo canes. A word of warning – wear gloves as the bougainvilleas have vicious barbs that are quite capable of drawing blood.

## BOUVARDIA (*Rubiaceae*)

Fragrance can add much to the conservatory and the evergreen and compact bouvardias will oblige agreeably in this respect. A further bonus is that **B. jasminiflora**, white in colour, and **B. ternifolia** (syn. *B. triphylla*),

scarlet, will flower over the winter months, the latter having a particularly long flowering period. After flowering plants can be cut back and potted on using a loam-based potting mix. Over the summer months plants can be housed in a storage corner out of the way but not over-neglected. Minimum winter temperature of 12 °C (54 °F) should be the aim, higher temperatures not being harmful.

## BRASSAIA umbrella tree
*see* SCHEFFLERA

## BROWALLIA (*Solanaceae*)

With shades of flowers through blues and purples these are small plants that will cheer the cool conservatory in early summer. Plants can be bought, but if one has a support greenhouse then this could be an interesting little chap to raise from seed sown during the spring. Keep them moist, in good light and as cool as possible to succeed. After flowering, plants should be disposed of.

## BRUNSFELSIA (*Solanaceae*)
yesterday, today and tomorrow

Interesting plants with a surprising number of fascinating common names. The best known alludes to the fact that individual flowers over the period of three days have a different colouring on each day – the plant given this name is **B. pauciflora 'Floribunda'**.

The plant that is most often offered for sale is **B. calycina** also having the same common name, but it should in fact have the equally amusing name of morning-noon-and-night, referring to the changing flower colour. It gives splendid value if properly cared for, and can well produce its short-lived flowers throughout the year. Leaves are evergreen on stout stems and flowers are rich purple and of good size.

Plants should be potted firmly into good rich mixture in the autumn. A minimum winter temperature of 12 °C (54 °F) is necessary and plants should have lightly shaded conditions. Keep moist and fed in summer, giving less water and no feed in winter. New plants are raised from cuttings a few inches in length taken in the spring and housed in temperature of around 20 °C (68 °F); in lower temperatures rooting will present problems.

## CALADIUM (*Araceae*) angel's wings

The conservatory that cannot offer a good amount of shade from the sun would be a virtual deathbed for these plants. The leaves are paper thin, and in the variety *C. candidum* almost translucent. Plants are grown entirely for their remarkable foliage, with colouring ranging from white through shades of green to rosy red. All are delicate and can suffer irreparable damage as a result of low temperature or exposure to direct sunlight, so care is needed, but there are compensations. When plants are reasonably at one with their surroundings they can be very impressive.

You must provide a conservatory with a good amount of shade and reasonable warmth; do not allow the soil to become waterlogged or bone dry. Having bought good quality plants (very important), you should be able to start with plants in early summer and have a wonderful show until the foliage begins to die back naturally towards early autumn. When this happens the soil should be kept bone dry and the tubers in the pot kept warm and dry through the winter until they are encouraged with watering to come back into life the following spring.

The most striking of these plants is without doubt the white leaved *C. candidum* and, besides its startling colouring, it is also the best plant to choose when seeking something that develops good shape and is reasonably tolerant in respect of care. If potting on is contemplated, a good houseplant mixture will be the most suitable. When plants are being bought they should be properly inspected. Do not purchase one with a protective paper sleeve cover where possibly a lot of problems might not at first be apparent.

Although seldom offered it might be possible to purchase tubers but these must be of good quality and unblemished. To start these off in the spring high temperature is needed.

## CALATHEA (*Marantaceae*) peacock plant

These are foliage plants grown purely for their decorative leaves; they will need more than a little care in order to do well. There are numerous varieties and all of them quite distinctive from one another. Main requirements are a well shaded location as direct sun will very quickly kill them. A temperature minimum of not less than 16 °C (61 °F) should be kept with higher temperatures being appreciated rather than harmful. Take care to ensure that plants don't remain saturated for long periods. Be sparing with water in winter and give no feed during the colder months of the year, but weekly at other times.

Of the numerous varieties there are probably no more than six that the commercial nurseryman attempts to grow. Few of these plants are easy to care for, but it must be said that the nursery standards in recent years have improved immensely. Some of the larger specimens of such plants as **C. makoyana** are superbly managed. The common name given to *C. makoyana* does not adequately describe the truly wonderful patterns and colouring present in the rounded leaves which are supported on slender petioles.

The principal reason for failure with this plant is low temperatures allied to overwatering. The other problem is that it is susceptible to attack by red spider mite so precautions have to be taken. Prevention being better than cure is an important adage as the tiny mites are very difficult to detect, being very much the same colour as the foliage.

There are numerous other species in the calathea tribe and all of them will need similar growing conditions to that described here. In a display bed they can be very effective, but it is wise to have an electric warming cable in the bed as calatheas are very touchy when it comes to growing in wet and cold conditions.

## CALLISIA REPENS (*Commelinaceae*) wandering sailor

Similar to the tradescantias, *Callisia* does not have the usual variegated foliage. Instead the leaves are small in size and a bright glossy green in colour. It freely produces small white flowers that give the plant much more appeal when flowers are seen against the green foliage. In small pots these are relatively poor plants, but as more mature subjects in small hanging containers they take on a new dimension and can be very effective when suspended from the roof of the conservatory. Little trouble, they should be protected from bright sun, be well watered while growing and have less at other times. Although it is not generally recommended to feed variegated tradescantia-type plants as they may revert to green, this will not affect the wholly green callisia so feed them at weekly intervals.

## CALLISTEMON CITRINUS (*Myrtaceae*)
bottle brush plant

Tough plants from Australia originally, these may well suit the larger conservatory where there is little or no heating. It is a plant that will tolerate very cool conditions and is hardy

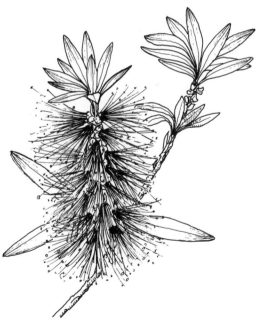

**Callistemon**
Almost hardy, these are tough old plants for the cooler conservatory and will usually oblige with bottle brush flowers.

out of doors in milder climates. In any event, it is better out of doors in a container for the duration of the summer. In time they become large, untidy plants needing lots of space. Plants can be lightly pruned after flowering and some of the prunings could well be used to propagate new plants in a mix of peat and sand. New plants can also be raised from seed but this is a slow process and not recommended if one is in a hurry to obtain plants of any size. The common name alludes to the flower which appears at the ends of the growing branches.

## CAMELLIA (*Theaceae*)

The common camellia is **C. japonica** from which many of the modern day plants have been derived. They require little description here as a result of their increasing popularity as evergreen decorative plants. The bright, glossy green leaves are an attraction throughout the year, but the plant comes into its own in the spring when fresh, clean flowers in a wide range of colours make their appearance. In the garden, plants are likely to be damaged by frost which can be a disappointment. It is usually best to grow plants in tubs so that they can be potted into a suitable mixture.

The conservatory is the perfect location for protection and in here one can admire and appreciate the unblemished flowers in comfort. The flower colouring ranges from white through many shades of pink to deepest red. There are also multicoloured flowers, such as in **C. 'Tricolor'**, to add a little spice.

Plants may be purchased as little more than rooted cuttings, often sporting a flower, or as mature plants. A spring visit to any garden centre will provide one with a surprising choice of varieties, some in decorative pots and simply asking for a conservatory location where they can show off a bit! Alternatively, one can consult the lists of the specialist grower – at least one of whom lists the camellia as being as hardy.

New plants can be raised from cuttings, and it is not so difficult as we are sometimes led to believe. Firm tip cuttings a few inches in length are taken in mid autumn and inserted in a peat and sand mix, either in trays or several to each small pot. To encourage rooting the cuttings can be treated with rooting powder, but the most important requirement is that they should have what is termed bottom heat. That will mean placing the cuttings in a pot or box on a bed of peat with a soil warming cable running through it. Once rooted the cuttings can be potted into small pots filled with an ericaceous mixture to grow on – but be warned that it takes time for plants to mature. Very large pots, or containers are not necessary and once plants have been potted into pots of reasonable size they can remain there for many years if fed occasionally during the growing season. Top dressing of the soil in the pot is another way of providing the plants with additional nourishment. Do this after flowering by removing some two or three inches of old soil from the top of the pot and replacing it with fresh to nourish the plant and to improve its appearance generally.

The appearance of plants will also be improved if, when they are brought in from the garden, the leaves are cleaned with a soft, damp cloth. Dirty leaves may be acceptable in the garden, but not when the plant is sitting by your elbow in the conservatory.

## CAMPANULA ISOPHYLLA
(*Campanulaceae*) star of Bethlehem

A relatively hardy plant that never amounts to much when growing as a garden plant, when treated as a hanging container subject in the conservatory it takes on an entirely new dimension.

Plants are raised from cuttings of non-flower tip growth taken early in the year as soon as plants are of sufficient size. If well grown the plant will seem never to be without flowers in summer and autumn. To get them off to a good start put five or six cuttings into a small pot filled with houseplant potting soil and keep them reasonably warm until rooted. Put three plants in a decorative hanging container with a drip saucer attached. Do not plant into an unsightly large wire container lined with moss – such traditional baskets, so beloved by the purist, are of no value in the conservatory as they drip water everywhere. When potting

the plant into its hanger, use a mixture containing some loam and not all peat.

From here on you simply keep the soil moist and occasionally fed and your campanula will do splendidly. If the flowers are allowed to go to seed the plant will hardly be worth bothering about, but if the withered flowers are removed several times each week the new flowers will keep on coming right through the summer months.

If there is a choice, the white flowers of *C. isophylla* **'Alba'** are much superior to that of the more common blue form. Actually, the flowers are both attractively star-shaped, but the growth of the white form is much more prolific and more pendulous in habit, trailing to 1 m (3 ft) or more, even in quite small containers, if feeding is not neglected.

For the summer months it is a lovely fresh plant to have hanging in the conservatory where it will appreciate protection from bright sun and airy rather than stuffy conditions. After flowering cut the plants right back to the rim of the container and keep them fairly dry until the following early spring when it comes into life for another season. A further blessing of this lovely plant is that pests are not a problem.

## CAMPELIA ZANONIA (*Commelinaceae*)
Mexican flag

In the old days this rather majestic member of the tradescantia tribe was known as *Dichorisandra albo-lineata*. The lance-shaped leaves that form in clusters atop stout stems 2 m (6 ft) in height are the main attraction, and are coloured cream, white and green. The assorted colours form lengthwise along the leaf give very good effect.

Plants need warm and light conditions to do well and ample space in the container which will have to be fairly large for the amount of foliage growth that will be produced. The pale coloured stems of the plant are not unattractive in themselves which is a blessing as the plant tends to shed lower leaves as it matures.

To propagate new plants the rosette, or cluster of leaves at the top of the stem should be removed complete and the severed end of

should be stored warm and dry at a temperature around 5 °C (41 °F).

New plants can be raised from seed which will need to be soaked for 24 hours and chitted (breaking the hard outer skin) to encourage germination. Alternatively, the roots of plants can be divided when plants are being potted for the new season in early spring.

**Canna**
Much used as centre-pieces in summer bedding, the canna will also offer good service in the conservatory as an attractive flowering plant.

**Campelia**
Related to the tradescantias, this is a fine plant for the connoisseur to add to a collection of interesting foliage plants.

the stem allowed to dry before inserting in a peaty mixture in pots that are about 13 cm (5 in) in diameter. Plants are in short supply, but they are fine for the back of planted borders if obtainable.

**CANNA** (*Cannaceae*)

These probably make too much leaf growth for the smaller conservatory, but their brilliant heads of flower throughout the summer months will add much to the larger room, particularly if they can be planted near to water. During the active months of the year, plants should be kept in good light and well watered with twice weekly feeding, or a weak feed at every watering. Over winter, plants

**CEROPEGIA WOODII** (*Asclepiadacaea*)
hearts entangled

These are wee, insignificant plants that at first sight in small pots would not seem to have any place in the modern conservatory, but, with the benefit of hanging containers and their ability to add another dimension to the garden room, the ceropegia could well come into its own. It is the most natural of hanging plants with fragile stems that will trail, for a good many metres when growing in containers of reasonable size. The small mauve coloured, tubular flowers are comparatively insignificant, but the succulent heart-shaped leaves are more than a little interesting. These are produced in great numbers and, as the common name suggests, they can become an entangled mass if the strands of growth have to be gathered together at any time so that the plant can be moved.

Grow in light shade and keep moist and fed throughout the summer months for plants to do well. New plants can be raised from cuttings with two leaves attached at any time during the spring or summer. Put several cuttings in each small pot and when established, plant several pots in a hanging container. The growing tips can be removed to encourage plants to branch, or new shoots can be pegged down in the container so that they too will produce roots and give a much fuller and more attractive plant. There are no pest problems to worry about.

## CESTRUM (*Solanaceae*)

There are several varieties of cestrum with the one most often sold being **C. elegans**. The cestrum are evergreen or semi-evergreen plants that are better suited to the larger conservatory where their climbing/spreading growth can be trained to a wall or pillar as it develops. Flowers of *C. elegans* are produced in drooping clusters and are a rich wine red in colour.

High temperature is not necessary and can go down to 5 °C (41 °F) in winter. No harm will be done if the soil is kept very much on the dry side. In summer they will take their chance with whatever temperature might be possible, but plants should be well watered and fed if they are to do well. The potting mix must contain some loam, and any potting on that is needed should be undertaken in the spring. The basic framework should be maintained but any unwanted or untidy growth can be pruned out in late winter. Towards the end of the summer new plants can be propagated from pieces of stem 10–15 cm (4–6 in) in length. Remove from the plant with a piece of old stem attached and plant in a very sandy mix in a cool and shaded location.

## CHAMAEDOREA ELEGANS (*Palmae*)
parlour palm

This is one of the more compact indoor palms that will be well suited to the smaller conservatory, whereas many of the more vigorous palms would quickly outgrow their allotted space. When purchasing plants it is well to seek those that have several small plants in the pot as opposed to solitary ones. As plants develop the larger clumps will give a much bolder and more impressive plant. In time with good care these are plants that could well attain a height of 2–3 m (6–10 ft) but they are not so spreading and space-demanding as many of the palms are.

In the conservatory they will need shaded conditions and a minimum temperature of around 16 °C (61 °F) with ample water in spring and summer and less in winter; occasional feeding is needed during the active months of the year. New plants are propagated from seed sown in high temperature, preferably in spring, but it must be said that seed is very seldom made available outside the nursery trade. A watchful eye must be kept for red spider mites on the undersides of leaves and for the possible incidence of scale insects on the stems of the plant rather than on the leaves. Plants suffering from red spider mite will develop pale discolouration of foliage. Treat early and thoroughly with recommended insecticide as soon as pests are detected. Precautionary treatment with insecticide is often better than trying to eradicate pests once they have a hold.

## CHAMAEROPS HUMILIS (*Palmae*)
European palm

This is a tough old plant that will only be suitable where there is ample space for overwintering – in summer it can be stood out of doors to decorate the garden or patio. Leaves are coarse and spreading and attached to stout fibre-covered trunks (a principal feature of the plant). Plants will eventually have to go into large pots and should be potted into a mixture containing a good proportion of loam. They should be thoroughly watered and allowed to

**Chamaerops**
Very tough palms that will serve well in the conservatory where only minimal heat is provided in winter. In time it needs ample space.

dry reasonably before repeating. Alas, seed is not freely available, but plants can be propagated by removing young plants from around the base of the parent so that they may be potted as individuals, late summer being a good time to tackle this task.

## CHLOROPHYTUM COMOSUM
(syn. *C. capense*) (*Liliaceae/Anthericaceae*) spider plant

Another of our more common houseplants normally seen struggling to grow in small pots that are totally inadequate for the amount of root and top growth these plants are capable of achieving. Knocking almost any chlorophytum from its growing pot will disclose the fact that they do have the most robust root system imaginable. The reason for most of these plants suffering and developing brown tips to their leaves is that they become starved of nourishment. This can happen when plants are being fed but not getting as much nourishment as they require.

One of the most fascinating aspects of the chlorophytum is the way in which it produces stalks of growth from the centre of the plant, to which are attached perfect miniature plants of the parent. The best way to display plants carrying babies to full effect is to place them in a hanging container where the plant and plantlets can spread in all directions and have the light and fresh air that they desire. The container should be reasonably large and the potting mixture must contain some loam as all-peat preparations are not suitable for these vigorous subjects. Ample watering is an essential requisite in spring and summer, with less in winter, although plants should never be allowed to become too dry. A watch should be kept for aphids during the spring and summer. These get down amongst the more tender small leaves where they might not appear to be all that harmful, but they do cause unattractive blotching of leaves as they mature.

Although they are very common, you will derive much pleasure from growing large and unblemished plants, if only to see the look of astonishment on the face of the visitor who struggles with weedy plants in pots that are much too small for the job.

## CHRYSALIDOCARPUS LUTESCENS
(*Palmae*) butterfly palm

A mouthful of a name and one that is not favoured by all growers of these plants, they are often incorrectly given the name of *Areca lutescens*, which the average purchaser finds much more easy to manage. This is a lovely plant with delicate pale yellow stems and, for a palm, small and attractive leaves. Plants will attain an eventual height of 2–3 m (6–9 ft), but will always retain their elegant appearance. Plants can usually be purchased in quite small pots for growing on and will very often have a surprising number of what are virtually seedling palms in the pot. Needless to say, when shopping for plants one should keep an eye open for the pot that is well filled with plants. The newly purchased plant, or any plant being potted, should go into a slightly larger container using a good quality houseplant potting mixture.

Offer shaded location and a reasonable temperature and take care not to water too freely during the colder months of the year. Feed weekly during spring and summer with a liquid fertilizer. Besides being good individual specimens, when large enough these will also make fine centre-pieces for a formal planting scheme in the larger conservatory.

As with most palms it will attract red spider mites and scale insects. The mites are barely detectable with the naked eye, hence their ability to become established before one detects their presence. Pale discoloration of the otherwise green leaves is an indication that mites have become well established. Taking the preventative measure of regularly treating one's plants with a systemic insecticide will do much to deter these troublesome pests.

Scale insects are found on the stems and undersides of plant foliage, and an indication of their presence is a sooty mould deposit on the upper surface of leaves, underneath where the pests are at work. The mould is unsightly and the pests will weaken the plant so some action is necessary. Where only a few plants are involved the best action is to wear a pair of rubber gloves and to make up a preparation of liquid insecticide recommended for scale treatment, and to use a firm sponge soaked in the solution to forcibly wipe the pests from their anchorages on the plant. The mature pests are blackish brown in colour and easily detected while the younger members are flesh coloured. The best technique with the sponge is to hold one hand on the opposite side of the leaf while the hand holding the sponge is used to clean the pests thoroughly from their perches. For all the many other plants that are susceptible to scale attack this treatment will be a much more positive method of getting rid of pests than simply spraying on the insecticide with a syringe, as the hard shell of the parent scale provides a perfectly sealed haven that is almost impossible to penetrate, regardless of how efficient the spraying equipment may be.

## CHRYSANTHEMUM (*Compositae*)

To become addicted to the growing of chrysanthemums is something of a disease more than a hobby when you see the sort of blooms, quite astonishingly large and perfect, at any good exhibition of these plants. Exhibition specimens would have little place in the modern conservatory, other than when they might be brought in as a temporary potful of blooms.

In fact, these are essentially temporary plants as far as the conservatory is concerned, the best example being the Pot Mum, produced annually in millions to be sold in 13 cm (5 in) pots in a wide array of colours. Everything about these plants is controlled as far as the nurseryman is concerned: the eventual height of the plant is controlled by applying carefully controlled doses of growth retarding chemicals and the flowering time by manipulating the amount of light that is available to the plant. He produces like clockwork a crop of plants every ten weeks or so of the year. The result is a compact, free-flowering plant in a wide range of colours that is virtually guaranteed a six-week life on the windowsill once it is brought indoors. After flowering the plant can be disposed of or it can be planted in the garden in the hope that it will go on to flower another day.

*C. frutescens* (now *Argyranthemum frutescens*) is a plant with typical white daisy flowers that appear in late summer/autumn. Besides the white there is a lovely yellow form, *C. frutescens chrysaster* which has the common name of Boston yellow daisy, and the pink marguerite, *C. frutescens* 'Roseum'. All of these have lovely fresh colouring that will do much to brighten the conservatory scene as autumn approaches. Plants may be bought as bushes or as standards – the latter being very impressive when growing in a decorative pot and given ample space for the spread of foliage and flowers on top of the stately stems. After flowering these can be transferred to the cool greenhouse to be grown on for the following year.

Another favourite among these plants is the Korean chrysanthemum, *C. sibiricum*, which can be started by taking cuttings in late

*Aechmea fasciata.*
An easy-care
bromeliad provided
the central 'urn' is
never allowed to
dry out and the
temperature
remains
reasonable.

*Agave*. With bayonet-sharp points to its stout leaves this is a plant that requires ample space in which to grow if more robust forms are chosen.

*Bougainvillea*. One of the kings of conservatory plants once it is established and producing cascades of flowering branches in the upper reaches of the room.

*Opposite: Ananas.* The decorative pineapple in its variegated form is one of the most striking of potted plants when bearing colourful fruit.

146

*Opposite:*
*Codiaeum.* Better known as croton, there are many varieties, producing plants with the most brilliant colouring, but only if temperature is adequate.

*Clivia miniata.* Evergreen, leathery leaves sprouting from a bulbous base and brilliant orange flowers make a handsome combination on this fine plant.

*Calathea.* Grown almost entirely for their highly decorative foliage these are plants for the experienced plant person with a warm and shaded conservatory.

149

*Cymbidium*. Spectacular orchids that are among the easiest of these plants to care for, but they do respond best to careful attention.

*Opposite: Datura*. With trumpet-shaped flowers in many shades of colouring these are fine plants for the larger room. Pay attention to pest control.

*Dracaena*. A diverse range of plants of upright habit. Excellent plants when employed as background subjects in the larger room (species shown: *D. fragrans*).

*Echinocactus grusonii*. An aristocrat in its field, the barrel cactus is very slow to develop but matures to a superb rounded specimen in time.

winter/early spring. Tip growth about 8 cm (3 in) in length should be inserted in a peat and sand mixture in seed boxes or pans and watered in. In modest warmth they will root with very little bother, and once rooted they can be potted into 13 cm (5 in) pots (three or four cuttings per pot) and grown on in good light and ample fresh air. They can be fed once established, but it is often better to pot plants on when roots have become well established. By August they can be in 20 cm (8 in) pots standing 60 cm (24 in) from the floor with a wide head of fresh green foliage. You can bring plants on earlier by using black polythene to reduce the amount of daylight available to the plant, but they are better left to flower naturally in late autumn when there is not all that much to offer for colouring the interior of the conservatory. The bright yellow button flowers of this plant will completely obscure the foliage and provide a really cheerful display for the effort that has gone into their preparation and handling. After flowering cut them hard back and store the plants in a cool greenhouse in readiness for the following spring when the process begins all over again.

## CISSUS (*Vitaceae*)

An early favourite when houseplants were becoming popular was *C. antarctica* (kangaroo vine) with its evergreen leaves and coarse stems that would oblige by climbing or trailing depending on whether it was fixed to a support or not. In recent years it has been supplanted by numerous more decorative subjects. For the modern conservatory the only practical use for this old favourite is to use the plant as a background of foliage tied in on a wall or pillar, as it is not a natural climber.

Only suitable where the conservatory conditions are warm, humid and shaded, the rex begonia vine, *C. discolor*, can become a spectacular free-growing plant, but with less than the suggested growing conditions, you will have a miserable plant that will do little to enhance its surroundings. This is a plant grown purely for its fine foliage colouring with a lace pattern of silvered venation. The reverse of the leaf is a rich maroon. Given the correct

conditions and care the growth can become very vigorous during the spring and summer months of the year. Although plants will climb naturally it will be wise to train some of the shoots to the desired position so that a more pleasing effect may result. It will never be easy, but it can be said that in the right hands these make marvellous plants, but the winter months can be very testing and great care should be taken not to overwater. Use water at room temperature rather than water direct from the cold tap. As with all the more delicate plants it is well to remember that a combination of cold and wet conditions will often be fatally harmful.

Early spring is normally the accepted time for propagating exotics such as *C. discolor*, but if temperature and conditions are suitable propagate fresh plants towards the end of early autumn when cuttings will be generally firmer and more suitable. Cuttings should be prepared from a single mature and undamaged leaf with a piece of the main stem about 2.5 cm (1 in) above and below the node attached. The cutting should be treated with a rooting powder and inserted in pure peat in either trays or shallow 13 cm (5 in) diameter pots – the latter probably being better where only a few plants are needed. They will root on an open bench in a warm greenhouse, but only if there is a misting unit in use. Otherwise employ a heated propagator maintained at temperature of not less than 20 °C (68 °F). Thereafter you should keep the cuttings out of direct sunlight and cross your fingers! Once rooted the young plants in their pot can be moved intact into a slightly larger container using a good houseplant potting mixture. Almost half the pleasure of growing plants is to raise your own by whatever means of propagation, but this one will test your skills.

The Cape grape, *C. capensis* (syn. *Rhoicissus capensis*), is a very free-growing vine which will quickly fill an area where it can climb and sprawl over the supporting frame. Leaves are evergreen, large and glossy. It is an ideal subject in the new and larger conservatory where one is endeavouring to provide a quicker answer to the problem of covering bare surrounding walls or pillars in the least possible time. A very easy plant to manage, it asks for little more than reasonable warmth, moisture and regular feeding while in active growth.

## CITROFORTUNELLA MICROCARPA
(*Rutaceae*) Calamondin orange

A true miniature in citrus terms is calamondin orange, which is available in either green or variegated form. Besides being small, it is also capable of bearing scores of small orange fruits. Another attribute is that prior to fruiting you will be treated to the magic fragrance of the plentiful white flowers. Keep them out of doors in their pots on the patio during the summer to encourage flowering and fruit setting, and bring them in before the outdoor conditions become too cold. In the conservatory they will do best in light, cool conditions, and will require careful watering that avoids erring on the wet side. Feed with a tomato fertilizer while plants are actively growing. Fruit bearing will vary from mid winter through to late spring to provide decorative plants for many months.

## CITRUS (*Rutaceae*)

In northern Europe, as elsewhere, there is considerable interest being shown in the production of citrus plants of all kinds as decorative pot plants with the conservatory owner in mind as the eventual purchaser. Before rushing out to buy up all the available stock, the conservatory owner should, however, be warned that attractive though these plants may be while in fruit or flower they leave much to be desired when occupying valuable space as purely foliage. There is ever the promise that plants will soon be bearing fruit again, but you could well have a long wait. Where there is plenty of sun around, plants will be better out of doors during the summer months, and as a result of being exposed to the sun and the elements they will often oblige by flowering and fruiting more freely.

Some of the citrus are much too large for the average conservatory, but will grow well and tolerate savage pruning if planted out in a deep bed of soil. Two that could be considered are *C.* **'Ponderosa'** (American wonder lemon), which produces very large lemon-yellow fruits, sour but edible, that will bring a gasp from every visitor. The other that is usually obtainable is *C.* **× *paradisi*** which is capable of fruiting very heavily.

For the more modest conservatory plants should be smaller and more manageable, and there is a reasonably good selection of these (see also *Citrofortunella microcarpa*).

Besides getting plants to bear fruit, two other main problems with these plants are red spider mites and scale insects. A careful watch must be kept for both of these debilitating pests and remedial action should be taken immediately they are detected. Rather than attempting to eradicate these pests once they have taken up residence it is much better to make a practice of regularly giving plants a preventative spraying over with suitable insecticide.

## CLEOME SPINOSA (*Capparidaceae*)
spider flower

Growing to a height of 1 m (3 ft), these are annual plants that give a splendid show when

**Cleome spinosa**
From a packet of seed a fine display of these exotic annuals may be had – ideal for providing exotic colour at little cost.

planted in groups either in the formal bed in the conservatory or in large containers. One of the blessings is that they are inexpensive, being reasonably easy to grow from seed that is sown in early spring in warm conditions. As they become plants of substantial size it will be important to ensure that they are not allowed to become rootbound in the early stages of development. Pot plants on into slightly larger containers as roots fill their pots, using a loam-based mixture for preference. In the conservatory they will need good light, but not direct sun, and airy conditions in which to grow.

## CLERODENDRUM (*Verbenaceae*)
bleeding heart vine

In the conservatory heated all the year round there is a much greater opportunity for growing more varied plants and, obviously, plants of more tender disposition. Many of these will be in containers while others will be planted in the ground, perhaps in a border around the perimeter of the interior of the building. When planting out such beds it might well be necessary to have soil warming cables in the soil to reduce the possibility of plants becoming too cold during the winter months.

There are numerous meritorious plants that might be considered for covering part of the wall as permanent plants in the conservatory, and **C. thomsoniae** is a plant that might well fit the bill. When happy this is a plant that will attain good height of some 4 m (12 ft), but it will need careful attention, particularly during the settling-in period. The evergreen leaves are coarse in appearance and attached to stout stems that will require supporting: a neat framework can be made with trellis, or at more reasonable cost with strained wires attached to the wall. Principal attraction of the plant are the large red and white clustered flowers that appear in spring and go on for many months.

Plants need a minimum temperature of not less than 18 °C (64 °F), shade from bright sunlight and some care with watering, ensuring that the soil does not become saturated for long periods – this is more important with plants that are growing in containers as opposed to those that are planted into the ground.

## CLIVIA MINIATA
(*Liliaceae/Amaryllidaceae*) kaffir lily

Among the more expensive flowering plants, the clivia has achieved considerable popularity. The leathery evergreen leaves emanate from a bulbous base, with the appearance of the plant being much enhanced by the arrival of clustered orange flowers atop stout stems. In conditions that are warm, lightly shaded and moist, these are very easy plants to manage and will go on producing their showy flowers regularly each year. In large pots they can be moved around within the conservatory, occupying a prominent location while in flower and less conspicuous spots when flowers have gone over. Potted plants are fine, but if you really want to see what the clivia can do in the way of flowering then the plant should be planted in the ground where it will have a free root run. You will then see plants of much more robust appearance and capable of producing virtually dozens of flowers all at the same time.

When potting plants on, or when preparing a bed where they may be planted, use a rich mixture containing a good proportion of loam. When plants are being potted it is also a good time to think of dividing the clumps of root and potting them up individually to make further plants. Clivias are not much troubled by pests.

## COBAEA SCANDENS (*Polemoniaceae*)
monastery bells

A free-growing climbing plant that, though perennial, is usually grown as an annual and disposed of at the end of its season. Violet-coloured bell flowers are freely produced and the plant is provided with tendrils that simply require a framework to which the plant can cling and spread over a large area in comparatively little time.

The green-foliaged form will not be difficult to raise from seed sown in warmth in the spring. There is also an attractive variegated form 'Aureomarginata', that must be propagated from cuttings of young shoots in warm conditions in early spring. Plants need ample water and feeding while in active growth, but any that are being overwintered should be kept on the dry side with no feeding from late autumn until new growth is getting under way. Don't forget that it is likely to be more practical to dump old plants so that fresher and more vigorous ones can be introduced the following year.

**Cobaea**
Grow from spring-sown seed and never overpot this very vigorous climber that will quickly cover a wall of the conservatory.

## COCOS (*Palmae*) coconut palm

Grown throughout the tropics for their edible fruit, the coconut palm, particularly its more miniature forms, are interesting decorative plants for the conservatory. Producing coconuts on conservatory grown plants is, however, out of the question. In recent years we have seen the introduction of pot-grown plants growing from the coconut lying on its side on top of the pot. Although highly decorative, this is not the easiest of plants to maintain, the plants seeming to be highly sensitive to fluctuations of any kind, and in

particular radical changes in the amount of water given. Plants should have reasonably steady temperature ranging from 13 to 18 °C (55–65 °F). When watering endeavour to keep the soil moist and avoid extremes of wet and dry. In low temperatures plants will be very vulnerable if the soil is excessively wet. A light location with some protection from direct sunlight will suit them best.

In good conditions with proper care plants will generally fare quite well if left in their original pots with little need for frequent potting on. If the conservatory boasts a planted bed of decorative plants the plant pot can be half buried in the soil with the result that roots will find their way through the holes in the bottom of the pot to enjoy the nourishment that is available in the soil below. The plant can then be watered and fed into the top of the pot and the surrounding soil can be treated in the same way. The difficulty with this approach is when it comes to potting the plant on – the answer is not to bother, as the plant will go on for years with this sort of treatment and not seem to object unduly.

## CODIAEUM VARIEGATUM PICTUM
(*Euphorbiaceae*) Joseph's coat, croton

If the conservatory cannot be maintained at a minimum temperature of not less than 12 °C (54 °F) then there is little point in attempting to grow these plants for anything other than the warmer months of the year. The codieaum is really much better known by its common name of croton, but there should be little difficulty in obtaining plants by mentioning either name. The flowers of this plant are very insignificant and should be removed when they appear. The foliage is the main attraction and there can be few groups of plants that can match the brilliance and variation of colouring found in the leaves of the croton. There are many varieties, some with broad leaves on vigorous plants, while others have extremely narrow leaves by comparison.

Given the right conditions and care these are plants that will grow quite strongly, but will almost surely lose lower leaves as time goes on – this seems to be almost a natural characteristic of these plants. In poor light plants will lose much of their colouring, so the answer is to provide a light, even sunny location. The only difficulty with sunny locations is that the plants dry out much more rapidly, and the incidence of red spider mite will be much increased. Plants should be treated regularly with suitable insecticide to discourage mite; when syringing plants give particular care to the undersides of leaves where the majority of these minute mites will be at work.

Crotons can be planted out in deep beds of rich compost or they will look equally fine as individual plants in decorative containers. Appearance of plants will be considerably enhanced if the leaves are cleaned with a damp sponge or cloth at regular intervals. As mentioned the incidence of red spider mite will be greatly increased if plants are grown in hot and dry conditions, so to offset the possibility of dry atmosphere and dryness in general it is advisable to spray frequently the foliage and surroundings with water.

Cuttings will root at almost any time of the year, but they must have a temperature in the region of 20 °C (68 °F) in order to succeed. The cutting can comprise of nothing more than a single leaf with a piece of stem attached, but the best cuttings are prepared from the top sections of stem. The stem should be sturdy and the cuttings will need to have at least two firm leaves attached. Insert them in a peat and sand mix and keep them in a propagating case until rooting takes place. Propagating exercises of this kind are invariably less successful if a solitary cutting is placed in the propagator. It is very much better to do a batch of cuttings (nor necessarily all crotons) so that propagator is well filled and a nice atmosphere is created with the unit. It may seem odd, but plants do appear to do better when growing in the company of other plants!

## COFFEA ARABICA (*Rubiacaea*)
Arabian coffee

Growing and blending your own coffee from the odd plant or two that may be housed in the conservatory is perhaps being a little over-ambitious, but there is no reason why well cared for plants should not produce their crop of coffee beans on the plants once they have well matured. When berries appear the coffee plant with its naturally glossy, evergreen leaves is much enhanced: the berries are coloured in many shades of orange and yellow and remain on the plant for a considerable time. Pot grown plants will attain a height of some 2 m (6 ft) with a 1 m (3 ft) spread, so ample space is needed to house them.

In respect of care they are not too temperamental, but a minimum temperature of not less than 12 °C (54 °F) should be kept. Lightly shaded conditions and regular feeding will be needed while it is producing leaves. When watering err on the side of dry rather than wet conditions, as prolonged periods of wet root conditions will invariably result in loss of plant leaves. When potting on, use a good house-plant mixture, but never pot on too frequently. In fact, once plants are in pots of around 25 cm (10 in) in diameter, they will rarely need further potting and can be sustained by regular feeding.

## COLEUS flame nettle
*see* SOLENOSTEMON

## COLUMNEA (*Gesneriaceae*) goldfish plant

In *C. microphylla* we have one of the most spectacular of all plants for growing in hanging containers. Growth is naturally pendulous with relatively small, rounded leaves. When it is in large hanging baskets of around 35 cm (14 in) in diameter, it is possible to have plants with trailing stems 2 m (6 ft) in length. In mid summer when these stems are laden with scarlet and yellow flowers you then have a hanging plant that is virtually second to none. To do well the plants need to have a minimum temperature of 16 °C (61 °F) and a lightly shaded location. As with all hanging basket plants, it is essential to place much importance on watering, and on feeding once plants have become established. Also important with these larger hanging baskets is to remember that when they are well watered there is considerable weight which will entail provision of a really stout anchor point from which baskets can be hung.

Less spectacular, but a very fine plant nevertheless is **C. x banksii** which has the added advantage of being very tolerant and able to contend with very variable conditions other than wet and cold. This variety comes into flower in mid winter when there is little else available in the way of flowering basket plants. Stiffish stems are more sprawling than trailing, but mature plants produce their eye-catching scarlet flowers lasting well into the spring. Offer these the same attention as advised for *C. microphylla*.

New plants can be raised from cuttings taken after flowering. Almost any firm piece of stem will produce roots in warm and moist conditions protected from the sun. When rooted, several cuttings should be potted into small pots to grow on and when these have established, at least five plants should go into hanging baskets and allowed to establish at bench level (easier to manage) before they are suspended from the ceiling, or attached to a bracket on the wall of the conservatory.

There are numerous other columneas, including a variegated form (*C. m. variegata*) that will be perfectly suited to the heated conservatory.

## COPROSMA (*Rubiacaea*) mirror plant

Although the conservatory is very much part of the living area of the house it is often shut away for much of the time in winter with the result that the heating of the extension is often neglected. Where tender plants are concerned it is obvious that resulting cold conditions could be fatal. The answer is either to provide higher and more constant temperature or to select plants that will be tolerant of the cooler conditions. In this respect consider plants that are referred to as half-hardy, the sort of plants that will get through a mild winter but will be vulnerable when temperatures are low.

Indigenous to New Zealand, there is at least one coprosma, **C. robusta 'Williamsii'**, that will be ideal for the cooler conservatory. This is a compact, woody shrub, which is slow-growing and very easy to care for. The small rounded leaves are cream and green in colour with a gloss to them that seems to suggest that they might have been varnished. It is unlikely that the plant will flower whilst growing in a pot, but the year-round glossy foliage will more than compensate for the lack of flowers.

Provided it can enjoy cool and light conditions, it will be little trouble in respect of care. Over-winter watering will have to be done with care, ensuring that the soil does not remain overwet for long periods. During the milder months of the year the plant can be transferred to the garden where it will be a welcome addition to the patio plants. In summer the coprosmas will require more water and will benefit from the occasional liquid feed. When plants are brought in from their garden location it will almost be inevitable that some lower leaves will turn brown and be shed, but this should not give rise for undue concern.

## CORDYLINE (*Agaraceae*) dragon tree

The majority of cordylines are often mislabelled with the name *Dracaena* which can lead to confusion when plants are being selected from a catalogue of names, as opposed to seeing the actual plant at the retailers. To add to the confusion it will also be found that *C. australis* will often be labelled as *Dracaena indivisa*; the latter should now be labelled as *C. indivisa*.

Some of the cordylines will develop into substantial plants in time, plants that would only be suitable for larger conservatories offering ample headroom. Even then it will be wise to confine plant roots to a container rather than plant them freely in a bed. There are numerous varieties of **C. australis**, some with reddish colouring while others are variegated. These are plants seen to best effect when planted in ornamental tubs and growing in well drained soil containing a good amount of loam. Offer them good light and water and feed well during the milder, growing months of the year, giving no feed and less water in winter.

There are many varieties of **Cordyline fruticosa** (syn. *C. terminalis* and mislabelled *Dracaena terminalis*) that will provide brilliant colouring to enhance one's plant collection. As

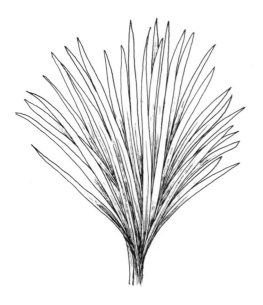

**Cordyline**
Tough plants, often confused with dracaenas, they are seen at their best when growing in pedestal containers as single specimens.

is so often the case the price we pay for much brighter colouring is greater care and much better growing conditions. Currently the most popular of the fruticosa types is *C.f.* 'Atom' with very bright red leaves normally offered as tight rosettes of foliage on stems of around 45 cm (18 in) tall. In the conservatory these are plants that should be left in their pots so that they can have individual attention in respect of watering and feeding.

Plants are not too much troubled by pests, but they do have an unfortunate tendency to develop leaves that are brown at their margins, a problem that is aggravated by excessive watering. All members of the cordyline and dracaena family have a natural tendency to shed lower leaves as they increase in height, so there is little that can be done about the problem. The fruticosa types have natural high gloss leaves, so will benefit from occasional cleaning, but it is important to remember that too frequent use of leaf cleaning chemicals can be harmful, as will application of such chemicals when plants are exposed to bright sunlight.

**CRASSULA** (*Crassulaceae*)
money plant, jade plant

For the cactus garden within the conservatory there are numerous low-growing crassulas that will do excellent service and not be any great bother to care for provided they are kept sunny, warm and not too wet, particularly in winter. Of all these, however, the plant that has most caught the attention in recent years is *Crassula argentea* which seemed to have a new lease of life when the common name of jade plant underwent a change to that of money plant – something to do with one owning a plant and being lucky as a result. Whatever the common name it is a rewarding plant, which will be very easy to manage if grown in good light and given a holiday on the terrace out of doors during the summer months. The evergreen leaves are glossy green and succulent, and grow from stout stems that become an interesting feature with age.

With smaller leaves and of less vigorous growth there is a fine variegated variety in *C. portulacea* 'Hummel's Sunset' which has an overall bronzed appearance that will be much enhanced if the plant can stand out of doors in full sun during the summer months.

*C. coccinea* are succulent plants much favoured for their colourful scarlet tube flowers that are carried in clusters on short stalks in mid summer. They are plants that respond to sunshine, and should be placed very close to the glass in a sunny part of the conservatory.

Water is given freely during the spring and summer with gradually less in the autumn, with very little in winter. A minimum winter temperature of 13 °C (55 °F) should be the aim, bearing in mind that at this temperature the soil in the pot should be very dry if plants are to survive.

For *C. coccinea* following flowering, plants should be trimmed hard back to within a few inches from their base. The following year new plants can be made from cuttings taken from the first shoots that appear in the spring. The cuttings, like the parent plant, love the sun and should be left close to the glass for a few days following removal before they are inserted in a sandy mixture. Even after insertion the cuttings do better if they remain in their position near the glass in the greenhouse or conservatory. Once rooted they can be potted on into slightly larger pots in a sandy mixture. The parent plant will also have to have some fresh soil once it has begun to grow for the new season. This can either be achieved by potting the plant on into a bigger pot, or the plant can be removed from its pot so that much of the old mixture can be removed before it is repotted in the same container with fresh mixture filling in the gaps from where the old soil was removed. Feeding is not important.

Propagation of other species is relatively simple and can be undertaken at almost any time of the year if conditions are agreeable. Top sections of stem a few inches in length make the best propagating material and should be removed with a sharp knife and left until the severed end of the cutting had dried before it is inserted. Put individual cuttings, one per small pot filled with any reasonable well drained mixture, in good light but not direct sun. In no time you will have baby plants growing but it will be some years before they attain an interesting size.

## CRINUM (*Liliaceae/Amaryllidaceae*) swamp lily

There are numerous varieties with the best known being **C. × powellii** which in itself has given rise to several cultivars. This is a hardy plant which does well against a south-facing wall and produces a wealth of foliage and striking pink flowers during the summer.

The red **C. amabile** and the white **C. sanderianum** are suggested as plants for the conservatory offering reasonable warmth, and for the cooler interior **C. asiaticum** with white flowers and decorative foliage is a very desirable plant.

Plants are seen to best effect when growing in large tubs, and once planted in these in good soil they will go on for several years without need for disturbance provided they are fed regularly while in active growth. Bulbs should be bone dry and rested over winter, and the best place to do this is with the containers placed on their sides underneath the bench in a

warm greenhouse. Placing containers on their sides will prevent the soil becoming watered inadvertently, so upsetting the necessary winter rest.

New plants can be raised from seed but this is a very slow process; it is much more rewarding to remove offsets so that they may be potted up individually.

## CRYPTANTHUS (*Bromeliaceae*) earth star

This is not the most spectacular of bromeliads in that the flowers are very inconspicuous, and the plants are comparatively small. They are also different from the majority of bromeliads in that they do not form upright rosettes of leaves in watertight vases. The cryptanthus rosette is much flatter and, as the common name suggests, star-shaped, in many varieties. In time they will form into fairly large clumps of rosettes, but when purchased are little more than a single neat rosette – many of them being offered as suitable plants for a glass container where an important requirement is a slow growth rate.

A generally scarce plant, but one of the very best is **C. fosterianus** which produces very robust leaves and intricate partridge-breast colouring from base to tip of each leaf. With the brightest colouring we have a pink-foliaged plant with the odd name of **C. 'It'**.

By themselves these are plants that are comparatively insignificant, but they can be particularly interesting when grouped with other plants of the bromeliad family, and also when filling odd clefts on a bromeliad tree.

In respect of care they require a temperature of not less than 16 °C (61 °F) to do well and where possible it will be advantageous to use rain water when watering. Potting on is needed only very occasionally. Use a mixture that is peaty with some fine grade chipped bark to keep the mixture open and free-draining.

To propagate new plants, simply remove small rosettes from around the base of the parent to pot them individually. Some of these will be very small and difficult to keep in position without using a large wire 'hairpin' pushed into the soil on either side of the plant to hold it in position until roots develop, when the pin can be removed. Pests are never a problem with members of the bromeliad family.

## CTENANTHE (*Marantaceae*)
never never plant

The actual never never plant is **C. oppenheimiana 'Tricolor'** which is indigenous to tropical South America and one of the easier ctenanthes to manage. Best grown in a tub it will in time develop into a substantial low-growing plant. Long, narrow leaves are brightly coloured on their upper surface and wine red on their reverse.

Of the many tropical plants one may acquire, this one is reasonably tolerant and not likely to collapse at the slightest sign of mismanagement. Ideally, the plant should have temperature minimum of not less than 16 °C (61 °F) with higher temperature a benefit rather than a

**Ctenanthe**
Low growing *C. oppenheimiana* is the easiest to manage, with multicoloured foliage on compact plants that are best in shallow tubs.

problem. Provide a shaded location and keep the soil moist, also the surrounding area: damp with a watering can or syringe the foliage. Feeding with a liquid fertilizer once a week during the time the plant is in active growth will be helpful but must not be overdone.

Another fine ctenanthe is to be found in **C. lubbersiana**, leaves of which are carried on long petioles to give the plant considerable distinction. The yellow and pale green variegation looks outstanding when it is grouped with other warmth-loving subjects.

When new plants are wanted, older clumps of growth can be separated and potted individually at any time of the year other than mid winter – even then if growing conditions are warm and agreeable.

## CYCAS (*Cycadaceae*) sago palm

Said to be the oldest plant in the world, the cycas grows into a magnificent specimen when seen in its natural habitat. Plants are slow to grow and form stout, gnarled trunks topped with spreading, rich green foliage. On very rare occasions one may be able to purchase a mature plant growing in a container, but the cost will be very high. The alternative is to make do with one of the smaller plants that periodically come onto the market, and to hope that you live long enough to see something resembling maturity in the plant!

Plants need a light location with conditions that are never too wet during the winter months. Although very slow growing these are not especially difficult plants to care for, and may stand out of doors during the milder months. What they really need is time in which to grow, and there seems to be no way of hastening the process.

## CYCLAMEN PERSICUM (*Primulaceae*)
alpine violet

These lovely plants in many bright colours are guaranteed to brighten up the dreary winter months. There was a time when it took a full eighteen months and an autumn seed sowing to produce a quality plant in a 13 cm (5 in) pot.

With the advent of modern methods and intensive hybridizing, it is now possible to sow seed in late winter and to have superb plants ready for sale the following winter.

Although a plant that relishes cool, light conditions, the seed is sown in high temperature to encourage germination. This is really the only time in the life of the cyclamen when cool, light and airy conditions are not the order of the day. If plants are bought there should be few flowers showing colour and lots of buds in evidence underneath the foliage. The leaves should be turgid and there should be no signs of rotting at the base of the leaves – this sort of rotting is the fungus botrytis, and it is well worth giving plants a reasonable inspection before parting with one's money.

Plants that are earmarked for the conservatory should be purchased as a group rather than individually – a group of half a dozen or so placed in a shallow container (not too closely together) will provide a much more striking effect. As mentioned it is essential that plants should grow in good light, as close to the window light source as possible. At all costs avoid placing them on the floor in the shadow of other plants. Fresh air is another must, so windows must be opened wherever possible. Many cyclamen succumb to the effects of overwatering, very often as a result of standing plants in dishes of water and forgetting them. The best watering practice is to lift the leaves on the edge of the pot and to pour a little water onto the surface of the soil and to wait for this first small application to soak away before giving the plant sufficient water to see the surplus draining through the holes in the bottom of the pot. It is then very important to allow the soil to dry out quite appreciably before any further water is given: allow the leaves to become perceptibly limp to the touch before watering again.

When they die, the flowers of cyclamen should be pulled out so that the entire flower stalk is removed; any pieces that are left will rot and possibly damage the plant. When flowering is over the plant will begin to develop yellow leaves quite naturally and this should be a sign to reduce and eventually stop watering so that the plant can be stored warm and dry until new growth is seen developing in the centre of the corm. When this happens the plant should be watered and then removed from its pot so that much of the old soil can be removed and replaced by a fresh mixture using the same containers. It is never wise to pot cyclamen into very large pots.

## CYMBIDIUM (*Orchidaceae*)

These are extremely adaptable plants that will tolerate wide variation in temperature and, on the whole, are not difficult to manage. There are many, many different varieties that one can choose from, although it tends to be more run of the mill plants that become available with general plant retailers, but it is probably better to start with something ordinary before progressing to the more exotic.

Producing their flowers mainly over autumn through until spring, these are especially valuable plants for the duller months of the year. Cool and airy conditions will suit them best, and they can spend the summer months in the garden; the cool and light shade of an apple tree is ideal. If plants are to remain under glass during the summer they must have maximum air and will benefit from regular syringing with water.

New plants can be made by removing older back bulbs, preferably with a new bulb developing. These can go direct into pots just large enough to accommodate the bulb; the potting mixture should be one that is specially prepared for orchids, i.e. an open, well drained mixture. With luck you could have a spike of bloom during the spring following the year of propagation. In respect of feeding there are special preparations which are formulated for feeding orchids, and these should be used as directed.

## CYPERUS (*Cyperaceae*) umbrella plant

Provided they are never allowed to dry out these are among the easiest of plants to grow. They are also easy to propagate by dividing clumps into sections and potting them individually at almost any time of the year. Alternatively, once established, plants can be allowed to go to seed so that fresh young plants sprout up in all directions – they grow like the proverbial weed.

There are several varieties with **C. diffusus** and **C. involucratus** (syn. *C. alternifolius*) being the most compact, and **C. papyrus** the giant among them. Both of the more compact plants have variegated and very attractive forms, but these are generally in short supply. Being natural waterside plants they are ideally suited to the margins of pools, or they can be very effective when seen growing on a miniature island in the middle of the pool. There is no problem in respect of care provided it is not too cold in winter.

## CYRTANTHUS PURPUREUS

(syn. *C. speciosa*) (*Liliaceae/Amaryllidacaea*)
Scarborough lily

Tender bulbs with evergreen leaves, producing scarlet trumpet flowers during the summer, these are old-fashioned plants that have been favourites on the windowledge for countless years, but for some reason are not so much in evidence today. Their former name was *Vallota speciosa*.

When bulbs are available they can be planted in the autumn or spring. Use a mixture composed of equal parts leafmould and loam with a little sharp sand added when potting bulbs firmly just below the surface of the soil. Bulbs need a good soil mixture as they must remain in their pots undisturbed for several years. When potting on is undertaken you can then remove small offsets from the base of parent bulbs in order to increase stock.

Water plants sparingly over the winter months, but increase the amount in spring to early summer for the period March, with very little from then until early autumn. A minimum temperature of 5 °C (41 °F) is necessary, and while plants are not in flower they can stand out of doors provided the temperature does not fall below the suggested minimum.

## CYRTOMIUM FALCATUM
*see* POLYSTICHUM

## CYTISUS RACEMOSUS (*Leguminosae*)
florist's genista

Compact, spring flowering plants with small leaves and bright yellow flowers. They must have cool and light conditions in order to succeed and in particular, they must have these conditions if plants are to reach their best and not go over too quickly.

Plants are normally bought in flower and should have the lightest position in the conservatory when they are brought home. It is often neglected, but an important requirement immediately after flowering is to cut plants hard back to a few inches from the base of each stem – new growth will soon appear and result in a much more attractive plant the following year. During the summer months plants can be out of doors but must not be neglected in respect of watering.

If potting becomes necessary this should be done soon after the plants have been cut back following flowering. Once established in their pots plants can be fed with a weak solution of liquid fertilizer.

## DATURA (*Solanaceae*) angel's trumpet

Finding adequate space can be a problem with these as there are varieties that can attain a height of some 2.5 m (8 ft) with a 2 m (6 ft) spread of branching leaves. The most manageable in respect of size are **D. suaveolens** with white coloured flowers and height of around 2 m (6 ft) tall, while **D. sanguinea** (now classified as *Brugmansia sanguinea*) with pale orange flowers attains a height of about 2 m (6 ft).

The pendant trumpet flowers of many of the daturas are fragrant and ought to be raised on a pedestal if the plants are short so that the flowers may be fully appreciated. In time the plants will need fairly substantial containers and should be potted into a mixture that is not too light and peaty. Cuttings can be taken at almost any time while there are non-flowering tip growths available. In any event, cuttings will be on the large side but larger leaves can be reduced by half using a pair of scissors – cuttings will root with no trouble in reasonable warmth. White fly and red spider mite can be troublesome pests and must be dealt with as soon as noticed, or by taking the precaution of treating plants with a systemic insecticide at regular intervals to dissuade pests.

## DAVALLIA CANARIENSIS (*Davalliaceae*) hare's foot fern

There are other davallias offering different common names, but this is the one that is most likely to be on offer. The common name derives from the peculiar manner in which new growth hugs the pot, very much resembling the paw of a hare or rabbit. The resemblance is there both in colour and shape. The creeping rhizome adds much interest to the plant, and is seen to best effect when the plant is growing in a hanging container. From the rhizome dark, wiry stalks appear to which are attached the finely cut and attractive leaves.

These are plants that are well suited to the cooler conservatory as they are not unduly perturbed by lower winter temperatures. Besides being fine and tolerant plants when suspended overhead they are also useful at floor level in more shaded parts of planted beds where other subjects would be struggling to survive. Moisture and shade from direct sunlight are their most important requirements.

When potting on becomes necessary, they should have a slightly larger container using a peaty houseplant mixture. Potting on plants in hanging containers can be much more complicated than it sounds on account of the peculiar fashion in which growth develops. When hanging specimens become too large for their containers it could be more sensible to wait until the spring of the year and then to water the plant well prior to removing it from its container in order to divide the roots. New plants can also be brought on by sowing spores on fine, moist peat in warmth at any time of the year – a shaded location will also be important. Spores appear on the undersides of fronds and should be removed when ripe and placed in a paper bag to dry and fall from the fronds before they are sown. The result could well be an abundance of baby hare's feet padding around the conservatory!

## DIEFFENBACHIA (*Araceae*) leopard lily

There was a time when the dieffenbachias, and there are many of them, came under the general common name of dumb cane; leopard lily is now favoured by the producers of these plants. It should be stressed that the reason for the dumb cane appendage is a reference to the poisonous qualities of the sap of this plant. The sap causes the tongue to swell up; however, when the stem is broken, it gives off a very unpleasant odour which makes it highly unlikely that one would be tempted to consider eating the plant. Plants if handled when wet can cause an irritating rash on sensitive skin, so a pair of rubber gloves should be worn when handling plants to clean them over, or when taking cuttings.

Despite this, among the dieffenbachias we find some of the finest decorative foliage plants that one could possibly wish for. All of them are of upright habit and may have small leaves as in *D.* 'Camille' or large highly patterned leaves as in *D. seguine* 'Tropic Snow'. Both *D. seguine* and its sport have very large leaves requiring ample space for them to be seen to best effect – they are also very easily damaged if handled inconsiderately. When being transported the leaves can be drawn upwards to facilitate packing but if the bending is overdone the leaf will crack along the midrib and the section beyond the crack to die soon after. When purchasing keep a watchful eye for damage of this kind.

There are numerous other dieffenbachias with spotted leaves, green leaves, golden leaves and one, *D. oerstedii*, which has a very dark green leaf with the exception of the midrib which is a striking ivory white. The latter is also a much smaller plant that will be fine for limited space. The best plant, however, for cramped conditions is *D.* 'Camille', a remarkable plant that has leaves almost entirely creamy white with only the margins of leaves being green. This one is by far the most popular and is produced in hundreds of thousands annually in 13 cm (5 in) diameter pots.

All these plants have one thing in common and that is they must have minimum temperature of at least 16 to 18 °C (61–64 °F).

They will also benefit from shaded and damp conditions, needing more water in summer than in winter. Feed them while they are adding fresh leaves and when potting use a good quality houseplant mixture in spring. These are plants that are not too much troubled by pests – their worst enemy is cold and overwet conditions during the winter when growth is inactive. In the conservatory that includes only a few specimen plants in attractive containers as opposed to a jungle effect the dieffenbachias with larger leaves do make the most splendid plants and should be considered for prime locations.

## DIONAEA (*Droseraceae*) Venus fly trap

Not all conservatories are splendidly isolated retreats with a jungle of exotic plants providing the perfectly tranquil setting. Many of the modern conservatories will have to, among other things, contend with the presence of children of all ages, and if plants are to be part of the scene then the children ought to be encouraged to take an interest. One obvious way of doing this is to introduce a collection of cacti which for some odd reason younger offspring seem to find very fascinating. Another way is to get them interested in something else peculiar in the plant world and that is carnivorous plants – tell the babes that the plants eat flies and you will immediately have an interested audience.

Your starter plant could well be the Venus fly trap, that peculiar plant with leaves that seem to be hinged along their midrib. They also have odd claw-like growth along the leaf margins, with amazingly sensitive hairs in the centre of the leaves. For the child (adult too possibly!) the fascination will be complete when a fly is seen to alight on the centre of the leaf and for the hinge to be activated. The leaf folds, the claws come together to imprison the insect, and the plant has caught its supper. The plant will attract flies naturally and needs no other form of nourishment. There is always the temptation to poke at the leaves with a finger or stick in order to see them close but this practice is harmful to the plant and the temptation should be resisted.

Most of these plants die because they are given hard water when watering. There should be a firm rule to use rain water only, and this should be poured into a shallow dish and kept topped up so that the plant is permanently standing in an inch or so of water. These are perfectly hardy plants that can remain out of doors if desired, so it is wise to keep them as cool as possible should they be in the conservatory.

When the need comes for potting plants on, which is not often, a mixture of equal parts peat and fresh sphagnum moss should be used. Plants can be propagated by dividing older clumps in the spring or by sowing seed on the surface of the mix suggested for potting on.

There is a form with more reddish colouring to its leaves, and there are numerous other carnivorous plants becoming freely available as more and more interest is being taken in these fascinating plants.

## DIOSCOREA DISCOLOR (*Dioscoreaceae*) ornamental yam

Not a plant for the beginner, and also one that will be in short supply and only available from the specialist nurseryman or importer of ornamental bulbs. There are other varieties that vary in their growing requirements, but *D. discolor* is a very decorative foliage plant that will suit the smaller conservatory, maintained at a minimum temperature of 16 °C (61 °F).

The tubers should be planted in peaty houseplant mixture as early in the year as possible, at a temperature of around 18 °C (64 °F) to get them under way. Plants should be kept under control by training them to a supporting cane which will also be advantageous in setting off the exquisitely patterned leaves when they appear. In warm, shaded conditions where plants are kept moist and occasionally fed, the growth will be lush and attractive – certainly something different.

The leaves of this plant are paper thin and can be easily damaged if roughly handled so care is needed. If exposed to bright, direct sun they will also scorch very easily, so some form of shading in the conservatory is of prime importance.

**Dioscorea**

A variegated climbing yam that must have good temperature to do well, especially important when plants are started into growth in early spring.

## DRACAENA (*Agavaceae*)
dragon tree, song of India

These are among our most rewarding of tropical plants for indoor decoration, and ideally suited to the conservatory that is warm and offers reasonable headroom for the taller growing kinds. Some would be much too tall but we shall avoid these and concentrate on the varieties that you can accommodate and hope to care for without too much bother.

Beginning with smaller plants the best known is probably **D. marginata** which is sold as small plants in vast quantities throughout the world; nevertheless it will attain a height of some 2.5 to 3 m (8 to 10 ft) in time. Growth is relatively slow, with many years transpiring before plants bought when young are pushing their heads against the glass roof!

In common with almost all dracaenas this one will shed lower leaves as the plant attains some height, and the tendency will be for rosettes of tufted growth to develop atop woody stems. By removing the leading growth when the plant has attained some height it can be encouraged to branch to provide a standard effect which will be more practical in the smaller conservatory.

Another of the smaller leaved plants that will take many years to reach any size is the lovely **D. surculosa surculosa 'Florida Beauty'**, which develops rounded leaves having an overall golden colour. Individual plants take a long time to make anything worthwhile, so it is better to buy several plants at the outset and to plant them together in shallow pans (with drainage holes) so that they form into a low-growing bush as opposed to a spindly single plant.

Where there is ample head room **D. fragrans** and its numerous varieties will be a tough plant that will add character to the setting. The best of these is D. fragrans 'Victoriae' which has a stout stem and radiating leaves that are an overall golden yellow in colour. This is a slow-growing plant that will be both expensive to purchase and in constant short supply. When considering the purchase of any major plant for the conservatory you must go to the supplier to inspect the plant just to be sure that it is going to fit in and suit your particular taste.

The real queens of the dracaenas are the numerous cultivars of **Dracaena deremensis**; In particular, **D.d. 'Bausei'** and **D. 'Souvenir de Schryver'** (of Belgian origin) will draw gasps of disbelief from visitors when these are seen and growing well. All D. deremensis grow in typical dracaena fashion with tall, stout stems on top of which will be the rosettes of growth, but this is not unattractive if more bushy plants of some other kind are placed at the base of the dracaena to hide some of the sparseness.

**D. reflexa 'Variegata'** (song of India) is a fine plant and, grown well, will be a real gem. The leaves are a rich golden yellow with touches of cream and green and are attached to twisting stems that in older plants will droop over very attractively at their extremities.

When grown in a container the plant will attain a height of some 2 m (6 ft), but it is very slow growing and plants of this size will be of considerable age, in excess of twenty years. Like all dracaenas this one will have a tendency to shed some of its lower leaves as the stem increases in height but this is not a great problem as the plant branches freely with many stems once established.

To grow dracaenas well, they must have good light with protection from strong sunlight only, and the temperature should not fall below 16 °C (61 °F) in winter. Plants will need ample watering and occasional feeding during the summer months with less water and no feed in winter. Most dracaenas do not object unduly to a little neglect in the way of feeding and potting on.

When potting on use a loam-based mix that is free-draining and put some drainage material in the bottom of the container before introducing soil. If plants are to be grown in a bed it is often better to plunge two thirds of the growing pot in the bed rather than take the plant from its pot to plant it out. Left in the pot roots will soon find their way into the bed of soil. Dracaenas are not too much troubled by pests or diseases.

The success rate when attempting to propagate plants by means of cuttings is very low, and it should only be attempted if the plant is well provided with growing stems that can be cut. The song of India is indigenous to South India and Sri Lanka, and from this source in recent years there has been keen interest in supplying young rooted plants for growing on. Acquiring young plants from the retailers of such imported plants would seem to be much more sensible than attempting one's own propagation when additional plants are required.

## ECHEVERIA (*Crassulaceae*)

The metallic blue grey colouring of the leaves of many of the echeverias have no equal anywhere in horticulture. Leaves are formed in low-growing rosettes, large or small depending on the variety. They will also oblige with arching stems of small and interesting flowers.

We often hear of collector's pieces in the world of antiques, and in the field of echeverias there are some fine varieties that are scarce enough to qualify as collector's pieces. If the conservatory is small with little space for plants, the echeverias could well provide an interesting specialist collection where only these plants would be grown.

They all like to have lightly dappled shade and must at no time be too wet, particularly in winter. When one has a collection of these plants there is good reason for selecting more attractive terracotta pots in which to put plants when they are potted on in the spring. Use a specialist cactus mixture when potting, but never be tempted to put plants into containers that are too large.

Mentioning varietal names would seem rather futile here as plants are never very freely available – it is much better to select a specialist grower and to see what he can spare from his treasures (it won't be a lot if past experience is anything to go by!)

## ECHINOCACTUS GRUSONII (*Cactaceae*)
golden barrel

Even if you should be one of those people who have an aversion to cactus in general there is little question that you would be impressed on seeing mature specimens of this truly wonderful plant.

As the common name suggests the plant is of rounded shape and golden in colour, with closer inspection showing that the golden colour is actually in the multitude of spines that completely cover the ball of growth. As a centre-piece in a formal bed of cacti there is absolutely nothing that can touch this plant as it sits there looking and surely feeling that it is king of the castle.

Slow to mature these are best purchased as young plants to be grown on. Good light is essential, as is careful watering with extreme care never to be in any way generous during winter. Water is naturally given more freely while plants are active (though they will show no visible signs of being so), when occasional feeding with a specialist cactus fertilizer will be beneficial.

**EPIPHYLLUM** (*Cactaceae*) orchid cactus

At first sight these have the appearance of the Christmas cactus that have become enlarged in respect of leaf size, but there the similarity ends as these are quite different plants that in time will produce the most magnificent inflorescence that you could ever wish to set eyes on. Flower colours range from white through yellow to brilliant red, and are in evidence from late summer into autumn depending on the variety.

For plants that can flower so wonderfully they are incredibly tolerant, very often seeming to thrive on neglect. Minimum winter temperature of 5 °C (41 °F) is needed when the soil in the pot should be on the dry side but not bone dry. During spring and summer more water is needed, also a little feeding of established plants, but neither should be overdone. When potting use a mixture that contains loam, peat, leafmould and sand, with a greater proportion of loam and leafmould. These are plants that need a richer mixture than cactus to which family they belong, but it is never wise to pot plants on too often or to have them in very large containers. Experience suggests that they will flower more freely when the growing pots are well filled with roots, which is the case with many flowering pot plants.

During the summer months plants are best placed out of doors. New plants are not difficult to propagate by using mature leaves cut into 8 cm (3 in) sections and firmed into a peat and sand mix in shallow boxes or pots. A heated propagator will be a considerable help in encouraging cuttings to root.

**EPIPREMNUM AUREUM** (*Araceae*)
devil's ivy (formerly *Scindapsus aureus*)

A long time favourite with the growers of indoor plants, the epipremnum has attractive yellow and green variegated leaves which stand up well to growing in conditions offering poor light. They are possibly seen at their best when trained to grow on an upright pole so that they can be placed as specimen plants within the conservatory. In warm, shaded and moist con-

ditions this plant can be put to numerous uses – as a trailing plant in a hanging container, as a ground cover plant amongst others in a planted bed, or as a wall plant. If it is to be grown as a wall climber then the container should be placed close by the wall and a framework should be arranged for the plant to be trained against. It could be planted out in a bed of peaty soil, but there you would need to provide a warming cable in the soil to prevent the roots of the plant becoming cold. If there is ample space the latter could be the best position, as this is a plant with capacity for spectacular growth – in ideal growing conditions the leaves of the plant are likely to become significantly larger and very much more colourful.

**E. 'Marble Queen'** has marbled white and green variegation but it is not well known; it is also a much more difficult plant to grow successfully.

For both of these plants minimum temperature of not less than 16 °C (61 °F) must be maintained and for the latter care is needed when it comes to watering. Never allow the soil to remain excessively wet for long periods of time, an especially important requirement during the winter months of the year. Feed both with liquid fertilizer once each week during the spring and summer, with none in winter.

**ESPISCIA** (*Gesneriacaea*) snowflake flower, flame flower

The queen amongst lovely plants is **E. cupreata** (flame flower) and her many offsprings. The type, *E. cupreata*, is a fine plant with a silver sheen to its leaves and small red flowers that are comparatively insignificant. Although generally listed as a creeper for covering the floor of the jungle, it is really at its best when growing in a hanging container. The term hanging container immediately suggests that the plant should be at or above head level, but this plant like many others has superb leaf surface that is better to look down on rather than up at. With this in mind, one should give some thought to providing the plant with a pedestal that is made to accommodate a hanging basket. You can then have the plant at the right height to look down on the lovely leaves, and you can also have the easy facility of being able to move the plants around, either to a better location or out of bright sunlight.

These plants need warm growing conditions, at least 16 °C (61 °F) in winter, and shade from direct sunlight. When propagating new plants for the ensuing year, it is best to remove a few of the longer, more mature strands of growth and to make cuttings from firmer stems. These should be inserted in small pots filled with peat and sand mix and then be enclosed in a heated propagator out of direct sunlight. If plants are propagated during late spring there will be sturdy plants for potting into hangers by the end of the summer.

Another and much easier species is *E. dianthiflora* (now classified as *Alsobia dianthiflora*) which has numerous common names most of which relate to the peculiar flower that is white in colour with ragged lips to the ends of the petals. The name snowflake flower seems to be a very appropriate description of this very easy plant, which is naturally pendulous in habit. Foliage is plain green and formed into neat rosettes that can be removed and planted in small pots at any time to produce new plants very easily. When suspended in the conservatory they will need ample watering and feeding during the summer, with no feed and less water in winter. The minimum temperature can drop to 0 °C (50 °F) in winter if the soil is kept very much on the dry side – remember that a cold and wet combination is the reason for most plant failures.

## EUONYMUS (*Celastraceae*) spindle tree

For the conservatory providing only shelter with no heating whatsoever there are a number of evergreen euonymus plants which when grown in pots, will provide pleasing colour yet need very little attention. There are both white and yellow variegated forms that form into neat bushes which can be trimmed to shape at any time should they be outgrowing their allotted space. Some can also be encouraged to climb if given some form of support, and the best of these is *E. fortunei* 'Variegatus' which has larger leaves and should be able to establish itself in the conservatory kept cool and light. To do well plants need to be in pots of at least 25 cm (10 in) diameter with modest watering over the winter months and no feeding. In summer it would be much too hot in most conservatories, therefore it is wise then to transfer plants to the garden where they must have attention in respect of regular watering and feeding.

## EUPHORBIA (*Euphorbiaceae*)
poinsettia, crown of thorns

This is an extensive family of plants offering several subjects well suited to conservatory growing, including many fine cacti. Here only a few are mentioned and the first of these is *E. fulgens*, a plant that is not easy to grow but is much used by florists during the early months of the year when there are not so many exotic blooms available. Bloom is not a very suitable description for a plant that produces arching sprays of bracts to which are attached lots of small orange-red flowers. These plants are best grown in containers in a warm conservatory that does not fall below 16 °C (61 °F) during the winter, and care should be exercised when watering at this time – never too wet. In June any stems that are left on the plant (many will have been cut earlier in the year) should be pruned hard back to within an inch or two from their base. At the same time, if necessary, plants can be potted on into slightly larger containers using a loam-based potting mixture.

A much easier plant to manage is *E. milii* which was at one time known as *E. splendens*, with the common name of crown of thorns. As this name suggests, the stems are indeed well endowed with spiteful thorns so careful handling is required. Bought as small plants normally, these should have good light in the conservatory with careful watering that is never excessive. More mature plants can be fed during the spring and summer. In time plants can become quite large and if you want to produce really large specimens then it is wise, once they have developed a good amount of growth, to provide a framework around which the plant can be trained to give the plant a rough ball shape. Wear strong gloves when handling the plant in this way, and keep an eye open for the presence of mealy bug, a pest that can become an awful nuisance if it gets amongst the more inaccessible parts of the plant. Sections of stem about 10 cm (4 in) in length will be simple to propagate if the severed end of the cutting is allowed to dry well before it is inserted in a peat and sand mix – any time other than winter will be suitable for this task.

**Euphorbia**
Lots of different kinds of these, including the poinsettia, with something for everyone including easy and difficult plants.

The king pin of the euphorbias must be the **E. pulcherrima** (poinsettia), seen growing freely throughout the tropics as untidy large bushes. They are more often seen indoors or at the plant retailers where they will be growing in pots of anything from 13 to 18 cm (5–7 in) in diameter, and in colours ranging from white through to red with numerous interesting shades between becoming available in recent years. Considerable skill goes into producing these compact plants almost all of identical size and shape to be ready for the busy Christmas markets around the world. All the more compact plants will have been treated with a growth retarding chemical applied at critical

rates during the summer/autumn growing season of the plant. Producing these plants to such a high standard is very much the task of the skilled commercial grower who has devoted a lifetime to the care of the poinsettia.

What about the poinsettia for the conservatory scene? There is little doubt that their rich colouring does much for the interior of any building that is warm and light where water is given with care, ensuring that plants never become excessively wet. The most important initial requirement is to first of all purchase quality plants, as inferior plants will always be a problem when it comes to aftercare indoors or in the conservatory. Plants not treated with a growth retardant will easily grow to 2.5 to 3 m (8–10 ft) with their roots confined to large containers. This sort of plant could provide a colourful background to other plants in the conservatory. Tall plants of this kind will be the smaller plants bought at Christmas and potted on with their top growth as opposed to cutting plants back after flowering which is the usual practice. With large and small poinsettias there is a tendency for them to attract all sorts of pests, so a watchful eye must be kept to ensure that pests do not get a firm hold on plant foliage.

Poinsettias will not mind higher temperatures, but efforts should be made to keep the conservatory above 16 °C (61 °F) over the winter. If one has an experimental turn of mind it will be found that cuttings of these plants will not be difficult to root in a propagating case during mid summer if they are protected from direct sunlight. Cuttings are made from the top section of the plant with three or four leaves attached. When the plant is cut sap will run from the stem but this will not be harmful. The cutting should be immediately placed in water so that the severed end is sealed before being inserted in a small pot filled with peat and sand mix. It is of great importance to spray it over with water immediately after insertion, and this practice should continue frequently throughout the first week until such time as the limp and seemingly lifeless cutting becomes more turgid.

The appearance of the interior of the conservatory can be considerably enhanced over the festive season by introducing fresh poinsettias and arranging groups of them in decorative containers. The different colours can have splendid effect if they are arranged in groups of their own colouring with the containers at different levels in the garden room.

## x FATSHEDERA (*Araliaceae*) ivy tree

This is an unusual plant in that it is a cross between the humble green ivy and the broad-leaved *Fatsia*. The result is an upright plant with a strong central stem to which are attached glossy green leaves not dissimilar to stunted fatsia leaves. It is a very tough plant that can endure outside winter conditions in milder areas, so it is a good prospect for the room that offers only little heat during the winter months. When introduced to the conservatory it will be wise to plant several plants rather than one in a larger container with a view to training the group to grow on a framework against a wall. This will be one way of overcoming the difficulty of finding suitable wall plants that do not object unduly to winter temperatures in the cold conservatory room. New plants can be grown from cuttings prepared either from sections from the top of the stem of the plant or from sections of stem with a solitary leaf attached. This can be attempted at almost any time of the year when the temperature is reasonable, with a peat and sand mix and a propagating case. Leaves will have better appearance if they are cleaned with a damp cloth or leaf cleaner periodically, but avoid too frequent use of chemical cleaners.

## FICUS (*Moraceae*) fig

This is a particularly useful family of plants for both indoor and conservatory decoration including old favourites and some very fine new introductions. All are grown purely for their decorative foliage, but there are plants to suit all tastes and all situations from the creeping fig, **F. pumila** to the majestic **F. benjamina** and its numerous varieties. They will also vary in their growing requirements – some are relatively easy to manage while others will test the skills of the most accomplished plantsman.

They are used for many purposes indoors and not least as plants for interior landscaping of offices and public buildings, many of these with their acres of glass walls being not dissimilar to the heated conservatory. Many of our enclosed shopping malls with their overhead transparent roofs are virtually conservatories on the grand scale, and by studying the progress of chosen plants for the landscaping of such interiors one can learn a lot about the durability or otherwise of conservatory plants. A benefit that the private

**x Fatshedera**
Can be used as background climbers if tied to a framework, and will tolerate the low temperatures of cooler rooms if kept on the dry side.

owner will have over the public counterpart will be the absence of vandalism.

As the plants in this family are so varied in their requirement it is not easy to offer across-the-board advice on their care, hence the following list that deals with them all in detail according to their particular needs.

*Ficus benghalensis* is native to India where it is known as the banyan tree, and tree is the correct expression as this is a very vigorous plant that can easily attain a height of 6 m (20 ft) with its roots restricted to growing in a pot or tub. The leaves are dark green, hairy and have distinctive venation – they are also broad and some 30 cm (12 in) in length. The stems are very woody with plants gradually developing a very strong upright trunk. Also with age there is the likelihood that plants will produce aerial roots from their upper stems, and one might well wonder what this strange phenomenon might be. The aerial roots are, in fact, what are known as prop roots which in nature will reach to the ground and root so that they act as a support for the plant in much the same way as a guy rope does for a tent. These roots can be cut off if you feel that they are un-attractive, or they can be tied in neatly to the stem of the plant so that they run naturally into the pot of soil when long enough.

On account of their eventual size and their normally rapid rate of growth, these are not plants for the small conservatory; for a large building offering ample headroom they will be fine if you want to fill the upper area with spreading tree growth.

The most important aspect of care is to inspect the roots of a newly bought plant with a view to potting the plant on into a larger container using a loam-based mixture. Potting should be firm and the holes in the bottom of the pot should be enlarged, as the plant will most certainly push roots through these holes in time and it is as well that roots should not be too restricted. If you really want these plants to grow apace then the pot should be plunged to its rim in a bed of good soil; if they are planted out they will grow much too rapidly so the temptation to do so should be avoided.

In, respect of general care it needs a minimum temperature of around 16 °C (61 °F), a lightly shaded location, ample watering and occasional feeding while in active growth. It is not too much troubled by pests, but the main difficulty could be rapid growth; the overgrown branches can be lopped at any time to keep the plant within bounds.

*Ficus benjamina* has surely established itself as the favourite of all the indoor figs and has won for itself the common name of weeping fig on account of the graceful manner in which the arching branches spray in all directions from the central stem. It is one of the most popular plants for interior landscaping and one that is particularly handsome with its glossy green leaves when placed as an individual specimen. In time the plant will develop into a fine small tree of compact appearance, and will not object unduly to the pruning of overgrown branches.

Although not in any way a difficult plant, there could well be a worrying shedding of leaves when the plant is first introduced to its new situation – this is caused by the change in conditions and is only temporary until the plant has settled in. However, this problem can continue if the plant is placed in a location where it is getting inadequate light; it is important that the weeping fig should have a lightly shaded location and not a dark corner. Mealy bug on the leaves may also present difficulties with taller plants that are mostly above head level and difficult to inspect. The best defence against these messy pests is to treat plants periodically with an insecticide as a precaution rather than try to eradicate them once they are established. Bugs drip excreta on lower leaves where black fungus eventually forms, thus marring the appearance of the plant. Scale insects may also prove a problem and the same advice is offered to deter these with precautionary treatment at regular intervals. Scale insects can become established almost without one noticing as the limpet-like bodies attach themselves to stems of the plant that are very much the same colouring – sooty mould deposit on leaves will be an indication that pests are there. Use a sponge to clean the upper surfaces of leaves and at the same time firmly sponge away any pests that are noticed. If rubber gloves are worn the sponge can be soaked in diluted insecticide before attempting to clean the plants.

*Ficus deltoidea* (syn. *diversifolia*) has the common name of mistletoe fig and forms into a neat bush of some 1.5 m (5 ft) in height when being grown well in a container. The small evergreen leaves are attached to woody stems, the leaves being spotted brown and of paler colouring on their undersides. The principal attraction is the pale berries that are present throughout the life of the plant – the berries are purely decorative, and not to be eaten.

A more difficult plant to care for than the general run of ficus, it needs a slightly higher temperature not falling below 16 °C (61 °F) in winter, with temperatures of higher level not being harmful. Greater care is also needed when watering as this is a slow growing plant that will take up less moisture than the more vigorous kinds. Water should be given sparingly over the winter months and at other times a good watering is advised, with the soil allowed to dry out quite appreciably before repeating. Similar advice is given for feeding – none in winter, but weekly liquid fertilizing during the spring and summer. Plants do best in a lightly shaded location.

*Ficus elastica* is an old-fashioned sort of plant to which the common name of rubber plant was given when indoor plants first became popular. Times change, tastes change and, though often going unnoticed, the plants themselves change. *F. elastica* is seldom seen these days, having been superseded first by *F. decora* and then by the now popular **F. robusta**. As the name suggests the latter is a much more vigorous plant with broad leaves that are carried on stout stems. It is also a much more tolerant plant doing well in a wide variety of locations and temperatures. As a young plant this is not really a conservatory specimen, but as a maturing small tree in the conservatory it will hold its own with many of the other more exotic inhabitants. The plant has a big advantage in that the leaves are broad and naturally glossy and, when cleaned, can be particularly attractive.

Plants are dormant in winter when little water and feeding will be needed, but at other times one can be generous with both water and feeding. Leaves can be cleaned with chemical cleaners but it is often just as well to use a soft cloth and soapy water. When cleaning avoid new leaves at the top of the plant as these are very easily damaged. A positive signal that the new season's growth has begun is when the spike enclosing the new leaf at the top of the plant begins to expand to produce its first leaf of the year. Offer plants a light location out of direct sunlight.

Purchased plants will vary in height depending on how much they cost, but if plants are needed for important positions in the conservatory then plants of reasonable size should be acquired at the outset. A plant that is 1 m (3 ft) tall and growing in a 18 cm (7 in) pot will often establish in its new location much more readily than a small plant – this applies to the majority of plants that one might contemplate purchasing. In agreeable conditions the rubber plant can put on 1 m (3 ft) of growth each year, such growth being much too much for the average conservatory. The answer to very rapid growth is to remove the growing top section of the plant with a pair of secateurs so that several growing branches are encouraged to develop from the leaf axils immediately below where the stem is cut. You then have a small standard tree that can be a pleasing addition to the conservatory scene, and one that can be periodically pruned to keep growth under control.

There are numerous figs with variegated foliage that will be a great asset in the conservatory when plants are growing next to green foliage and providing a contrast. At one time the only variegated form available would have been **F. elastica 'Doescheri'**, a plant with long and narrow leaves similar to that of *F. elastica*. The colouring of this plant is a well defined creamy yellow and pale green with intricate patterns of colour adding much to the overall appearance of the plant. The one drawback is that this is not an easy plant to care for, needing very careful attention over the winter months when the temperature must never drop too low and great care is needed to guard against excessive watering. This is also a plant that is invariably in short supply.

There are several other broad-leaved ficus with variegated leaves and the present favourite would seem to be **F. elastica 'Belgica'** that is no more difficult to care for than the ordinary rubber plant. Leaves are variegated green, pale brown and cream and can be very effective when a group of young plants are growing together as a feature in the conservatory, either planted out or in a container of good size.

Not so popular these days another broad-leaved plant with variegated leaves is *F. schryveriana* which has dull yellow and green colouring on plants that will attain good height in time. However, it is not the most attractive of plants, having a somewhat hard appearance.

The green leaved *F. benjamina* has already been mentioned as a fine plant, and it must be said that its several variegated forms are among the finest of purely foliage plants. These are plants that have been gaining prominence in the past decade or so and we now have three varieties that seem to be leading the field in respect of popularity: *F.b.* **'Golden Princess'** was one of the first to appear with white and pale green colouring, but since its arrival we have seen two remarkable plants in *F. benjamina* **'Starlight'** and *F. microcarpa* **'Hawaii'** both of which have glistening white appearance with very little green in their colouring. These are both plants that will add much to the plant selection in the conservatory, all of them needing the same sort of conditions and treatment as suggested for the weeping fig.

*F. lyrata*, the fiddle leaf fig, has quite a different appearance to all the others in that the leaves are shaped like the body of a violin. The leaves are broad, large and pale green in colour with very prominent lighter coloured veins. Provided it is given reasonable warmth and a lightly shaded location with ample feeding and watering while in active growth this is one that will indeed become an indoor tree with stout branches pushing out in all directions. Not a plant for limited space in the smaller conservatory.

The extreme opposite is offered in the creeping figs – *F. pumila* and its variegated form, *F.p.* **'Sonny'**, both of which need a good temperature and damp, lightly shaded conditions in which to grow. Any drying out and both of these will shrivel up alarmingly, so moisture is a key word with both plants. One supposes that they could be described as indoor ground cover plants in that they will creep over almost any surface that is damp enough for the roots produced along the stem to obtain a hold. It is not often appreciated but these are also nice plants for covering a wall in similar fashion to ivies. If several plants can be planted in a bed of good soil at the base of an internal wall they will soon begin to fan out if the wall is kept damp. The foliage which is pale green in *F. pumila* and variegated in its counterpart will make a fine backcloth for plants placed in front of them. Plants in hanging containers should be avoided as it is almost impossible to keep plants moist when growing in elevated positions.

There are numerous other *Ficus* varieties on offer and, although they do not flower, the majority will offer support and contrast to more colourful subjects. It should not be forgotten that these plants offer interest all the year round while flowering kinds will be seasonal often followed by dull foliage.

## FITTONIA (*Acanthaceae*) snake plant

Small plants growing at ground level in a conservatory would be something of a nonsense, but there is a definite place for these smaller plants when they are used for decorating tables or other pieces of furniture, and very fine such plants can be when carefully chosen and arranged.

There are three fittonias normally on offer with *F. verschaffeltii* var. *argyroneura nana* being far the most popular and possibly the easiest to care for. Its big brother is *F. verschaffeltii argyroneura*; both have silver grey foliage colouring with attractively netted venation. Identical in every way to the last mentioned is *F. verschaffeltii* with the exception that the leaf colouring is red as opposed to green in the other two.

Of the three, the easiest to manage is the dwarf variety which is sold in rather small pots; here they will be difficult to manage as plants do not have sufficient nourishment and the wee pots will present problems with watering. The best answer is to be found in buying several plants rather than one and to plant these in a shallow container in good houseplant potting soil. The outcome will be a pleasing carpet of foliage and plants that will thrive on account of the fresh mixture that will provide them with the additional nourishment needed.

As with all more tender plants, the most difficult time will be winter when care is needed to ensure a temperature of not less than 16 °C (61 °F), higher if possible. If higher temperatures are not possible it could be wise to start some fresh plants from cuttings at the end of the summer and to keep these over winter in a propagating case; this will not be so costly to heat to a higher temperature compared to heating the entire conservatory. When watering it is best to use tepid water and to be very sparing in winter. Select small pots and fill them with moist peaty potting mixture, being sure to water the surface of the soil with a fine rose using tepid water once the pots have been filled – it is always preferable to strike several pots of cuttings rather than single ones that will be difficult to care for. The cuttings should be taken from the ends of the growing shoots and ought to have at least two firm leaves attached. Treat the severed end of the cutting with rooting powder and use a pencil to make shallow holes in the soil into which cuttings, three to each pot, are inserted. From there you again water them gently over the leaves with tepid water before placing them in the propagator. Keep the lid of the propagator closed and shaded from direct sunlight – a sheet of newspaper will do if the plants are being exposed to direct sunlight. After about four weeks check for root development, and when the cuttings are seen to be well rooted the young plants can be potted on into a slightly larger pot using a good houseplant mixture.

## FUCHSIA (*Onagraceae*) lady's ear drops

Fuchsias are everybody's favourite and are among the most popular of all plants for growing in containers out of doors and in glassed areas. Two of the main reasons for their popularity are their plentiful and colourful flowers and their ease of culture. There are both hardy and tender fuchsias: the hardy kinds can be left out all the year (although some may succumb in very harsh winters), but they will be cut down to ground level when temperatures fall. All the top growth that is made in one year dies back and in the following year the plant produces fresh growth from ground level to flower from mid to late summer.

However, being hardy does not preclude these plants from being grown as subjects for decorating the conservatory – indeed, in the small flowered variety *F.* **'Phyllis'** we have one of the most floriferous of plants. An interesting aspect of this plant is that when grown in the conservatory it can be trained to grow up a wall or trellis against a pillar so that a framework of strong growth develops. If the conservatory is kept from freezing the mature wood will not die back in winter and the plant will come into flower much earlier in the year and will be capable of producing a stunning display of fuchsia red flowers right through into the autumn. There are not many conservatory flowering plants with this capability.

Making a choice from the thousands of fuchsia varieties is not easy and the best possible starting point is to visit a good flower show in the early summer to see what the professional growers are offering – you may well be more confused than ever to see the array of plant varieties that are available. Before making your choice you should know what sort of plants you actually require. You can have fuchsias that make good standard plants, those that are naturally trailing and ideal for hanging baskets, and those that develop into neat, rounded bushes. In the catalogues of the commercial growers plants with these various growth habits will be clearly indicated. You may well want a plant or two for growing against the wall of the conservatory, in which case you should talk to the man at the show and get his recommendation for a vigorous plant capable of developing sufficient growth to make a good wall specimen when tied into position.

Alternatively there is no reason why you should not start at the beginning by propagating your own cuttings and taking it from there. When it comes to producing plants from cuttings the fuchsias are very accommodating with almost any sound piece with a leaf or two attached being capable of rooting. The very tiniest pieces from the tip of the growth can be taken with two tiny leaves and encouraged to root. Such small cuttings will usually be too small to have attracted anything in the way of disease or pests and will be all the better for it.

The easy way is to put fresh peat into the smallest pots available and to water the pots with a rose before treating the cuttings with rooting powder and carefully inserting them singly in the centre of the small pot. Once inserted the cuttings should be watered with a fine rose using tepid water, after which they can be completely enclosed by a piece of creamy white polythene – a cut down shopping carrier bag will be both ideal and cheap! If the cuttings are kept warm and out of direct sunlight they can virtually be left untouched within the polythene for a month; the polythene can then be removed and every cutting should be well and truly rooted. Leave them in the little pots, minus the polythene, to establish before potting them on into slightly larger containers using a good potting mixture. If pots are not available the cuttings can go into seed boxes, but small pots are preferred.

Growing the plants on will not be difficult but they may be better in the conservatory feeder greenhouse as opposed to being among the decorative plants in the conservatory. Tiny plants tend to be a bit lost, and are often neglected when there are too many large plants around them. It is important to keep plants on the move when young by not allowing them to become pot bound before moving them on to the next pot size up. At every stage it is wise to maintain a watchful eye for the presence of whitefly that can be devastating if allowed to get out of hand.

When growing them on, fuchsias need to be in reasonable warmth and shade from strong sunlight – too much direct sunlight can be very detrimental. High temperature will also be detrimental, as will stuffy airless conditions so provide ample air when the weather is warm. Another important requirement is a good potting mixture that will sustain plants over the summer months, and feeding at least once a week when they have become established. In terms of watering they will soon let you know if this aspect is being neglected when the foliage flags alarmingly – you should avoid this problem by regularly watering your plants.

Over the winter months plants should be housed in a frost-free greenhouse, but keep on the dry side with no feeding. In early spring new growth will be seen developing on the overwintered plants and this should be a signal for increasing the supply of water. Once the soil is well wetted the plant should be removed from its pot; remove much of the old soil before potting into the same container using fresh mixture. Unlike the outdoor fuchsias which die back to the ground in winter, those that are kept frost-free will sprout growth from the old stems of the previous year. Plants develop gnarled, hard woody growth in time, but this does not in any way affect their flowering ability. Old favourites such as *F.* **'Celia Smedley'** will produce a wonderful show year after year if treated as suggested and grown as a standard or large bush.

It is not necessary to have these plants growing up the wall in order to appreciate their beauty – they also make superb basket plants and many conservatives are much better suited to displaying this sort of plant as opposed to free standing or as plants trained to a trellis. If dead flowers are regularly picked off the hanging basket fuchsia in the conservatory will go on for months with masses of flowers if kept watered and well fed.

The most troublesome pest is white fly that is mainly found on the undersides of leaves, and is generally at its worst during the summer months. Where do they come from is a question that is often asked, and the simple answer is that they are always about and the fuchsia is part of their natural source of nourishment. They can also be brought in by buying plants that are already infested with this pest – a check on the undersides of plant leaves should always be made when plants are acquired to ensure that they are clean. White fly will also be more prevalent when the growing conditions are dry, so frequent misting of the atmosphere is advisable. The important thing is to be vigilant and to deal with these pests as soon as they are noticed, and before they get out of hand.

In hot, dry conditions there will also be the prospect of red spider mites attacking plants.

These are tiny mites that get onto the undersides of leaves causing them to turn pale brown in colour and to eventually shrivel and die. Again, dry atmosphere will encourage them so spray around the plants regularly to maintain desirable moist conditions. There are many pesticides available for the control of these pests, but one must be assiduous and not expect one treatment to be fully effective.

The other and less troublesome problem is rust which causes brown irregular patches to appear on the undersides of leaves. If not controlled with a fungicide, rust will have a serious weakening effect on the plant. Badly affected plants should have their leaves stripped off and disposed of, and plants ought to be segregated until the problem has been cleared.

## FURCRAEA (*Agavaceae*) false agave

In their natural habitat these plants form large rosettes of leaves, which individually can attain a length of some 2.5 m (8 ft) with particularly vicious barbs along the margin of the leaf. So it is not a plant for the small conservatory but the variety **F. sellowiana 'Variegata'** could well form a splendid centre-piece in the larger cactus collection. Like most plants that tend to become very large it is wise to keep this one in check by growing the plant in a relatively small container, that should have the appearance of being too small for the top growth of the plant. In the cactus display bed the pot can be plunged to its rim in the soil.

The leaves are large and attractively variegated and the plant itself is particularly tough in respect of neglect, going for long periods with no water whatsoever. A very light location is preferred, but it will also tolerate lower light levels if this is all that is available. There are no pest problems and water and feeding should be an occasional summer task and a very infrequent activity during the winter. New plants are propagated very easily by removing offsets from around the base of the plant and potting them individually in any reasonable mixture. Temperature of around 5 °C (41 °F) will be tolerated if the soil in the pot and surrounding area is dry.

**Furcraea**
Of Mediterranean origin, these produce large spreading rosettes so are only suitable for larger rooms. Good light and dry conditions needed.

## GARDENIA JASMINOÏDES (*Rubiaceae*) Cape jasmine

There are other gardenias but *G. jasminoïdes* is far and away the most popular with the commercial grower, so it is the plant that is almost always offered for retail sale. The leaves are evergreen and richly dark in colour on plants that may be grown as short standards or compact bushy plants, or they can be planted out in the border in the warm conservatory. It is quite a difficult plant to care for, so not a practical proposition for the beginner.

Plants should have a lightly shaded location and temperature that does not fall below 16 °C (61 °F) at any time. It is also necessary to maintain a moist atmosphere without actually getting the soil in the growing pot too wet – maintain the moistness by damping the area around the plant and by misting the leaves when the plant is not in flower. The flowers are by far the greatest attraction and are creamy white in colour and either double or semi-double with the most stunning fragrance – a fragrance that is almost overpoweringly heavy.

Plants require a rich mixture when it comes to potting on which should be no more than every second year and only when plants are growing well. Keep the soil moist but never saturated, giving less in winter. During active growth in the summer give an occasional feed with liquid fertilizer, but be sparing rather than generous. In a temperature of not less than 22 °C (72 °F) propagation of cuttings about 10 cm (4 in) in length can be attempted in early summer, but be warned, it is not an easy plant to root. Use fresh peat for inserting cuttings and a propagating case to maintain the right conditions.

## GERBERA (*Compositae*) Barbeton daisy

Seen in the florists shop these are among the most beautiful of all the daisy-type flowers, and are available in the most wonderful range of colours. When grown by the professional nurseryman the stems are long and the flowers unblemished, which might give one the impression that these would be something different for the conservatory indoor garden. However, they are very difficult to manage, needing all the skills of the grower to nurse his plants along and to keep them producing flowers.

Numerous attempts have been made to popularize this plant as a pot plant with much excitement being shown when the new introduction **G. jamesonii 'Happy Pot'** came on the scene some years ago. Although the flower stalks are shorter than the 100 cm (2 ft) length of the ordinary Barbeton daisy the new introduction is not particularly wonderful and is not the easiest of plant to care for. Also, as with all gerbera, the foliage is nothing to get excited about and leaves one with a very unattractive potful of foliage when the flowers are no longer in evidence.

However, for anyone wishing to take up the challenge of growing gerbera successfully there is seed available that can be sown in early spring in a temperature of around 16 °C (61 °F) to produce plants for growing on. At all times other than when very young they will need good light and very careful watering, ensuring that no water is allowed to get amongst the leaves which may cause botrytis rot – this will mean an almost instant finish to the plant.

## GLECHOMA HEDERACEA (*Labiatae*)
ground ivy

Variously described as ground cover or a hanging basket plant, this is a plant that is quick to grow and spread and should only be used as ground cover in an indoor bed if the custodian has ample time to ensure that it does not become too invasive. Much better by far is to grow the plant in with other subjects in a hanging basket where growth will be restricted and can be much more easily seen and trimmed when necessary. The leaves are kidney-shaped and attached to pendulous wiry stems; the colour is grey and white variegated.

Almost any piece of stem with a leaf attached will root if placed in a pot filled with a house-plant potting mix. To make better plants it is best to put a good number of cuttings in the pot rather than a solitary one. Allow the first growth to develop to a few inches then remove the growing tip to encourage the plant to branch – it will never be a wonderful plant, but pinching out tips will help it along! Almost any growing conditions will be suitable, other than cold and dark.

## GLORIOSA ROTHSCHILDIANA
(*Liliaceae/Colchicaceae*) glory lily

Grown from elongated tubers that lie dormant over winter, these should be started into growth in late winter to provide exotic climbing lilies for a long period during late spring and summer. Where growing space is limited one tuber should be planted in a 18 cm (7 in) diameter pot, but where there is ample wall space three to five tubers can be planted in pots of 25 cm (10 in) diameter. Rich potting mixture is needed and it is essential that a high temperature of not less than 22 °C (72 °F) be maintained to get the tubers started and to keep plants subsequently on the move. On reading the foregoing it should be clear that this is not a plant for the beginner in a small conservatory where the heating arrangements are inadequate.

There are several other gloriosas but *G. rothschildiana* is the variety that is most often offered for sale. Besides growing from tubers, plants can be purchased at better plant retailers, but it is important to ensure that plants have a green and healthy look about them as they can be very easily chilled while in transit, or at the retailers if his premises are inadequately heated. Care is needed when transporting plants home as it only needs a very short cold spell in even the boot of the car for irreparable damage to be done.

In the conservatory, plants should remain in their pots and be placed close to the wall where the framework is to be placed to enable plants to climb by their natural tendrils that are, in fact, an extension of the growing leaf. Purchased plants are usually grown on a horseshoe wire frame which is not very attractive, so one should carefully unwind the plant and tie it neatly to the framework to give the plants a start. They prefer to grow in a lightly shaded location and it is most essential that they enjoy very warm and slightly humid conditions – the minimum temperatures while plants are actively growing should not fall below 22 °C (72 °F), higher levels not being harmful, provided it is not above 30 °C (86 °F) for prolonged periods. The sight of bright red and yellow flowers set against dark green foliage will make the effort of caring for these fine plants well worthwhile.

During their natural growing season they will have to be kept moist but not totally saturated for long periods, and they will benefit from weekly feeding once established. At the end of the season when foliage yellows and dies naturally this will be a sign that watering should be reduced and finally stopped so that tubers may be stored dry and at minimum temperature of not less than 16 °C (61 °F) until the following late winter when the tubers can be potted into fresh soil and, perhaps, baby tubers attached to the parent can be removed to propagate fresh young plants.

These can be very rewarding plants when grown well, but they are not the easiest of subjects to manage. Should they be managed really well it might be possible to train the growth along strained wires overhead in the conservatory – you could then have a really mouth watering display.

## GREVILLIA ROBUSTA (*Proteaceae*)
silk oak

These are indigenous to Australia, with *G. robusta* being the plant that is most often offered for sale. Robusta would seem to be an appropriate name as the silk oak will develop leaves and branches at a surprising rate once it gets under way. Young plants will not be difficult to purchase, but it is equally easy to raise one's own plants from seed that will germinate very readily if sown in agreeable conditions in the spring of the year.

This is the ideal plant for the conservatory owner wishing to fill space quickly with foliage in a room that is provided with just a modicum of heat – a minimum temperature of around 5 °C (41 °F) will suit these plants fine if they are fairly dry at their roots. They will quickly attain a height of 2–3 m (6–9 ft) so plants should have a location at the rear of the room or against a wall. Being tough, the branches of the grevillia can be cut back at any time of the year in order to reduce its size. To promote more bushy growth it is also wise to remove the growing tips of plants once they have become established and are seen to be growing well.

When potting on use a loam-based mixture and pot into terracotta pots so that plants retain their equilibrium. Although they are not much troubled by pests one should keep a watchful eye for the presence of mealy bug; the white waxy cottonwool-like substance in which they enshroud their young will make detection fairly easy.

## GUZMANIA (*Bromeliaceae*) flaming torch

These are mostly smaller rosette-forming bromeliads developing a wide range of colourful bracts that, besides bright colour, can be of fascinating shape, often with branching heads.

Most have glossy green leaves but there are more colourful forms and in particular **G. 'Omar Morobe'** has soft leaves that are multicoloured and very striking. Alas, the latter is a plant that is generally in short supply, but others among the guzmanias are generally more freely available.

The biggest plus factor with these plants is that they are particularly easy to care for if given reasonable warmth and careful watering that errs on the dry side. Plants can be fed occasionally but it is not important. When you pot plants on, a peaty mix should be used but, like feeding, frequent potting is not required.

**Guzmania**
Becoming more popular, these bromeliads produce, in the main, elegant flower spikes that are carried well above the foliage.

One of the best uses for these very tolerant plants is in decorating a bromeliad tree that is made from a stout branch covered with sphagnum moss into which the plants are placed then secured in position. In this location, given frequent misting and regular watering, plants will often go on for years with little attention. In the conservatory these plants need light shade and a temperature not falling below 16 °C (61 °F) for preference.

**GYNURA** (*Compositae*) velvet plant

This plant must be grown in good light if the brilliant purple colouring of leaves and leaf hairs are to be fully appreciated. Possibly the best location in the conservatory is a hanging container located about head height where plants when catching the light will be at eye level. It will trail naturally in time but can look rather thin if the hanging container is not well filled with plants at the outset.

Providing lots of plants for the container should not be difficult once one has acquired a plant of reasonable size as the gynuras will root like the proverbial weed. Fill pots of reasonable size with houseplant potting soil and insert several cuttings so that plants with a full appearance will be the result once they have rooted. In warm shaded conditions in the spring they will root with very little attention. Once they have got under way the growing tips of each should be removed and the hanging container should be potted up, again using houseplant mix, with enough plants for one not to be able to see any soil. This way you have an instant plant that will be much more impressive than a plant made from a single pot of cuttings.

The gynuras have most attractive leaves but be warned that the clusters of small orange coloured daisy flowers when they appear have the most abominable smell – the answer is to remove those as soon as buds appear, not allowing them to open.

Keep plants warm, in good light, well watered and fed and they will be little bother. There are two forms that one might acquire, **G. aurantiaca** which has larger leaves and is more vigorous and **G. sarmentosa** which is the smaller of the two and much the better plant.

**HAEMANTHUS** (*Liliaceae/Amaryllidaceae*) shaving brush plant

This is a really fun plant that will always excite interest on account of its odd habit of growth and the peculiar brush-like flower which appears in the centre of the strap leaves emerging from a large bulb set at soil level.

The plant most often seen is **H. albiflos** with white brush flowers, but there are other colours that may occasionally be available.

Plants are undemanding in their requirements, needing good light, moisture and reasonable warmth to succeed. New plants can be simply provided by removing small offset bulbs that form around the base of the parent and putting them individually into small pots filled with any reasonable potting mixture. To attract interest plants do not necessarily have to have exotic flowers – there is often more excitement over something that is a bit odd rather than your most carefully cultivated most exotic flowers.

## HEBE (*Scrophulariaceae*)

These originate from New Zealand and include hardy and half-hardy plants. Perhaps better known by their old name of veronica, there are green and variegated forms among them and they will oblige with interesting flowers in a range of colours. There are low-growing ones such as the hardy **H. pinguifolia 'Pagei'**, and quite splendid taller kinds such as the half-hardy **H. 'Andersonii Variegata'**.

What this has to do with the conservatory might be a touch puzzling – it is simply that the hebes make splendid plants when grown in pots on the patio and there is no reason why they should not be utilized as plants for the cool and light conservatory. The half-hardy kinds only need a little protection to get through most winters so it should be perfectly possible to have them in the conservatory that is virtually unheated overwinter. This can only be a bonus for comparatively little effort and virtually no cost in respect of heating bills.

These plants are very accommodating in respect of treatment, needing good light, fresh air and the usual needs in respect of watering and feeding. Pots of reasonable size will be needed and the potting mix should be loam based. A range of these plants can usually be seen at the premises of the good plant retailer where you will also get advice on the hardiness and suitability of the plants that are stocked. Once plants have been acquired it will be found that they are very easy to root from cuttings a few inches in length, taken from growth at the top of the plant stem.

## HEDERA (*Araliacaea*) ivy

The ivies are often passed over as being too common for inclusion in the conservatory collection of plants, which is unfortunate, if only on account of their ability to adapt to all sorts of situations, but in particular because of their tolerance of low temperatures. Also, in recent years, there have been numerous new and interesting cultivars introduced.

Ivies can be used as ground cover plants, for walls, and in hanging containers. Many of them will grow at a surprising rate in the conservatory during the summer months when they should be fed, watered and regularly misted over to deter red spider mites. Over winter they do little in the way of growing so watering should be considerably reduced and the feeding should cease.

The common name of **Hedera algeriensis** (syn. *H. canariensis*) is Canary Island ivy and the best variety is **'Gloire de Marengo'**. This is a very fine plant with large cream and green variegated leaves and an almost unmatched capacity for clinging to moist walls and covering them with bright foliage. A further bonus is that this plant is perfectly hardy out of doors. One of the best wall climbing plants of all is **H. helix ssp. helix 'Goldheart'** (in the past *H.h.* ssp. *h.* 'Jubilee') which has very bright golden foliage; this will add colour to the interior of the colder conservatory. When seen growing in a pot and perhaps being offered for sale this can be a poor looking plant with thin strands of growth, but this should not be a deterrent as the plant comes into its own once it has been planted out.

In a planted bed on the floor of the conservatory there are endless ivies that will provide ground cover but, a note of warning here, these can be very invasive when planted in rich soil in agreeable conditions. However, they can be harshly pruned at any time with the result that growth is more compact and easier to manage.

In hanging containers they can also add

much to the general scene. (Note the mention of hanging containers and not hanging baskets – the latter can be very cumbersome and unwieldy in the conservatory where flexibility in the use of plants can be an important factor.) If lightweight plastic containers are employed it will be found that they are much easier to maintain as the plastic unit does not dry out nearly as rapidly as, for example, a basket lined with moss. These plastic hangers are also much easier to plant up and move around when necessary.

The other big bonus is that, in spite of the scepticism of the more traditional gardener, the plants do amazingly well if watered and fed well in a lightly shaded location. Ivies are not too much troubled by problems, but the hanging ones will shrivel alarmingly if they are allowed to become dry in sunny locations – the answer is to give them more shade and more water. The other problem is red spider mites which can be very troublesome in hot and dry conditions. Keep the foliage syringed over on hot days and spray the foliage regularly with insecticide to deter these pests. Pay special attention to the undersides of leaves where pests are normally to be found.

Cuttings made from two leaves attached to a firm piece of stem will root with little bother and should be placed at least seven cuttings to a pot of 8 cm (3 in) diameter.

When growing plants in hanging containers it is best to fill the container with all one variety rather than a mixture. One of the most attractive for this purpose is *H. helix* **ssp. helix** 'Goldchild' which, as the name suggests has rich golden colouring. Ivies are also lovely when all one variety is planted in a shallow dish for placing on a table – pinch out the growing tips periodically and they will retain a compact and pleasing shape.

## HELICHRYSUM PETIOLARE
(*Compositae*)

With the growing popularity of hanging baskets for house decoration this is a plant which has become surprisingly popular, though not much seems to be known about it. One of the first things to learn about growing a

basket of assorted plants, watered and fed regularly, is that a plant will develop an amazing mass of growth over the summer growing season. This plant is principally grown for its foliage which is entirely grey in colour with branching stems, providing a pleasing foil for other plants in the basket in its early stages of growth; as the plant digs its feet into the soil it grows at a surprising rate, often dwarfing other plants. Yellow daisy flowers are of little interest compared to the foliage.

Being perennial, plants can be carried on from one year to the next if desired, but it is very much better to take cuttings from pieces of stem some 10 cm (4 in) in length and to root these in small pots filled with a mix of peat and sand. It is also advisable to use a heated propagator as this plant, though very vigorous in growth, can be something of a problem when it comes to getting cuttings to root so one needs to mollycoddle them a bit. Put several cuttings in a pot when getting them under way and keep them warm and on the dry side over winter ready for planting the following spring. In common with other plants in mixed planting, the helichrysum will need rich compost to ensure that it does well.

## HELIOTROPIUM (*Boraginaceae*) cherry pie

An old favourite, this is probably better known as heliotrope, and much favoured on account of its very fragrant clusters of purple coloured flowers. Although normally sold as window-sill-sized plants that would not be suitable for other than table decoration, in the conservatory they can be trained to be much more impressive plants.

New plants can be grown from seed sown in March or they may be propagated from cuttings about 10 cm (4 in) in length taken in the spring. Insert cuttings in small pots filled with a peat and sand mixture and provide the warm temperature of a propagating case to encourage root development. Cuttings are subsequently potted into slightly larger pots using a good houseplant potting compost, but they should not be expected to do very much in their first year. Keep a minimum temperature of 13 °C (55 °F) to see them through the winter, raising the temperature in late winter to get them under way for the new season. Plants should be grown on in the conservatory, potting them on as required until the early summer when they can be planted in a prepared, sheltered bed out of doors, where they will make much more growth than they would if restricted to a pot inside.

The plants should be lifted from the garden early to mid autumn with the roots trimmed in order that the plants can be potted into a container of appropriate size using a loam-based mixture that is not too heavy. While the plant is outside, growth should be trained to grow up a supporting cane, or trained on a trellis framework so that in future years it can become a feature in the conservatory, as opposed to just another pot plant.

While in the conservatory they should as far as possible have a lightly shaded location in a cool temperature. Water sparingly in winter, giving more as new growth becomes active, and feed established plants while in active growth. Any untidy or unwanted shoots that are growing away from the central framework of the plant can be trimmed back in early spring.

## HELLEBORUS (*Ranunculaceae*)
Christmas rose

Probably the best known of these hardy plants is **H. niger** which has the common name of Christmas rose. It is not often that this plant obliges with its flowers at this time of year, as it is usually a little later on. For a conservatory it might be thought that they are not the most suitable of plants, yet any plant that flowers during the bleaker months of the year must be acceptable.

To use these in the conservatory it would be necesssary to have several clumps of them in the garden so that alternative plants could be lifted. Clumps should be lifted in mid autumn with care being exercised to ensure that there is not too much disturbance of the root system, which is something that these plants abhor. To avoid disturbance it is necessary to use large pots to accommodate the roots. Ideally when lifted they should go into a cold frame in the garden where they can be kept cool, or they may go into the greenhouse to be maintained at a minimum temperature of around 5 °C (41 °F). With a bit of luck, you should be able to bring potfuls of flowering Christmas roses in to decorate the conservatory, possibly maybe for Christmas! New plants are made from carefully splitting established clumps in the spring.

## HELXINE see SOLEIROLIA

## HEMIGRAPHIS (*Acanathaceae*) red ivy

When well grown these are attractive plants having violet leaves with a silver sheen on their upper surface and reddish purple on the reverse in the variety **H. colorata** (often labelled *H. alternata*). The common name of red ivy is also confusing as the plant is not related to the ivy and there is little in its appearance to suggest that it is one.

Not the easiest of plants to maintain, it must have a minimum temperature of at least 10 °C (50 °F) with careful watering erring on the side of dry rather than wet conditions. Feed only when plants are producing fresh growth and no more than once a week with a weak solution of liquid fertilizer.

When potting on becomes necessary use a good houseplant mixture and never be inclined to pot plants into containers that are excessively large. The best time for potting on will be early summer when plants are starting to grow well.

In the conservatory plants can be utilized as individuals growing in pots for placing wherever they will be most appreciated, or they can be planted in a bed for ground cover; stems will naturally develop roots that will find their way into the soil. Warmth is an important requirement of this plant and if planting them in a bed of soil it would be sensible to provide an electric warming cable to prevent the soil becoming too cold in winter. Offer plants a lightly shaded place to live in the conservatory.

## HEPTAPLEURUM see SCHEFFLERA

## HIBISCUS ROSA-SINENSIS (*Malvaceae*)
rose of China

This is almost the perfect plant for the average conservatory as it has so many good qualities, not least among them the fact that the plant is able to adapt to many different environments. The leaves are glossy green and are lightly serrated along their margins. Woody stems can be allowed to develop naturally into attractive bushes or they can be encouraged to develop to become a standard – a shape that will give the plant a very distinctive appearance. The object here is to allow a single stem to grow to some 1 to 1.5 m (3–5 ft) and then to remove the growing tip of the plant so that it will branch to form a head of growth. The branching pieces should then be allowed to grow to 15 to 20 cm (6–8 in) before they too have their growing tips removed; this will produce a head of foliage forming the standard shape. It will take several years before this sort of plant matures and looks its best.

The rose of China is a plant sold in vast numbers throughout the spring and summer months, and is available from literally every good plant shop. The trumpet flowers come in a wide range of colours from white through orange to red with interesting multi-colours to add flavour. The only fault with the flowers, if there is a fault, is that they open in the morning to close and finish by the same evening. But the hibiscus when well cared for has a fantastic ability to produce a continuous display of flowers – healthy well grown plants will never seem to be without flowers or buds. Plants and the surrounding area will be more attractive if dead flowers are picked up or removed from the plant as a daily chore. When this duty is being performed one can at the same time make a quick check on developing buds for the presence of aphids which seem to favour this area. Insecticides can be applied but the easy way of getting rid of these pests is simply to wipe them carefully from the buds with a tissue.

New plants are begun from firm stem cuttings of top sections removed in early spring and inserted in small pots filled with fresh peat and placed in a constant temperature around 24 °C (75 °F). Use of a propagating case will help considerably in maintaining this high temperature and will also help maintain a close and humid atmosphere around the cuttings. The cuttings should be allowed to become well established in the propagator before being removed in preparation for potting on. Where possible the change from the very warm conditions to the cooler, more open conditions of the conservatory should be gradual by lowering the temperature in the propagator for a week or so before plants are removed. The first potting after the rooting stage should be into only slightly larger pots using a houseplant potting mixture. Potting on should be done in gradual stages from one pot size to the next and not in one massive step to the largest container that one possesses. In the early stages of their development the young plants will need to be nursed along carefully, ensuring that they are kept warm, moist at their roots and sheltered from strong, direct sunlight. Wherever possible a small collection of plants should be propagated at the same time rather than single plants which is invariably a much more difficult problem when it comes to providing care. What to do with the surplus could be thought of as a problem but in fact it can be an advantage as planting several vigorous young plants in a larger container gives a more pleasing effect.

Once established the hibiscus plant will love to be in the sun, but will still benefit from some protection if the sun is very bright and the conservatory is not provided with some form of protective shading in the way of blinds to temper the midday sun.

Plants can be grown very successfully in attractive containers, which is clearly the sensible approach when the conservatory is fitted out more as a lounge area than a plant room. In containers the plants can be moved around to change the scene or simply grouped together when more space for other inhabitants is required. In the conservatory of reasonable size geared to growing plants, the hibiscus is more adaptable in that it can be planted in a prepared bed of good soil, perhaps close to a wall so that the resultant more vigorous growth can be trained to a framework offering quite a different sort of hibiscus display.

In respect of care, in hot conditions that go with sunny locations, plants will dry out quite rapidly, so ample watering becomes an important requirement. Plants obviously need to have water in the pots around their roots, but where conditions in the conservatory permit they will also benefit from the floor area around them being damped down in warm conditions.

Much less water is needed in winter when plants may become deciduous and shed their leaves as a result of being dry at their roots. If plants do shed an alarming number, even all of their leaves in the autumn, it is not necessarily the end – they will often begin to grow again in the early spring when the new season gets under way.

No feeding is needed in winter, but once plants have begun to develop new growth in the spring they will need to be fed every ten days or so. When growth has started, this is a good time for potting on any plants that are well rooted in their pots from the previous years growth. Being vigorous plants, they will need a rich potting mix.

Difficulties usually result from wild fluctuations in the use of the watering can – they either have far too much or not nearly enough when a good middle of the road approach should be the aim: keep soil moist all the time in spring and summer and very much on the dry side when inactive.

The main pest problems are aphids, which have already been mentioned, and red spider mites. The latter can have devastating effect on young foliage if precautions are not taken. Light brown discolouration of leaves is an indication that these pests have become fairly well established and probably at a stage when they will be difficult to eradicate. The old adage, prevention is better than cure is one that must be taken into account when it comes to pest control. So, don't wait for the pests to arrive – it is much better to give them a regular protection treatment throughout the season. These are pests that thrive in a hot and dry atmosphere, so it is important also to maintain high humidity by keeping the conservatory floor wet (if possible!) and by syringing frequently the foliage of all the plants in your collection.

## HYDRANGEA (*Hydraneaceae*)

Although well known for their colourful addition to the garden scene during the summer months the main attraction for the conservatory owner will be when potted plants are available in the spring. The professional grower takes his cuttings in the spring of one year for plants to flower the following year. Cuttings are normally prepared from top stem sections of shoots that are blind (non-flowering); the cuttings should have a firm pair of leaves and two less mature leaves. To reduce transpiration, the nurseryman will reduce the larger pair of leaves by half, simply by cutting them across their width. The cuttings are inserted individually in small pots filled with a peat and sand mixture and placed in a lightly shaded greenhouse maintained at a temperature of around 16 °C (61 °F). Once cuttings have rooted they are potted into 13 cm (5 in) pots filled with a loam-based potting mixture. Alternatively, pink-flowered varieties can be potted into acid soil (ericaceous), in order to produce plants with blue flowers. When done in this way the blue colouring might not be as bright and strong as desired; more positive results will usually be obtained by using one of the proprietary chemicals that are sold for the purpose of changing the colour of pink hydrangeas to bright blue. There are many varieties of these plant and some will 'blue' better than others; it is impossible to change the colour of white varieties.

The propagation of one's own hydrangeas from cuttings should be a comparatively simple task for the greenhouse owner who can offer modest facilities. It is important to ensure that the cuttings are removed from healthy plants. A propagating case is not necessary when rooting hydrangeas; they will usually do better when covered with a piece of clear polythene and placed in a lightly shaded spot in the greenhouse. The polythene will reduce transpiration and need only be removed when the plants have obviously rooted; thereafter you should syringe the cuttings frequently, or simply give them a quick damp over at regular intervals with a fine rose fitted to the watering can.

Once they have been potted on and become

established plants can be placed out of doors, once the risk of frost has passed. Select a lightly shaded area of the garden and ensure that plants never dry out. In early autumn they can be returned to the greenhouse for their dormant winter period, during which time plants will need very little attention. New growth appears during early spring when plants should be well watered; any that have done really well can be potted again, but one should avoid excessively large pots during the early stages of development. With luck plants will flower during their first year, but it may well be the ensuing year before plants achieve their true fullness and flower more freely. During spring and summer plants must have very light location and abundant watering with feeding regularly once plants have come into leaf.

Plants will flower over a long period up to late spring and they will be excellent plants for the decoration of the cool conservatory – light, air and water being their most important requirements. Plants bought in flower are best left in their original pots until the following spring when they can be potted into, perhaps, a decorative container that will grace the conservatory while the plant is in flower and will not be out of place as a foliage plant on the patio until it is time to bring the plant into a frost-free greenhouse or frame for the winter months.

Plants are available in many superb colours ranging from the brightest white, set off by dark green foliage, in the variety **H. macrophylla 'Soeur Thérèse'** to the deepest red with many fine forms of pink as seen in **H. macrophylla 'Alpenglühen'**. The much favoured lacecap varieties are excellent plants for pot culture, with blue, pink and white forms available and all needing the same light, air and ample water conditions.

## HYMENOCALLIS
(*Liliaceae/Amaryllidaceae*) spider lily

A scarce commodity, these are plants for the warmer conservatory where the minimum temperature can be maintained at not less than 16 °C (61 °F). Plants develop a bulbous base

not unlike that of the clivia with radiating fresh green strap leaves that in some varieties will be 1 m (3 ft) or more in length. The flowers are the main attraction, being most intricately fashioned and of the purest white colouring with a fragrance that sets this plant in a class of its own.

**Hymenocallis**
Plants for the warmer room, these are known as the spider lily and produce stems of clustered white flowers that are very fragrant.

A lightly shaded location is essential and a warm, humid atmosphere, the warmer the better provided plants are not exposed to direct sunlight. During the summer months ample watering and regular feeding will be needed with a reduction in the amount of water in the autumn and very little water during the dormant period in winter.

New plants are produced from offsets that develop around the base of the parent plant, but it is some years before these become plants with an ability to flower well. In their early years plants which have developed sufficient root system should be potted into slightly larger containers using a rich, loam-based mixture. Once plants have attained pots of 25 cm (10 in) in diameter they can remain in these pots for several years as plants will flower more readily when their roots are well massed in the growing container.

## HYPOCYRTA *see* NEMATANTHUS

## HYPOESTES SANGUINOLENTA
(*Acanthaceae*) polkadot plant

Easily raised from seed there is not a lot that can be said for the parent plant by way of recommendation as it is of poor colour with growth that is always thin and unattractive. As with many plants, the tired parent often produces a sport, a different sort of growth which can be removed, propagated and generally encouraged should it have sufficient merit. In respect of hypoestes, an attractive pink sport appeared some years ago which completely revolutionized this humble plant; it has become one of the most popular small foliage plants. Small plants are seen at their best when several are planted in a shallow dish so that a carpet of pink foliage develops. Or they may be put to very good use when combined with other plant varieties to make a decorative arrangement.

They must have good light and reasonable warmth with moist conditions at all times. Occasional feeding of established plants will do no harm but it should not be overdone as plants are more attractive when compact rather than straggly lengths of growth resulting from too much feeding. Use a good quality houseplant mixture when potting plants on; very large containers are never necessary. New plants can be raised from cuttings taken at almost any time when firm pieces of stem are available and there is reasonable warmth for encouraging rooting.

## IMPATIENS (*Balsaminaceae*) busy lizzie

The plant which has improved so amazingly in recent years is **Impatiens walleriana** (syn. **I. holstii**) which everyone knows so much better by its common name of busy lizzie. If they are kept shaded from the sun, moist and airy, there is nothing that can touch them when it comes to colourful continuity of flowering from late spring right through into the autumn. Keep them moist and fed with a liquid fertilizer once they have become established and they just go on and on.

Possibly their best contribution to conservatory colour is as hanging plants forming globes of amazingly bright colour. For real eye-catching effect moss-lined traditional hanging baskets can be made up as soon as young plants are available in the spring. The soil in the top of the basket should be mounded up before planting and young plants should be planted through the sides of the basket as well as into the soil in the top of the basket. In a 25 cm (10 in) basket you could fit in up to 100 plants, choosing all the same colour rather than a hotch potch of reds, whites and pinks. This may seem extravagant, but the end result is a real show-stopping effect for all who set eyes on it. The side walls of the conservatory are ideal for baskets, but they can also be suspended from arms that may be attached to upright supports within the building. With moss-lined baskets it is important to take plants down from their brackets so that they can be watered more conveniently and surplus water draining from the basket will not prove troublesome.

Other varieties include the New Guinea hybrids which can be permanent residents in the conservatory, with cuttings taken and rooted at almost any time of the year if new plants are needed. These are very strong growing plants needing rich compost and reasonably large pots once they have become well established.

Ample watering and frequent feeding is important, during active growth – a tomato feed being ideal for encouraging flower development. These hybrids are available in numerous colours, some of the varieties having attractively variegated foliage. Plants that are growing vigorously can be potted on several times in the same season with no ill effects; in fact, their growth will hardly be affected and plants of surprising dimension will usually be the result.

**IPOMOEA** (*Convolvulaceae*) morning glory

These are hardy annuals with truly brilliant blue flowers giving much pleasure over the summer months of the year. Plants should be provided with a framework for growth to climb naturally. By providing some form of support the plants can also be encouraged to fill in the overhead area in the conservatory. They may also be used to frame the doorway of the conservatory by placing a potful of plants on either side of the door.

Plants are started from seed sown in houseplant compost in temperature of around 18 °C (64 °F) in early spring. If there is a bed of soil in the conservatory they can be planted out as opposed to growing in containers; in beds they will be less of a problem in respect of watering. Should there be surplus plants as a result of the

**Ipomoea**
Morning glory has flowers that are very short lived but produced with great frequency. Raise from seed to get fine climbing plants.

seed sowing some of them can be hardened off to be planted around the doorway on the outside of the conservatory once the weather has become warm enough. The presence of red spider mite can be a major problem, so it is wise to check plants regularly for signs of leaf discoloration and to take remedial action.

There are also perennial ipomoeas with the same climbing habit; these can be trained to a framework and left in position. Untidy growth needs to be trimmed to shape in the early part of the year. These do well when planted in beds of rich soil and trained against the wall of the conservatory.

**IRESINE** (*Amaranthaceae*) blood leaf

These easy-care plants are grown solely for their foliage, *I. herstii* being rich wine red in colour and *I.h.* **'Aureoreticulata'** having yellow leaves with attractive venation. Both are equally easy to manage if given light and airy conditions during the summer months. Being vigorous plants they will also require ample watering and frequent feeding while producing new growth. Plants acquired in small pots should be potted on at the first opportunity using a rich potting mixture.

Plants can be propagated from cuttings at any time during the spring and summer months; there is little difficulty in encouraging them to root in reasonable temperature. Place three cuttings around the outer edge of 8 cm (3 in) pots filled with houseplant potting soil in order to produce stocky plants.

**IXIA** (*Iridaceae*)

Something different in the way of bulbs, these are indigenous to South Africa, and bear attractive flowers on slender stems. For the conservatory, bulbs are best raised in 13 cm (5 in) pots. Plant the bulbs in early winter, placing five bulbs at about half the depth of the pot and using rich potting mixture. To establish a good root system the bulbs should initially go under the staging of the greenhouse and be covered with peat, sand or chipped bark. When growth is evident the pots can be removed from their covering and placed on the greenhouse bench to grow on. When in flower they can be transferred to the conservatory for the fragrant flowers to be fully appreciated. Keep soil moist and occasionally fed until such time as the foliage is seen to be dying back naturally when water can be withheld until the soil is dry and bulbs are in a suitable condition for storing frost-free for the winter months. Additional plants can be made by removing small bulbs from around the parent and potting them individually.

## IXORA (*Rubiaceae*)

There are numerous varieties of these fine plants but they are only very occasionally offered for sale. A minimum winter temperature of 18 °C (64 °F) is preferred, with higher temperature and humidity being essential in summer. A lightly shaded location is required and every effort should be made to dampen around the plants. The latter can be achieved either by syringing the foliage or, where conditions permit, by damping the floor area around the plant with a fine rose attached to a watering can. Flower colours range from white through orange to red, and there are plant varieties with attractively variegated foliage. To increase stock, plants should be propagated in a heated propagating frame in the spring. Firm cuttings some 10 cm (4 in) in length should be placed in small pots filled with clean peat; cuttings must have protection from direct sunlight.

## JACOBINIA *see* JUSTICIA

## JASMINUM POLYANTHUM (*Oleaceae*)
jasmine

There are other species of jasmine but *J. polyanthum* is by far the most popular choice for growing in the conservatory, because of its heady fragrance. Another plus factor is that the plant flowers during the winter months of the year, generally a little after Christmas and for many weeks thereafter.

Very easy to manage, it will require a frame-work for the abundant foliage. Young plants trained to fan-shaped supports are freely available during the first months of the year. These have considerable appeal with their white fragrant flowers flushed with pale rose colouring. It is best to purchase such young plants and to enjoy them in their pots while still in flower and then to consider transferring the plants to a more permanent position. If you plant them in a bed of good soil in the conservatory be warned that there are extremely invasive plants that will more than likely get out of hand when given a free root run. A better alternative might be to pot the plant into a decorative container so that the roots and this growth are restricted. Plants in pots with a large amount of root will also flower more freely than plants that are growing too vigorously.

Jasmine is very tolerant of changing conditions and will put up with temperature fluctuations, although cool and airy conditions will suit them best. Shade from direct sunlight and give ample watering while in active growth. Plants should be fed occasionally, but not too much as plants can become too vigorous. They can quickly take over the conservatory to the detriment of other plants, so cutting back unwanted growth is an important chore and can be undertaken at almost any time other than when plants are in flower. Trimmings of firmer shoots can be used to make new plants which are not difficult to root inserted in pots filled with houseplant mixture, several cuttings to go into each pot.

Plants that develop a mass of almost impenetrable growth will almost inevitably become a home for many conservatory pests, so there is a need to be constantly on the look out for unwanted visitors.

## JUSTICIA (*Acanthaceae*)

There are both summer- and winter-flowering varieties of these fine plants which develop into compact shrubs of about 1 m (3 ft) with attractive heads of flower. For preference, winter temperature should be in the region of 18 °C (64 °F), but slightly lower levels will be tolerated if water is given with great care. In any event, winter watering of these plants should err on the side of dry rather than wet conditions. Following flowering plants can be pruned back to ground level, leaving only an inch or so of stem. When fresh growth appears in the spring it should occasionally be pinched out at the tips so that plants are encouraged to grow in compact fashion.

These are greedy plants, and it is important to ensure that they are well supplied with nourishment when in active growth – twice weekly with liquid fertilizer is not over generous. New plants can be propagated in the spring from firm cuttings placed in small pots filled with peat and subsequently placed in a heated propagating case.

**J. brandegeeana** (syn. *Beloperone guttata*) is a much underrated plant that is well known, as the shrimp plant, but seldom very well grown! The paper-thin foliage is attached to wiry stems and is evergreen, but not particularly attractive; neither are the small tubular flowers, so what is the appeal? The attractive

**Justicia brandegeeana**
The shrimp plant has had a name change, but it is still one of the best flowering plants for the conservatory if fed well.

part of the plant is the orange coloured bract that gives the plant its common name.

To grow these well it is of paramount importance to ensure that they are well fed and that they are potted on into a slightly larger pot using good quality potting soil. With this sort of treatment and warm, lightly shaded surroundings you can grow bracts of brilliant colouring and surprising size; they can reach 1.5 m (5 ft) tall and become quite magnificent, so be generous is the recommendation. Given proper care, these plants can be expected to produce a crop of bracts throughout the year.

## KALANCHOË BLOSSFELDIANA
(*Crassulaceae*) flaming Katy

On account of its tough qualities this has become an exceptionally popular plant with the florist and other retailers. Sold in vast numbers throughout the year they are available in red, pink, orange and yellow colouring. Foliage is fleshy and evergreen but not especially attractive on its own. Flowers form in clusters on short stems and seem to be forever present on plants enjoying reasonable care. General care of these plants amounts to little more than offering good light in which to grow and a watering programme erring on the side of dry rather than wet conditions. Provided they are not subjected to very cold conditions these are plants that will tolerate a wide temperature variation with no harm done.

By controlling the amount of light to the plant the commercial grower can programme his plants to be available throughout the year, regardless of the fact that these are natural summer-flowering plants.

If left in the tiny pots in which they are purchased plants will do little growing so pot them on almost as soon as purchased at times other than mid winter. Plants can be potted even though in flower, and should be advanced into pots of slightly larger size using a good houseplant potting mixture. Give the soil a thorough watering immediately after potting, then keep it on the dry side until plants are obviously settled and growing away in the new mixture. It may well be then discovered that the kalanchoe is a much more impressive conservatory subject than was at first thought when the plant was confined to its tiny pot.

Besides growing these as container subjects they can also be put to use in the decorative bed of plants. If you have a low retaining wall in front of the bed in which plants are to be grown, the kalanchoë is a fine plant for covering some of the ground and creeping over the edge to soften the hardness of the brick-work.

## KOHLERIA (Gesneriaceae)

In the conservatory there is much to be said for specializing in a particular type of plant, or in a family of plants. In the latter respect plants in the family Gesneriaceae could well offer colour and interest all the year round if you can maintain a minimum temperature of not less than 16 °C (61 °F) with 20 °C (68 °F) being better for some of the family. Although not freely available, there are several kohlerias that could add both interest and colour to the warm

conservatory collection. These are plants with both interesting foliage and colourful flowers, some varieties having lax and spreading habit of growth while others are more upright. Flowers are shaped like narrow tubes with a splayed, speckled mouth, an interesting contrast to the reddish orange colouring of the tube part of the flower.

Plants are grown from scaly rhizomes that are started into growth in warm conditions in late winter by placing several of these scales in a 13 cm (5 in) diameter pot filled with good houseplant potting mixture. Growth will soon be apparent and when growing vigorously pot the plant on into an 18 cm (7 in) pot if the plant is to be sustained through the season. At the end of the season when foliage begins to die down naturally, water should be withheld so that the potful of tubercles can be stored warm and dry until the following late winter when the growing procedure starts again.

Place plants in a shaded location that is warm and moist. Moisture at their roots is important but so too is moisture in the atmosphere and around plants generally. Once they are established in their pots, regular weekly feeding will be necessary.

**Kohleria**
Attractive plants for growing in pots – nodding flowers are delicately coloured. Keep almost dry over the winter and start fresh plants in spring.

## LACHENALIA (Liliaceae/Hyacinthaceae)
Cape cowslip

These bulbous plants are indigenous to South Africa, which is often an indication that they will have a growing season at odds with those from other parts of the world. Lachenalias indeed do have a growing season running from September to June in the northern hemisphere and a dormant period extending from June to September when the bulbs in their containers are kept bone dry.

Bulbs are started into growth by placing at least five to half the depth of a 13 cm (5 in) pot filled with good potting soil, best done towards the end of summer. Following planting the soil should be watered and the pot than placed in a cool location for roots to become established before removal to warmer conditions.

Flowers are a dull yellow in colour and are seen to best effect when the plant is growing in a hanging container. Here the bulbs can be planted direct rather than first going into a conventional pot. Following flowering the plant will die down naturally and should then be kept cool and dry until the new season gets under way.

In the conservatory, plants do best in cool and airy conditions, with no special requirements other than regular watering and feeding while in leaf.

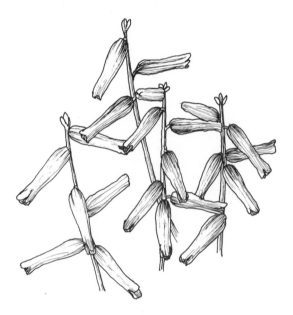

**Lachenalia**
Bulbous plants from S. Africa and ideal for growing in small hanging containers where their tubular orange flowers will be seen to good effect.

**LANTANA CAMARA** (*Verbenaceae*)
shrub verbena

These are very free-flowering shrubby plants ideally suited to the cool conservatory offering good light and fresh air. Leaves are coarse and not particularly attractive, but the verbena-like flowers more than make up for this deficiency. Not only are they free flowering over a long period during the summer months, they will also quite naturally produce flowers of many different shades of red, orange and yellow on the same plant!

Plants tolerate cooler winter temperatures of around 10 °C (50 °F) if you are careful to ensure that the soil in the pot never becomes too wet. Any potting that may be necessary should be attended to in the early part of the year with a loam-based potting mixture that is well firmed in the pot. Feed plants regularly and keep the soil moist over the summer months, with care taken to allow the soil to dry a little between each watering. Soil that remains very wet over long periods can be very detrimental to these plants.

The lantanas can be grown as compact bushes that are lightly trimmed to shape in the early part of the year, or they can be trained to grow as standards with mop heads that can be very impressive when seen in an attractive container. New plants can be raised from seed sown in early spring in high temperature, or they can be propagated from firm cuttings a few inches in length taken at almost any time during the spring or summer when cutting material is available.

**LAPAGERIA** (*Liliaceae/Philesiaceae*)
Chilean bellflower

When well grown, there are few better climbing plants than **L. rosea** for the cool conservatory where minimum temperature can be kept at around 10 °C (50 °F). Plants need to be placed near a wall so that growth can be trained to a trellis framework with the prospect of further training growth overhead on a light framework. The waxy, pendulous bell flowers are seen at their best when thus trained. Although growth 6 m (20 ft) long is a possibility, it is not the easiest of plants to manage.

Essentials are a lightly shaded location in a cool environment, careful attention to potting and soil mixture and a careful watering programme. A suggested mixture for potting is three parts peat and one part good loam with charcoal and sand added. The latter is to encourage good drainage which is very important to these plants. The containers must be generous in size and a good amount of drainage material must be placed in the bottom of the container before the soil is introduced.

Plants are seldom freely available, but if you

*Gloriosa*. Grown from tubers these are colourful
plants when attached to trellis frame and growing
well, but they need agreeable conditions (species
shown: *G. rothschildiana*).

*Hibiscus.* Free-flowering, easy care plants that are ideal for the cool conservatory that offers good light and modest warmth in winter.

*Below: Impatiens.* Shaded from the sun but in good light the greatly improved busy lizzie is a splendid plant for bright summer colour in many shades (variety shown: 'New Guinea Hybrids').

*Justicia.* Deserving to be more popular, these are
neat pot plants that can be trimmed back after
flowering to retain their shape so saving on space.

*Passiflora*. Invasive climbing plants with exotic flowers. Restricting root development will deter too rampant growth. Seek out the better varieties when buying (species shown: *P. caerulea*).

*Below: Neoregelia carolinae*. A bromeliad with colourful rosette of flat rather than upright leaves, and spectacular red centre when flowers appear.

*Pyrostegia venusta.*
The flame vine is a
remarkable
climbing plant that
will find its way
into the upper
reaches of the
tallest of
conservatories.

*Saintpaulia*. Good warmth and good light are
essential needs for these superb flowering plants
that will always be a test of one's skills as a
grower of plants.

*Above:*
*Spathiphyllum.*
Dark green leaves
and white spathe
flowers provide the
perfect
combination – fine
plants that do best
in warm, moist and
shaded conditions.

*Sarracenia.* As
interest grows the
prospects of a
plant collection
composed entirely
of carnivorous
plants has much
appeal, sarracenias
being essential
(species shown: *S.
purpurea*).

*Stephanotis.*
Provide a
framework for this
natural climber to
ramble around and
to produce its
remarkably
fragrant white
cluster flowers.

see them buy them in early spring so that plants can be potted immediately. An alternative to containers would be to plant direct into the soil in the conservatory, but in this event it would be essential to dig out a generous hole and to fill the bottom with drainage material before infilling with the potting mixture suggested above. To plant lapagerias into just any soil that is part of the foundations of the conservatory would be a waste of time and a waste of a fine plant.

From spring through summer plants can be watered generously, but it is important to ensure that water drains almost instantly through the soil when it is applied. During this period it is also wise to syringe foliage regularly – a practice that will benefit the plant and at the same time deter such pests as red spider mites. In respect of pests it is important to maintain a regular watch for their presence and to deal immediately with any marauders that may be present.

Any pruning that may be necessary should be attended to in the early part of the year, but pruning is rarely anything more than removing any dead or damaged growth that may be present. New plants can be produced by pegging down (layering) firm shoots in the soil, similar to that suggested for potting.

Besides the *rosea* variety there is also **L. albiflora** which is a white form. This is seen to best effect when both the white and the rose coloured form are grown together with their growth intertwined.

## LAURUS NOBILIS (*Lauaceae*) sweet bay

These are fine plants for the unheated conservatory offering good light and a modicum of care. The dark, evergreen leaves are much used for cooking and are produced densely on plants. They are seen at their best when grown as clipped specimens in containers. Belgium is the main source of these plants and they are available as mature plants that have been clipped and pruned to interesting pyramid and mop-head shapes.

Although perfectly hardy these plants may suffer unsightly leaf damage if exposed to severe weather, so it is wise to bring them into the conservatory during inclement weather. However, there is no reason why they should not occupy conservatory space throughout the year, even to the point of being planted out in formal beds where space permits.

During the growing season plants must be kept well watered and fed regularly, with less water and no feeding over winter. Scale insects can be troublesome pests so a careful watch is needed for these on both stems and the undersides of leaves. Thorough spraying with insecticide will kill them, but where there are only a few of these pests it is often better to use a sponge or cloth to clean them off manually.

When potting on it is best to use a loam-based potting mixture to sustain the plant, as it is likely that it will be growing in the same pot over a number of years. Potting is best done in late spring. Cuttings a few inches in length can be rooted in a sandy mixture by inserting them direct into garden soil to which sand has been added. A shady spot should be chosen and the cuttings ought to be covered with some form of glass protection. When striking cuttings, you should insert a good number so that a few failures are allowed for.

## LEPTOSPERMUM SCOPARIUM
(*Myrtaceae*) South Sea myrtle

There are several varieties of this fine plant, ranging from white through pink to crimson-coloured flowers. Generally listed as slightly tender when planted out of doors, this is an ideal plant for the cool conservatory offering reasonable space. If planted out and given a free root run they will develop into small trees which will be a mass of flowers over many of the summer months. When grown in tubs or any sort of large container the roots will be restricted and growth will be considerably reduced, which will be more acceptable where space is limited. These are tough plants which are not overparticular in respect of potting soil, but it is suggested that a good loam-based mixture should be used in order to get the best from the plant. Some shading will be required to prevent leaves being scorched under glass, but dark conditions should be avoided.

Large plants in containers will require a lot

of water and there should always be some space for holding water between the rim of the container and the surface of the soil – this area should be filled each time the plant is watered ensuring that surplus water is seen to drain through the drainage holes in the bottom of the pot before the watering can is put away. Simply pouring a little water onto the surface of the soil will do little for large plants with lots of roots. Care must be exercised in winter when plants are almost at a standstill.

Propagating new plants should be undertaken in the autumn when firm shoots can be removed from the plant and inserted in sandy mixture around the outer edge of a 13 cm (5 in) pot. If misted over regularly, cuttings should not be difficult to root in a cool greenhouse.

## LEUCADENDRON (*Proteaceae*)
nodding pincushion

Closely related to the protea, the South African national flower, these are exotic perennials that may be seen growing throughout tropical regions as robust shrubs. In their natural habitat flowers are produced in great profusion, but in conservatory conditions that are less than ideal one would not normally be able to produce plants with flowers in such abundance. Also it would not be wise to attempt to

**Leucadendron**
Fine plants for the cool conservatory that offers ample growing space. They have showy flowers.

grow these plants in conservatories that offer anything other than spacious surroundings.

The conservatory ought to be light and airy and plants in time will need tubs of substantial size. If smaller plants are acquired they ought to be potted on in stages as they fill their existing pots with roots and not introduced to very large containers as an initial step. These are plants that are particular in respect of potting medium, as they are when it comes to selecting and using fertilizers. For potting a mixture of peat incorporating a good percentage of sand and grit will be the most suitable, and when feeding it is advisable to avoid conventional brands and to obtain from the specialist supplier a fertilizer containing magnesium sulphate and nitrogen. Propagate from seed, or from firm cuttings placed in sandy mixture – a heated propagator will be an advantage for both operations.

## LEWISIA (*Portulacaceae*) bitterwort

These are hardy outdoor plants that at first sight might not seem to have any place in the conservatory, but there is quite a good case for concentrating perhaps on alpine plants in premises that are entirely unheated. Although described as hardy, the lewisias can be very disappointing plants when plants remain wet around their leaves over lengthy periods of time. In the light, well aired conservatory they will give a fine show of colour over many summer months, with several flushes of flowers on the same plant. They need good drainage, careful watering and in time should be grown in fairly large pots to ensure a good performance in respect of flowering. Flower colouring ranges from white through to deep pink with new colouring of yellow now becoming available.

Propagating plants from seed will present no difficulty as any seed falling on fertile soil will germinate almost as you look at them. A few large plants in reasonably substantial terracotta half-pots will be much more effective than having lots of smaller plants about the place.

Plants are at their most vulnerable when their leaves remain wet during cold weather, for any length of time. Therefore, it goes without saying that watering must be done with care, ensuring that the leaves are lifted so that the spout of the watering can is directed underneath them.

## LILIUM (*Liliaceae*) lily

Lilies can be especially rewarding plants as temporary members of the conservatory scene. Grown in pots, they can be brought in when in flower and returned to their place in the garden when flowers have lost their appearance. Bulbs can be purchased in the autumn, and the eventual quality of flowers will often depend on the quality of bulb bought.

When making your selection from the many lilies that are listed in trade catalogues, you should opt for those that are not going to be too tall as these will be difficult to move around without causing damage to the flowers. Lilies such as *L. auratum*, which grow to a manageable height of some 1.5 m (5 ft), will be ideal and, besides flowers there will also be the appeal of fragrance.

Potting mixture for lilies should not be composed entirely of peat as lilies do not take too kindly to this sort of preparation. Try to get as near as possible a mixture composed of equal parts of good loam, leafmould, well decayed manure and sand. The latter is important as lilies must have good drainage. For good results a 25 cm (10 in) pot should be used and three bulbs should be planted in autumn to about twice their depth (although this will vary depending on the bulb and its needs). Water the soil and place the pot outside in a sheltered location to grow on; transfer to a cold greenhouse if weather is inclement. Some bulbs are hardier than others. Provide canes when the growth is tall enough, and keep the soil watered and fed while the plant is developing.

Following flowering the plant can be returned to the garden where watering and feeding should continue. The stem of the plant should not be cut down following flowering. Bulbs in their pots should be stored in a sheltered dry place over winter. The following year some of the soil should be removed from the top of the pot and replaced with fresh.

## LITHOPS (*Aizoaceae*) living stones

These fascinating little plants are of South African origin and can almost be guaranteed to attract attention when imaginatively displayed in the conservatory. The common name of living stones fits them to perfection, as they are often very difficult to distinguish from the stones that may be surrounding them. Succulent growth develops into tight clusters that in both colour and appearance resemble pebbles. The lithops will be of particular interest to younger members of the family and it is another plant that can be introduced to a conservatory collection to stimulate a feeling for plants in general.

A miniature garden can be arranged in a shallow dish-type container by using a cactus potting mixture and covering the surface of the soil with pebbles. If the pebbles are carefully chosen they can be difficult to distinguish from the lithops of the same colour when they are planted together. Established plants will flower in early autumn and it may be possible to save seed from these in order to increase your collection of plants.

Good light and fresh air are essential needs of the lithops, with a winter temperature that does not fall below 16 °C (61 °F). The soil in which they are potted or planted must be very open and free draining – equal parts of sharp sand and loam will form a good basis for a potting mixture. If available, mortar rubble or crushed brick can be added to the mixture.

Careful watering is another important aspect of their care. Plants should be kept moist from late spring through to early winter and from then until the following spring they should have no water whatsoever. Done in this manner there should be attractive mounds of living stones to cause both amusement and interest.

## LIVISTONA (*Palmae*) fan palm

These are plants for the conservatory where the minimum winter temperature does not fall below 16 °C (61 °F), and where there is ample space. In the very large conservatory there is likely to be the temptation to remove the palms from their pots in order to plant them freely in the ground, but this urge should be resisted as plants are capable of attaining majestic size when given their head. It is generally much more satisfactory to confine the roots of plants to pots so that leaf development can be kept under control.

**Livistona**
The fountain palm is fine for the conservatory when the roots are confined to a container, but becomes too bold when free-planted in a border.

Although less popular today, the fan palms, such as **L. chinensis** (better known to the older gardener as *Latania borbonica*) were much favoured during the Victorian era of conservatories when buildings were generally higher and more spacious. Another reason for the demise of robust palms such as the livistona has been the popularity of the *Howea*, or kentia palm, which is much more decorative and less demanding in terms of space.

Lightly shaded conditions suit them best, and when watering it is essential that this is done thoroughly, giving sufficient to see surplus water draining through the holes in the bottom of the pot. As with the majority of potted plants in the conservatory the fan palms will need less water in winter. Plants will benefit from regular feeding while producing fresh leaves with no feed needed over the winter months. Misting, or wetting foliage with a quick douse will help to preserve a humid feeling around plants during the summer months and, at the same time, will help to deter pests.

Because the foliage is tough, plants are not too much troubled by pests, but scale insects can be a nuisance and must be watched for – an obvious sign of their presence is a black sooty mould forming on leaves below those where scales have attached themselves.

Seed is seldom available, but when it comes your way it should be placed in free-draining, well aerated material – it need not necessarily be soil. The seed is started in the highest possible temperature 22 °C (72 °F) in winter. This is a slow process that may well prove fruitless; the alternative is to purchase young plants and to grow them on in warm and agreeable conditions.

## LOTUS BERTHELOTII (*Leguminosae*)

Trailing strands of delicate grey foliage up to 1 m (3 ft) in length will add considerably to the colour and interest in the upper area of the conservatory when this plant is suspended from the ceiling. Scarlet flowers with the appearance of butterflies resting on the leaves will be present during the summer months. Added to these qualities is the pleasure of knowing that this is a relatively easy plant to care for.

Plants can be started from seed sown in warm temperature in early spring, or they can be grown from cuttings taken from firm shoots during the summer and placed in sandy soil in small pots at modest temperature. Grow them on in pots of good houseplant mixture until they have become well established and are ready for potting into their hanging containers. Provided they are not too clumsy, the larger the container used for planting the larger and more lush the eventual plant is likely to be, but it is important not to skimp: put several of the young plants in the hanging container and use good quality potting mixture when planting. Potting mixtures are now specially formulated for hanging containers and, if available, this is the sort of mixture to go for. These mixes will contain slow-release fertilizers which will sustain the plants over a much longer period than standard potting concoctions. After planting water the soil and keep the container (perhaps in the greenhouse) at bench level for ease of maintenance until plants are seen to have settled down. Then and only then should they be hung in their more permanent location.

Light, airy and reasonably cool conditions are best. All plants suspended from the ceiling of the conservatory will need ample watering and feeding while in active growth – twice daily watering not being overfrequent during hot spells. To encourage greater production of flowers a high potash fertilizer should be used, a standard tomato fertilizer being ideal.

## MACKAYA BELLA (*Acanthaceae*)

These are fine plants for the cooler conservatory where the winter minimum temperature need not be more than 7 °C (45 °F). They are large deciduous shrubs which will attain a height of 2 m (6 ft) when roots are confined to containers. Bell-shaped flowers are produced over a full three months from mid spring onwards, but it will be two or three years before plants started from cuttings are man enough to produce flowers. Clearly, in this event, patience is needed, but it will also be wise to have the benefit of a feeder greenhouse you could use for accommodating such plants in the early stages of development and for the period of their winter rest when they are dormant and contributing nothing to the conservatory display.

New plants are propagated from cuttings taken in early spring and inserted in small pots filled with a sandy mixture. In the warm and moist conditions that can be provided by a properly managed greenhouse or propagating case these plants will not be difficult to get under way. As soon as cuttings have begun to produce fresh leaves of their own they should be planted into larger containers using a good

houseplant mixture. At this stage three or four young plants should be potted together into a 13 cm (5 in) pot to ensure that resultant plants are full and attractive. Plants will quickly establish and should be further potted into 18 cm (7 in) pots when they have well filled their pot with roots.

**Mackaya**
Propagated from cuttings in spring, plants develop to some 1.8 m (6 ft) in height with pale lavender flowers over much of the year.

Plants should remain in light and airy conditions and kept on the move by regular watering and feeding. Feeding should not begin until some four weeks after the last potting exercise. From the beginning of autumn the amount of water given to plants should be gradually reduced until such time as there is virtually no water being given during winter. It may seem harsh, but towards the end of winter all the growth that the plant has made should be cut back to a few inches from the base. In subsequent years pruning in this way should follow immediately after the plant has flowered.

The trouble taken will be well rewarded as these are fine plants when in flower, and something very different to the run-of-the-mill plants generally seen decorating conservatories. The bell-shaped flowers are lilac in colour with attractive purple veins.

## MAGNOLIA (*Magnoliaceae*)

For the very large conservatory there are few more majestic plants than **M. grandiflora**, which can be grown as a free-standing small tree or planted against a wall when young eventually to form into a splendid wall covering of rich green leaves. In time they will produce their fragrant creamy white flowers that are as large as dinner plates and very impressive. Good light and cool conditions are necessary is plants are not to become thin and straggly.

In colder climates spring frosts can play havoc with magnolia flowers in the garden, but there is no reason why those plants normally seen in the garden, **M. × soulangeana** and **M. stellata** in particular, should not be grown in containers and be given the shelter of the conservatory in the spring when they are vulnerable to frosts. Ample space will be needed, but the plants need only occupy the conservatory area for a short time prior to and while they are in flower. The rest of the year they can become decorative foliage plants either on the patio or, still in their containers, placed as features elsewhere in the garden.

Whether plants are inside or out it will be important to ensure that they do not go without water and that they are fed regularly. When plants are in need of potting on one should avoid mixtures that are composed entirely of peat and use a loam-based mixture instead.

## MANDEVILLA (*Apocynacaea*)

Many of these are still offered as *Dipladenia*, in particular **M. splendens** which is an old favourite with the commercial grower and one of the few varieties that are produced in any quantity. Plants require good light and modest

temperature to do well. A considerable attribute is that they will flower over a long period and they make fine climbing plants if they are provided with some form of support.

Plants can be grown in containers with canes or a framework of trellis provided for plants to

**Mandevilla**
Often sold as dipladenia, these are fine climbing plants for the conservatory and should be grown in containers placed close to the wall.

be trained, or they may be planted in a border close to one of the walls of the conservatory so that growth can be encouraged to climb. Some of the varieties, such as **M. sanderi 'Rosea'** will seldom be without flowers during the course of the year and needs little attention other than the essentials of modest warmth, watering and feeding. Untidy growth can be trimmed to shape following flowering or, if plants become sparsely leaved lower down their stems, the pruning can be more drastic so that new growth is produced to refurbish the plant.

When potting on, preferably in the spring,

or planting out incorporate peat and leafmould in the mixture. Feed during active growth and water well during the summer, with less water needed in the autumn and very little in winter.

If available, plants can be raised from seed sown in warm temperature in the spring. Alternatively, they may be increased by means of firm cuttings inserted in very sandy mixture in a heated propagator during late spring and summer.

## MARANTA (*Marantaceae*) prayer plant, rabbit tracks

Marantas have long been fashionable as decorative plants for the home where they should enjoy warmth and shade in order to succeed. They are grown solely for their decorative foliage, the flowers being very insignificant. Those offered as indoor plants would, presumably, be ideal ground cover plants in their native jungle habitat, as creeping foliage can only be encouraged to grow upright if given a support. When grown vertically in this way the plants have a most unnatural look about them and one wonders why the practice is continued.

Leaves of the marantas are all attractively mottled with intricate patterns of colour further enhancing the attraction of the plant. The variety **M. var. kerchoviana** has attractive pale and darker green colouring with distinct blotches on each leaf said to resemble the marks left by a rabbit's paw, hence the common name of rabbit tracks.

In the conservatory shade from direct sunlight and keep warm and humid conditions. Normally seen as small plants growing in pots for the mass market, they may also be grouped in shallow containers so that a more impressive effect is obtained. Likewise, if a planted bed is being prepared in the conservatory it will be found that marantas are excellent plants for covering empty spaces. To enjoy shade effect they can be underplanted in the shade of taller subjects with more spreading foliage.

Provided conditions are agreeable, plants can be potted on at almost any time of the year. Use a peaty houseplant mixture and new pots that are not excessively large.

## MEDINILLA MAGNIFICA
(*Melastomataceae*) rose grape

This is one of the finest of all flowering plants for the conservatory, but it will also be one of the most testing of plants when it comes to care and attention. Large, leathery leaves are attached to coarse branches that protrude at all angles on plants which may eventually attain a height of around 1.5 m (5 ft). It is the flowers that are the wonder of wonders as they hang from the branches with their brilliant pink bracts and clustered florets of carmine-coloured flowers.

This is a plant for special treatment and should be provided with a pedestal so that the plant is lifted to head level in order to better appreciate the flowers.

High temperature is essential, with 18 °C (64 °F) as an absolute winter minimum. At the same time moist conditions are necessary, so floors of the conservatory should be wetted where possible and the foliage of the plant should be syringed with tepid water at regular intervals – this will mean several times daily in hot weather. During the summer season plants should be fed with a liquid fertilizer and watered generously. Less water is needed in winter and no feeding is needed unless plants are in flower.

The potting mixture should be rich: two parts peat, one part good loam and the fourth part made up equally of sand and well rotted manure. A potent and perhaps unpleasant concoction to handle, but plants potted into this will do well. Plants should be potted early in the year, given a good watering immediately then kept on the dry side until they are seen to be developing fresh leaves when more liberal watering can begin.

It will not be easy to root cuttings, but where cutting material is available, firm unblemished shoots should be removed and inserted into peat and sand in small pots before being placed in a heated propagator at 28 °C (80 °F) plus. To encourage rooting it will be necessary to mist the foliage of the cuttings continually. Where possible better results will follow if cuttings can be placed under a haze of moisture operating at very frequent intervals as the leaves of the cuttings dry out.

## MICONIA MAGNIFICA (*Melastomaceae*)
velvet tree

The flowers are of very little value, but the foliage of this plant seen on upright stems over 2 m (6 ft) in height will do much for the more exotic plant collection in the well heated conservatory. Some ability will also be needed in the handling of such tender subjects. Mature leaves will be over 60 cm (2 ft) long, very broad and coloured reddish purple on their undersides with an upper surface that is velvety green and beautifully veined.

Plants need to be renewed periodically and the best way of doing this is to sow seed in early spring in a peat and sand mixture in a temperature of around 28 °C (82 °F). Young plants must be kept warm and moist at all stages of their development. An alternative to seed would be to propagate plants from cuttings of any firm young shoots available in the spring. Again high temperature with frequent misting of the cuttings will be needed to maintain high humidity. The soil mix when potting on should be fibrous and open with equal parts peat and leafmould being ideal – a generous amount of sharp sand should also be added to assist the drainage. On account of their height and likelihood of becoming unbalanced it is wise to use the heavier terracotta pots as opposed to light plastic ones when potting on these plants.

Miconia should have a lightly shaded position with ample headroom. Moist conditions at their roots and in the surrounding atmosphere are also recommended as plants will quickly show their displeasure in bright, arid conditions.

## MIKANIA TERNATA (*Compositae*)
plush vine

This is another of the more unusual plants offered as subjects for small hanging containers. They are attractive in spite of the fact that they are grown purely for their foliage effect. Leaves are purple on the undersides and rich coppery green on the upper surface.

They are reasonably easy to manage when grown from cuttings taken at almost any

**Mikania**
With purplish-black leaves the mikania is a naturally pendulous plant, ideally suited for hanging containers.

favourable time. Once rooted, several cuttings should be placed in small plastic hanging containers to grow on. Given lightly shaded location and reasonably moist conditions they will soon develop into trailing plants with strands of growth 60 cm (2 ft) or more in length.

An alternative to growing these in baskets would be to start them from cuttings and to transfer them to 13 cm (5 in) pots when large enough, and then to plant them or put them into a decorative container near a wall so that supports can be provided for the growth to be trained as it develops.

The mikanias can also be employed as ground cover in the decorative bed of assorted plants. In terms of care they are very accommodating, needing to be kept moist and fed while producing leaves with less water and no feeding in winter. When potting on, a recognized houseplant mixture should be used.

## MIMOSA PUDICA (*Leguminosae*) sensitive plant

Another plant for the kids, the sensitive plant never ceases to amaze both old and young with its ability to collapse quite alarmingly when the plant comes into contact with any object. When children are about it will usually be a curious finger poked amongst the leaves to induce the plant to perform its peculiar reaction.

Not particularly attractive plants, they have pale green feathery leaves and small puffballs of purple-coloured flowers. Though perennials in the strict sense they are short lived and generally grown as annuals with fresh seed being sown each year in the spring. Plants can also be grown from cuttings if only a few are wanted as is normally the case. Cuttings can be struck at almost any time. Almost any soil, other than very heavy, will suit them.

## MIMULUS (*Scrophulariaceae*) monkey flower

There are both annual and perennial forms of these common plants mostly seen around wet areas in the garden. For the conservatory that boasts a water feature the perennial forms could well provide bright colour around the perimeter of a pool.

Named varieties are available and these would be the best to select if there is a choice. They can be planted at any time in moist, peaty compost, preferably in a lightly shaded location. Plants are available in a variety of colours ranging from yellow to deep red, with many flowers being attractively spotted in a different colour to that of the main part of the bloom. If planted in a moist bed they will creep quite quickly over the surface to provide very pleasing effect.

Cuttings can be taken at almost any time, and it is best simply to push them into the bed of peat where they will root and fill in any gaps that may be apparent. Alternatively, several cuttings can be put into pots filled with peaty soil to be used wherever their bright colouring might be thought necessary.

## MONSTERA (*Araceae*) Swiss cheese plant

These are very fine plants that do not come into their own until they have achieved reasonably mature size; when seen in smaller containers they show little sign of the majestic plants that they can become. There are numerous varieties – large leaves in **M. deliciosa**, which is a plant with numerous sports including both small leaved and variegated forms, and in the variety **M. friedrichsthalii** we have a plant with much smaller leaves liberally provided with holes that are large and natural to the plant.

The plant normally sold as a houseplant is *M. deliciosa* with glossy green leaves that in the early stages of growth are entire, but developing both serrations and perforations as the plant increases in size and the leaves become more mature. Besides young plants, mature specimens 2 m (6 ft) or more in height will also be available, and these are the sort of plants to acquire if an instant greenery effect is desired.

Pot-grown plants will always be slower to mature than plants that are removed from their pots and planted in deep beds of rich mixture, but the larger plants might well be too much for the average size conservatory. In pots or planted out the monstera will quite naturally produce aerial roots from the main stem of the plant with age. The best treatment for these is to tie them neatly alongside the main stem of the plant and to encourage them to root into the soil in the pots when these roots are of sufficient length.

In the conservatory a location offering ample protection from bright sun will suit them best, and they will respond to warm and moist conditions with regular feeding during the spring and summer.

New plants are propagated from seed sown in peat in high temperature, and this is the best method of increasing plants when large quantities are required. There are other ways and the best method is to root top sections of stem in peaty mixture in warm conditions. This form of propagation comes in handy when plants have become too tall for their available head-room – something that often happens. The top section of stem with two or three mature leaves attched is cut through just below a leaf joint and the cut end is allowed to dry before the cutting is inserted. Often taller plants will have become very sparse at their base; a way of covering up this bareness is to insert the cuttings from the top of the plant in the soil in the top of the pot so that the plant becomes much fresher and more attractive. The top section of the plant will in time produce new growth from the leaf axils.

## MUSA (*Musaceae*) banana plant

When seen throughout the tropics with so much commercial activity around them, these plants tend to be looked upon as very ordinary plants with little decorative value, but by choosing the right variety, **M. cavendishii** for example, you can have a plant of unsurpassed splendour. With its stout and colourful trunk sprouting very large, pale green leaves with ivory white midrib it is difficult to imagine a more splendid plant for the lofty and spacious conservatory. Spaciousness is the keyword as there is no point in growing one of these plants if they do not have at least 3 m (10 ft) of space from floor to ceiling, and almost the same lateral space to accommodate the wide spreading foliage.

They are remarkably adaptable, with an ability to tolerate high temperature, and temp-erature down to freezing provided the latter is of short duration, but a minimum temperature of around 16 °C (61 °F) would be more practical. The conservatory should be lightly shaded and not too hot and stuffy.

It would be foolish to remove plants from their containers to plant them in the ground with free root run as there is no telling just how rampant growth would become. It is much better to provide maturing plants with a large half-barrel container filled with good loam-based potting soil. The plant should be potted firmly leaving some space between the rim of the container and the surface of the soil. The soil will sink for a further few inches and this will then be right for filling with water so that the plant has an abundance of moisture at its roots. Keep the plant fed, watered and happy and you may well find one day that it is compensating you for your efforts by pro-ducing a hand of bananas!

Should the hand of bananas appear it will not be too long before the main plant dies down naturally, but all is not lost as fresh growth will be seen at the base of the parent; this growth will be your next banana plant.

The important needs of the plant are: ample space, good light, lots of water and frequent feeding.

## NANDINA DOMESTICA (*Nandinaceae*) heavenly bamboo

For the conservatory the average bamboo is much too vigorous and invasive a plant to consider, but the half-hardy *N. domestica* is less rampant and may be suited to the room that offers ample space.

It is best to restrict the roots of this plant to a container in order to control the amount of top growth that is made. Even so the heavenly bamboo will attain a height of 2 to 3 m (6–9 ft) as it develops into a thick clump of growth. The leaves take on a reddish tint in the autumn which gives the plant a little more appeal.

These are tough plants that will tolerate much ill treatment and varied temperature without seeming to be too upset. Light and airy conditions will suit them best and they need ample watering, especially during the more active summer months.

When potting on a fairly heavy potting mixture should be used. Plants will require large pots in time, but potting on should be a gradual process over a period of years. Bamboos are heavy and difficult to handle once they have become established in larger containers.

## NEMATANTHUS (*Gesneriaceae*)

Another member of the interesting gesneriad family, and one that is of vigorous habit if the growing conditions are to its liking. These should be warm, moist and shaded, with water given freely during the growing season and very much less at other times, the same applying to feeding.

Normally sold in small pots that do the plant little justice, *N. glabra* (clog plant) comes into its own when well matured and seen growing in a hanging container. The rounded dark green, succulent-like leaves are attached to wiry stems that will become pendant as the weight of foliage increases. The small, oddly shaped flowers nestle between leaf and stem to provide an attractive and compact plant when plants mature and there are lots of flowers in evidence.

Plants are propagated from sections of stem a few inches in length and placed in small pots filled with clean peat, and subsequently enclosed in a heated propagating case. Rather than a single cutting the pot should be well filled so that more attractive plants are the result when the cuttings have rooted. Following rooting the plant(s) should be grown on in its pot until well established before planting it in a hanging container. When propagating it is better to do a half dozen pots full of cuttings rather than the odd one; you can then plant several in the hanging container when they are large enough with the result that much more attractive plants are provided almost instantly.

The normal practice of pinching out the tips is not necessary as this plant branches naturally to provide solid clumps of growth.

Growing conditions should be well shaded as these are among those unusual plants that do not object to poor light. Keep them moist while in active growth with very much less water in winter. Feeding while in growth will add lustre to the foliage and should not be neglected.

When potting on, plants should go into new pots that are only slightly larger than the one that it is being removed from, and the potting mix should be of spongy texture rather than too heavy and restrictive to roots of the plant.

As with many of the more compact semi-trailing plants it is advisable not to suspend them at too great a height within the conservatory as much more pleasure will be derived if the container is about head level where plants are viewed to better effect.

## NEOREGELIA (*Bromeliacaea*) blushing bromeliad, cartwheel plant, fingernail plant

In some parts of the world the neoregelias will be seen bearing the common name of cartwheel plant which relates to the manner in which the leaves radiate from the centre of the plant like the spokes of a wheel. However, the spokes of this wheel are very broad, often highly coloured, and with water sitting where the hub of the wheel might be expeced to be! All the neoregelias are important members of the bromeliad family and originate from tropical regions of South America; they need more or less the same care and attention when grown in the conservatory.

Comfortable minimum temperature should be in the region of 16 °C (61 °F), although plants will not be unduly affected if temperature is at lower level. The difficulty with lower temperatures is that it is almost impossible to maintain a humid atmosphere in the conservatory, and humidity is something that these plants must have if they are to do well. The centre of the rosette of leaves is, in fact, a natural watertight urn that is formed by the overlapping base of the leaves. This feature gives the plant an immediate source of interest, as the urn must at all times be full of water. To prevent it stagnating the water should be periodically changed, and this is of particular importance when the plants are in flower as water remains fresh for a much shorter period. At this particular time the water may have to be flushed out with a jet of water from a hose-pipe. The soil in the pot should be only just moist, care being taken to avoid long periods of saturated roots, which is especially important should temperature be unavoidably low.

Feeding is not important, but plants will derive some benefit from feeding with a very weak solution of liquid fertilizer. Alternatively, they can have a foliar feed that is sprayed onto the leaves and absorbed by the plant. The growing location should be lightly shaded – the sort of shade that one might expect to find under a tree that is not too leafy.

The bromeliads in general and the neoregelias in particular are plants that come into their own when seen growing on a bromeliad tree. The plants can be affixed to the tree so that they are tilted slightly to 'look' to the front, or the tree's most pleasing aspect. (There is more information about bromeliad trees on p. 75.)

Perhaps the most important plant among the neoregelias is **N. carolinae** and its numerous varietes. The species has a spreading rosette of broad leaves, metallic green in colour, with toothed margin which means careful handing. Like its numerous relations, one of the most fascinating aspects of this plant is its ability to produce a central area around the urn that is a striking orange red when the flowers are about to appear. The shorter leaves in the centre of the urn and the base of larger leaves change colour to give the plant an entirely new appearance. The flowers themselves are purple and very short, only the tips of them appearing above the water level in the reservoir.

The variety **N.c. tricolor** has all the characteristics of the parent with the outstanding exception that the leaves are coloured bright cream and green and often flushed with pink – in poor light the pink colouring is either less conspicuous or absent. In Europe, Belgium is a major source of bromeliads of all kinds and the nurserymen there have not been slow in developing new cultivars. One of their most brilliant is a form of neoregelia that has been named **N.c. 'Flandria'** which has a splendid rosette of foliage of startling colour.

The variety **N. spectabilis** is one that has been around for a very long time and has the common name of fingernail plant, a name that alludes to the red tips on all of its olive green leaves.

As with the majority of bromeliads when they have produced their flowers, the main rosette of the neoregelia disintegrates and dies gradually following flowering. The old rosette should be cut away from the parent stump when no longer attractive. Care is needed to ensure that the young plants developing on the lower stem are left intact. The plant may have several or only one of these young plants: the larger and more healthy the rosette the more likelihood there is of getting a greater number of offsets. The offsets can remain on the parent to develop and eventually flower as a cluster of plants on the old stem, or they can be removed when large enough to be potted individually.

Those that are left undisturbed on the parent stump will usually produce their flowers in two years, whereas the plants treated individually will take a further year to mature and flower.

Many of the bromeliads are tree-dwelling epiphytes which indicates that an open free-draining mixture should be prepared when potting young plants or when potting on older plants. It will be more expensive, but the best ready made mixture to employ is one that is devised for potting orchids.

## NEPENTHES (*Nepenthaceae*) pitcher plant

For the conservatory where a warm and humid jungle effect is being created for plants, these are subjects that could make a fascinating contribution. The mere fact that they are carnivorous plants capable of catching and digesting all sorts of insects will be an immediate talking point and source of interest.

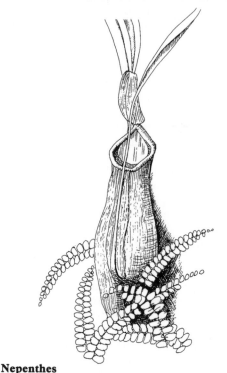

**Nepenthes**
The pitcher plant adds the exotic touch to the collection of carnivores as it is seen suspended from a hanging container.

They must have a minimum temperature of 18 °C (64 °F) or higher and humidity of the highest level. There are numerous varieties, but plants are only offered for sale spasmodically and when purchasing it is usually a question of accepting the best plants from those that are on offer. Dull green leaves are not attractive in respect of colour; it is the manner in which tendrils extend from the tip of the leaf eventually to produce the large pitchers which provide the main feature of the plant. The liquid in the bottom of the pitcher is pepsin, an acid into which insects are lured and digested. A further fascinating aspect of the pitcher is that it is provided with a natural cover, or lid, just above the mouth of the tube – this is nature's way of preventing rain entering the pitcher and diluting the pepsin. Mother nature thinks of everything!

The majority of pitcher plants are natural climbers, so will need some form of support to which the plant can attach itself. In large pots or hanging containers they can be hung on a trellis against a wall or, if the conservatory boasts a small tree the pitcher in its container can be suspended from the tree for the plant to climb more naturally through the branches.

It is not the easiest of plants to manage, but life will be easier for them if warmth and humidity is given priority. The potting mixture should be peaty and free draining, and should be kept moist at all times. There is a bonus with the pitcher plant in that it will find its own food by naturally attracting insects to its lair. Whever possible, rain water should be used when filling pots.

## NEPHROLEPIS EXALTATA
(*Nephrolepidaeae*) Boston fern

These superb plants grown the world over for their dense, lush green foliage, are indispensible plants for the floral decorator who will use them for all sorts of situations knowing that the foliage will prove sympathetic with almost every other plant that is part of the overall display. They will also prove to be useful in the conservatory – at ground level, decorating tables or when suspended from the ceiling in a hanging container. It is not the easiest of plants to care for: the most common fault is lack of water which causes foliage to become dry and eventually to shrivel up. Water should be applied so that the soil is saturated from the top to the bottom of the container and not just as a wetting to the soil surface, but it is important that the soil should then dry reasonably before further water is given. Soil that remains saturated over long periods can be just as damaging as soil that becomes excessively dry. Low temperatures are also harmful; a winter minimum of 16 °C (61 °F) should be the aim. Bright light is another reason for these plants shrivelling and losing their appearance, so well shaded locations ought to be chosen when housing them.

At the nursery where they are grown these ferns will grow at surprising pace with the result that, when sold, plants will have the appearance of being too large for their containers. Purchased plants if left in this condition will quickly deteriorate in the home or conservatory where the growing conditions are less favourable. The answer to this difficulty is to remove the plant immediately from its container (having watered it first), and to pot the plant into a slightly larger container using a peaty mixture. By attending to all the foregoing it should be possible to grow superb Boston ferns, the sort of plants that have spectacular effect when grown in large hanging containers or baskets suspended overhead.

New plants can be propagated from spores taken from the undersides of mature leaves. This can be done at any time provided a temperature in excess of 21 °C (70 °F) can be maintained. Perhaps the simplest method of increasing these plants is to plunge the growing pot to its rim in a bed of peat and to peg down the runners that develop naturally. Allow these to grow into manageable plants before severing them from the parent and potting them individually in small pots.

## NERINE BOWDENII (*Liliaceae/ Amaryllidaceae*) spider lily

Bulbous plants from South Africa originally, these are ideal plants for the cold conservatory. Like most South African bulbous plants they have a reverse growing season in the northern hemisphere extending from September to May, with a dormant period covering summer months from May to September. During the latter period plants must be bone dry with no water at all during this dormant period.

Bulbs are generally expensive to buy, but where possible it is best not to skimp by putting too few bulbs in the container – five bulbs to a 13 cm (5 in) diameter pot will give a good initial display. These should be potted into the soil with the nose of the bulb well exposed, and the time to do this is late summer. These are plants that must have a well drained fairly rich potting mixture. Drainage is particularly important.

During the summer months plants can be left out of doors in their pots in a sunny location, and at other times will do best on a high shelf in the conservatory where they can enjoy maximum sunshine and fresh air.

The flower spikes begin to emerge before the leaves, and their appearance is an indication that watering for the new season should commence if it has not already started. Flowers are very attractive in shape and a lovely shade of soft pink with a maximum height of about 45 cm (18 in). Plants multiply by means of offsets that form around the parent bulb and these can be removed to increase their numbers. Alternatively these can be left to fill the pot, only to be disturbed when the potful of bulbs is potted on about every third or fourth year. Provided the suggested watering routine is attended to these are plants that will go on for years with few if any problems.

## NERIUM OLEANDER (*Apocynaceae*)
oleander

These are summer flowering shrubs that will suit the cooler conservatory where it is only possible to maintain a winter minimum temperature of around 7 °C (45 °F). During the winter months, the soil should be almost bone dry – very important where low temperatures inevitably prevail.

Where grown as tub plants for the conservatory they will develop into attractive and reasonably compact shrubs with narrow, pale green leaves and flower clusters that are rose red in colour. Flowers are produced during the summer months when plants can be placed either outside or kept in the conservatory depending on the space that is available. While in the conservatory the plants will need good light and airy conditions.

Plants are propagated from firm young shoots removed at any time during the spring or summer when suitable cutting material is available. The end of the cutting should be allowed to dry before it is inserted in a peat and sand mixture, the cuttings to go individually into small pots. Rubber gloves should be worn at any time when the plant stem is being cut as the plant is poisonous in all its parts. In warm and shaded conditions the cuttings should not be difficult to root, and once well rooted they should be potted into 13 cm (5 in) diameter pots using a loam-based mixture. It will take some years, but as plants increase in size they should be potted into progressively larger containers until such time as they are in substantial tubs when they can be sustained by regular feeding.

Any growth that forms around the base of flower trusses in the summer should be carefully removed so as not to damage the flowers. In late summer the plant should be hard pruned by cutting back the shoots that have flowered to some six inches from their base.

## NIDULARIUM (*Bromelaceae*)
bird's nest bromeliad

Mention has been made elsewhere that there is much to be said for specializing in particular plants or in a particular family of plants, and the bromeliads are just such a family. There are many plants to choose from, and almost all of them are easy to care for if a minimum temperature of around 16 °C (61 °F) can be maintained during the winter months. Some are grown for their colourful leaves and interesting shapes while others are chosen for their striking flowers in many unusual colour combinations. The nidulariums are similar in shape to the neoregelias, forming a rosette of leaves, but it must be said that they do not have the same popularity.

The best known is **N. innocentii** and its numerous varieties, and is the plant with the common name of bird's nest bromeliad. The name refers to the deep funnel of leaves that could well form the basis of a nest. Bold leaves are broad and showy with purplish green colouring on the upper surface and rich maroon on the undersides. When plants are several years old they will come into flower, and as this happens the plant undergoes a complete change when the central area around the base of the leaves changes colour to become glowing crimson. The white flowers are comparatively insignifiant on their own, but the combination of white and red offers a plant of considerable interest.

The blushing bromeliad, **N. fulgens**, is a fine plant and an old favourite among plantsmen – the leaves are pale green with darker spotting on their upper surface and are viciously spined along the entire margin. The inflorescence in the centre of the cup is bright red with green tips; flowers are blue in colour. Although the main rosette of most bromeliads dies off following flowering there is the compensation of knowing that the plant remains in its colourful flowering state for many months. As the parent rosette deteriorates the plant develops replacement plants around the base of the main stem; these can be left in position to flower as a clump in about two years from the time the parent succumbs, or they can be removed to be grown independently, in which case they will take a little longer to flower.

Use an orchid mixture when potting up young plants, and keep the conservatory lightly shaded, moist and warm for best results.

selection, but it is important to locate these where they will not become a menace to anyone passing by.

It is also important with these larger plants not to be tempted to plant them freely into a bed of soil as they will simply take off and become more trouble than they are worth. They should be potted into smallish containers that will restrict their root development, and the mixture to use when potting should be loam-based with lots of sand added to improve the drainage. To further assist the latter the pot should have a generous amount of drainage material placed in the bottom of it before any soil is introduced.

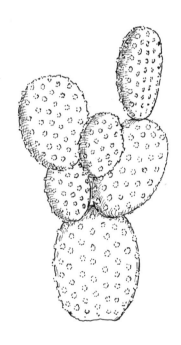

## OPUNTIA (*Cactaceae*) prickly pear

Smaller versions would normally come within a collection of cacti and would not be too conspicuous on their own, but there are much bolder plants among the opuntias that could well form part of the conservatory as individual specimens. For the real cactus feeling the opuntias with large pads of growth, generously endowed with spines, are the ideal

**Opuntia**
Given sufficient space and volume of compost these cacti grow to considerable size with lots of protective barbs that make handling difficult.

Following potting and locating the opuntia will require minimal care: fresh air, good light and dry conditions with a minimum temperature of around 10 °C (50 °F). Mealy bug amongst the foliage and root mealy bug around the roots should be dealt with as soon as detected. Watering the roots with suitable pesticide occasionally will be the best way of dealing with root bug, as there is no way that one would be able to remove the plant from its pot which is the customary practice when inspecting roots for this pest!

Almost any piece of stem taken from the opuntia will produce roots when potted, a propagating task which is best undertaken in the spring or summer.

## ORNITHOGALUM CAUDATUM
(*Lilaceae/Hyacinthaceae*) false sea-onion

In any plant collection you need to have a fun plant, one that will amuse the visitors and get them talking about plants. The false sea-onion is one of the easiest plants in the world to care for – not minding if the temperature is high or low, if it is wet or dry, and if it gets a feed of anything it will simply think that it's a birthday!

The first thing about the plant that will attract attention will be the large whitish green 'onion' that sits on top of the soil in the pot with long unattractive green leaves sprouting in ungainly fashion from the top of the bulb. But that is not all. In time it will produce its flower on the end of yet another ungainly stem that might be all of 1 m (3 ft) in length. On the end of this tall stem there will appear a raceme of flowers that are white and green in colour.

Another common name for this odd plant is healing onion: it is said that if the crushed leaves are placed over cuts and bruises they will speed the healing process. There is a healing onion recipe that claims to be a good protection against the common cold. There is not much more that one could ask of a common onion plant.

Even the propagation has been made as simple and foolproof as it could possibly be: mature bulbs produce offsets that lie on top of the soil around the parent bulb, and these have simply to be lifted and placed in a small pot of soil: the bulblets will soon root and new plants will be produced.

## PACHYSTACHYS LUTEA (*Acanthaceae*)
lollipop plant

Not unlike the aphelandra at first sight, the pachystachys has dull green leaves that are much less interesting than those of the aphelandra, although the style and colour of the flowers are very much alike. Where the lollipop plant scores is in the flowering period that will go on right through the summer months if the plant is properly cared for. The flowers are, in fact, white in colour and comparatively insignificant, it is the bract from which they emerge that is bright yellow and eye-catching.

In the conservatory, plants should have a lightly shaded location and minimum temperature in the region of 16 °C (61 °F). They

**Pachystachys**
With dull green leaves and upright yellow bracts these are easy care plants if kept warm, moist and fed frequently while in active growth.

will also approve of humidity and generally moist conditions, with regular feeding once they have become well established in their pots. An alternative to pots would be to plant them in a bed of rich soil where they will be less vulnerable should one be forgetful when it comes to watering. In the bed they will also grow more freely and there will be many more stems of growth producing flowers or bracts. Cuttings can be taken at any time when warm conditions can be provided and there are strong, non-flowering top sections available for cutting.

In both pots and planted beds they will need rich soil and regular feeding once established to keep them in good order. The growing tips of young plants should be removed periodically to encourage more bushy habit. When they have finished flowering in late autumn it will benefit plants in the following year if the stems are cut back, and it will make plants easier to care for and less space demanding over the winter months when the conservatory tends to be crowded with plants brought in for the winter from the patio.

## PANDANUS (*Pandanaceae*) screw pine

The common name of this plant derives from the manner in which the main stem of the plant twists as the plant ages. These are truly majestic plants that will only be suited to the warm and spacious interior where the plant can be placed out of the way of passing inhabitants.

The plant forms into a gigantic rosette of splaying leaves that are viciously spined along their margins and, for good measure, on their undersides as well. There are several forms with either white, cream or yellow colouring: in *P. veitchii* the colouring is predominantly white, *P. sanderi* has both white and yellow in its colouring and *P. baptistii* has colouring of blue-green and yellow.

Plants are never freely available and when on offer will generally be small offsets that have been removed from the base of larger plants (far too few are produced for large numbers to be on sale) and potted just long enough to produce roots of their own before being sold. It

will take some time for these to mature, during which time they can be easily accommodated in the average size conservatory, but they will grow to majestic size in good growing conditions. These should be light shade, minimum temperature of around 18 °C (64 °F) and the usual in respect of watering and feeding. Winter will be the difficult growing time when water must be given sparingly and feeding not at all.

This is another of the truly specimen plants, the sort of plant that should stand on its own, perhaps on a pedestal so that it can be appreciated to the full.

## PASSIFLORA (*Passifloraceae*) passion flower

There are all sorts of passiflora, with green leaves and variegation, with different leaf formation and with a wealth of differently coloured flowers, but the one most often seen being sold is *P. caerulea* with blue flowers. The latter is a plant that will survive out of doors if the winter weather is not too unkind.

The passiflora is frequently recommended for growing in the conservatory, but remember these are very invasive plants that could well take over the interior space of the smaller conservatory, and in a surprisingly short space of time at that. If you must have a passiflora in the conservatory then my advice is that it should remain in a container so that the root system, hence the leaf growth, is restricted. Curiously enough, if the roots are restricted the plant will be more inclined to produce flowers: it will certainly produce flowers in greater numbers once they begin to develop.

Being a natural, rampant climber, the plant should be placed close by a wall so that some form of support can be provided for growth to cling to. It should also have a position that offers good light, with frequent watering and occasional feeding during the summer, but less water and no feeding in winter. In late winter any weak growth should be removed and the length of growth generally should be considerably shortened. This is a good time also to remove any growth that might have been damaged as a result of colder conditions.

Plants can be propagated from seed sown in

warm conditions almost any time during the spring and summer. Cuttings can also be taken in warm conditions at any time over the same period.

## PAVONIA INTERMEDIA (*Malvaceae*)

An uncommon plant that will only be suitable for the conservatory offering warm and reasonably humid conditions, with shade from bright sun. Give these conditions, and assuming that you have been fortunate enough to track a supplier of the plant, you could have something different with which to regale visitors.

The leaves of the pavonia are shaped like the business end of a spear, bright glossy green, attached by slender petioles to upright stems. It also has blue flowers surrounded by very showy crimson-red bracts, the flowers sitting very attractively at the top of the plant stems so that they are displayed to very good effect. The most amazing aspect of this plant is that it literally flowers all the time, for a full twelve months of the year if the conditions are to its liking.

A plant with this ability must be listed as a considerable asset when it comes to stocking the conservatory. The bother with most plants is that they have a very definite season of, say, two months when they will be gloriously in flower and much appreciated, but one wonders about the other ten months of the year when you have to sit looking at a collection of leaves. When choosing plants it is advisable to consider the flowering period and to think of selecting those that are going to be in flower for the longest season.

There never seems to be many cuttings available for propagation purposes on the pavonia, but when they can be spared they can be removed at any time of the year and placed in a sandy mixture in small pots. Thereafter they must go into very warm and moist conditions with a temperature of not less than 22 °C (72 °F). It is usual to select cuttings that do not have any flowers, but in the case of the pavonia this might not be so easy as flowers are ever present; remove any flowers and buds that may be present before the cuttings are inserted.

Use a peat, loam and sand mix in equal parts

**Pavonia**
Unusual plants with upright stems and linear leaves, plus the added attraction that flowers are produced throughout the year.

for potting on the rooted cuttings. Plants will attain a height of some 2 m (6 ft) by which time they will have become rather thin lower down their stems. The only easy answer to this is to grow them in a mixed bed with a lower and fuller plant in front to hide the sparseness. If plants are being put into a bed they should be left in their pots and plunged to about half the depth of the container.

Keep the plant and the surroundings moist, but cut down in winter when it comes to watering. Feed with weak liquid fertilizer, but only in spring and summer unless plants are doing well and still producing new leaves, which well they might.

## PEDILANTHUS TITHYMALOIDES
### 'VARIEGATA' (*Euphorbiaceae*)
slipper spurge, zigzag plant

Growing to some 2 m (6 ft) in height, this is a weird sort of plant that produces the typical milky juice of the euphorbias, and has a distorted stem that seems to possess some of the variegation of the leaves; the stem, in fact, gives the plant one of its common names, the zigzag plant.

However, it has many blessings and not least among them is that it is tough with a preference for a sunny locaiton in the conservatory. It needs very little water, about once weekly in the summer and once a month to keep the soil just moist in the winter, but they can go without for longer periods and not be harmed. Feeding is something that you can forget as it can get by with no feeding at all. It has cactus qualities in that it wants to be warm, light and dry.

Even when being propagated, the cuttings would seem to wish to be mistreated in that they should be removed at a length of 10–15 cm (4–6 in), then placed on a shelf near the glass in full sun for a day or two before they are inserted in sandy mixture. An open, gritty mixture should be provided when plants or cuttings are in need of potting on.

## PELARGONIUM (*Geraniaceae*) geranium

For year-round colour in the conservatory there can be few plants that can match the pelargoniums. There are those with scented leaves, miniature forms, those with decorative leaves and free-flowering sorts that provide bushy, trailing or upright habit of growth, virtually plants for every taste. The majority of them are not difficult to care for provided they can have good light in which to grow, a minimum winter temperature of 5 °C (41 °F) and watering that is done with care, particularly over the winter months.

With proper care, the zonal types can be brought on to provide their best show of flowers either during the winter or the summer months. For a summer display cuttings are taken in late summer/early autumn of the previous year, and for winter flowering the cuttings are inserted in late winter/early spring of the previous year. Cuttings struck in summer will not be difficult to root in warm conditions if firm pieces from the top of the stem are allowed to dry at the severed end before they are inserted in a sandy mixture. Those taken in winter will also have to be cuttings of sound quality allowed to dry before inserting, but in this instance there will have to be a temperature of not less than 16 °C (61 °F) to get them under way. As roots develop the plants will have to be progressively potted on, and for those that are to form neat bushes it will be necessary to remove growing tips of the new shoots to encourage the plants to branch.

All the foregoing takes time and trouble, not to mention the right facilities in the way of heating and shelter to achieve the right results. An easy alternative could be to purchase young plants ready for potting on. In recent years much work has been done with pelargoniums, particularly in respect of young plants and there is now not so much need, as there was in the past, to keep stock plants overwintered in heated premises.

There is, however, good reason for retaining older plants if larger specimen plants are wanted, and this applies in particular to the cascade trailing types that can be so spectacular when seen trailing from a elevated location. Although these are naturally trailing plants they can also be encouraged to grow upwards if some form of support is provided. In a large tub with several canes tied in wigwam shape these can be very effective as free-standing units either on the patio or in the conservatory. Alternatively the plants can have a permanent position in the conservatory by placing them close to a wall to which they can be trained on supports. There are also the larger leaved types, such as **P. 'A Happy Thought'** with beautiful green margined leaves that are an attractive dull yellow in their centres. To get double value from some of these plants they can be grown against a wall or pillar in the company of another plant. For example, *Stephanotis* and *P.* 'A Happy Thought' make excellent companions providing colour and fragrance over a long period, in fact nice foliage all the year round.

The pelargoniums are another family of plants that would make an excellent specialist collection, and one that would provide a wealth of colour throughout the year, with not too much difficulty in respect of care. They are reasonably easy to increase by means of cuttings or seed sowing in early spring. Good light and reasonable warmth over winter are essential factors, plus a need for watering with care, especially during the winter months when plants should always be kept on the dry side.

Like the majority of plants, when they are growing well and established in their pots they will respond to regular summer feeding. When potting plants on it is advisable to use a loam-based mixture that is free draining, and to pot plants into pots that are only slightly larger than the ones they are being transferred from. Small plants in very large pots never do very well.

## PELLAEA ROTUNDIFOLIA (*Adiantaceae*)
button fern

This is a fern that in recent years has enjoyed greatly increased popularity as a houseplant, having small, dark green rounded leaves that are attached to creeping stems. They are much used by the plant decorator when preparing smaller containers for sale or display. In the conservatory their place would either be on a table as a small decorative plant, or as a ground-cover subject amongst other plants in a prepared bed. Whatever use they are put to, it should be borne in mind that these are shade-loving plants that will quickly deteriorate if exposed to bright sun.

Besides shaded conditions they will also require a minimum temperature of around 16 °C (61 °F), with higher temperature where possible. They also like to be kept moist with humid surroundings rather than dry, and when potting on a peaty houseplant mixture will suit them.

New plants can be made by dividing older clumps and potting them individually early in the year, or from spores sown on sandy mixture at any time provided a temperature of not less than 22 °C (72 °F) can be maintained.

## PELLIONIA DAVEAUANA (*Urticaceae*)
watermelon begonia

With greenish brown variegated foliage these are not the most wonderful plants in the world, but they are easy care plants able to adapt to all sorts of uses. One of the nicest things about the pellionias is that they will not object to fluctuating temperature provided it is not too low.

Shaded locations suit them best, and in this respect they can be employed, for example, as decorative plants under the staging in the greenhouse, or under plants or tables in the conservatory where they will spread, rooting into soil or gravel as they go. A further benefit of their adaptability is that they are fine plants in baskets in the shaded conservatory. Cuttings of almost any piece of stem with a leaf attached will root at any time of the year, or those that have rooted in as they creep along the floor can be lifted and potted. When preparing plants for baskets it is best to put several cuttings in small pots and to allow them to become well rooted before transferring them to hanging containers; put at least three or even five pots in the container if it is on the large side. Then simply water them in, feed them weekly and just watch them grow. Nice plants that deserve to be better known.

## PENTAS LANCEOLATA (*Rubiaceae*)
Egyptian star cluster

With rose-coloured flowers appearing in winter this is a plant that will make a useful contribution to the conservatory display during the dreary months of the year. There are other varieties with red and with white flowers, but these will be more difficult to obtain than the one mentioned above.

They all develop into sturdy plants about 60 cm (2 ft) in height with fresh green leaves topped by pretty star-shaped small flowers formed in attractive clusters.

Plants are started from cuttings taken from the top section of stem during the spring or summer. Cuttings are inserted in small pots filled with a peat and sand mixture, and placed in a temperature of not less than 22 °C (72 °F) to get them under way. Once rooted the cuttings are transferred to small pots using a good houseplant potting mixture. Thereafter the tops of growing shoots should be removed to induce bushy habit and the plants should have a lightly shaded location in which to grow. Provide an average temperature, ensuring that it does not fall below 13 °C (55 °F) during the winter months. Following flowering the plants can be pruned to shape, which could well be a good time for selecting cuttings for propagation.

Being a relatively easy plant to grow, besides being one that offers winter flowers, it is surprising that it is not more popular. It is worth seeking out in the lists of more adventurous growers of exotic plants.

## PEPEROMIA (*Piperaceae/Peperomiaceae*)
desert privet

As smaller plants for decorating the windowsill indoors these are very popular plants, and the majority are reasonably easy to grow provided they have a light location and the amount of water given is geared to dry rather than wet conditions. In the conservatory the smaller plants would tend to be a bit lost, but they can be made to look more impressive by planting several of the same variety together in a shallow dish-type container.

The majority form into compact and bushy plants but there are also varieties that are of trailing habit and these are very effective in the conservatory on account of their ability to be decorative throughout the year, as opposed to the plants that are seasonal and in need of annual replacement.

Perhaps the best of the trailing types of peperomia for basket culture is *P. scandens* **'Variegata'** which has attractive heart-shaped leaves that are brightly cream and green variegated – the green form is also a pretty plant, but is not so often seen. Both of these when planted in a basket or hanging pot will fill the container well to form an attractive mound of trailing foliage. *P. glabella* **'Variegata'** is another fine free-branching form that is cream and green in colour with similar habit to the *scandens* variety.

Of the more compact forms the best known is probably *P. obtusifolia* (syn. *P. magnoliifolia*) which has thicker and more succulent foliage bright cream and green variegated. There are several cultivars with either larger leaves or more variable variegation. In a decorative bed of plants in the conservatory this is a bright, perennial plant that will add year-round colour if planted in a group at the front of the border.

*P. caperata* is commonly known as emerald, or green ripple and has indented or rippled foliage that is a lush dark, metallic green in colour, and eventually produces rat's tail flowers, which are interesting but of little attraction. There is a variegated form, a much weaker sort of plant, that is less easy to manage. Another cultivar which is much more agreeable and easier to manage has reddish colourings suffused through the leaves. The watermelon peperomia *P. argyreia* (syn. *P. sandersii*) has highly glossy grey green leaves with attractive bands of silver, the whitish green rat's tail flowers not being of any great merit.

There are numerous other peperomias which in themselves could provide an interesting collection and perhaps an even more interesting assortment of propagation methods. All of them need lightly shaded conditions while growing or being propagated, and need reasonable temperature in which to grow.

For propagation the temperature needs to be around 20 °C (68 °F) and reasonably humid. Clean peat will be fine as a medium, and the propagating material should be from healthy plants and fresh and firm, as opposed to thin and weak. The *scandens* varieties can be done from sections of the stem of the plant with one or two leaves attached, the *caperata* kinds by removing individual leaves and inserting them, and the *obtusifolia* types from top sections of stem with two sound leaves attached. Perhaps the most interesting method, however, is employed when propagating the *argyreia* variety. With these, healthy leaves are removed and the petiole disposed of before the leaf is neatly cut into four quarters, across the leaf and down the middle. The cut edges are then placed in a peat and sand mix with just a small amount of the leaf buried, the cuttings standing quite close together. Wonder of wonders then when new growth identical to the parent is seen to emerge from the base of the cut sections. All of these, once rooted, can be potted into small pots filled with houseplant mixture. Thereafter provide good warmth, filtered light and not too much water in order to succeed.

## PERESKIA (*Cactaceae*) wax rose

With growth that is not at all like the conventional cactus, these plants will form into sizeable specimens when well grown, but for the average conservatory they will have a more interesting use: for grafting when you wish to give plants such as epiphyllum and zygocactus a different appearance.

The cuttings of pereskia are started in the spring and should be prepared from sections of stem a few inches in length that are inserted in small pots filled with sandy mixture, at a temperature of around 20 °C (68 °F). Cuttings meant to be used for grafting should be grown as single stems and should be staked almost from the time they begin to grow of their own accord. The supporting cane will have to be changed for something stronger and taller as the stem develops, with the intention in mind that a firm upright stem will be produced to the top of which the chosen cuttings are grafted by exposing the sap of both scion and stock and binding the exposed areas tightly to one another to form the graft. The result is that the grafted plants will be seen to much greater advantage when raised to higher level than one could ever hope to see them when the flowers are around the base of the growing pot. Not the easiest thing in the world to accomplish, but it will be a rewarding exercise if successful.

Light shade and reasonable warmth with careful watering will suit plants fine once they have got under way. Pot on as necessary and the standard-effect cactus that you have made will go on for years. Alternatively, these are plants that can be grown in pots of good size or the border in the conservatory where they are close to a wall. If a trellis support is provided they can be trained to provide interesting plants with colourful greenish gold foliage.

## PETUNIA (*Solanaceae*)

Although normally seen as colourful summer bedding and potted patio plants the petunias are also good value in the conservatory, offering lots of colour over a lengthy period for comparatively little effort. What is not always appreciated is the fact that these are perennial and not annual plants, and thus you can retain from year to year plants that are of special merit. Plants can be in pots, hanging containers or boxes in the conservatory where they can remain and do well if the conditions offered are lightly shaded, airy and reasonably moist. Plants need more water in spring and summer when flowers are present and less in winter while they are resting.

To retain plants from year to year, the old plants can be cut back either at the end of their flowering time or during late winter/early spring. If further plants of the more treasured varieties are needed cuttings can be taken in late winter a few inches in length from fresh young shoots. These are inserted in a sandy mixture in a warm greenhouse kept at around 16 °C (61 °F). Plants should be progressively potted on as root development dictates, and as growth is produced so the tips of early shoots ought to be removed to encourage more bushy and attractive plants. Naturally, plants may also be raised from seed sown in warm conditions in the early part of the year.

## PHILODENDRON (*Araceae*)
sweetheart plant

This is one of the most important of all the families of plants as far as those utilized for indoor decoration and conservatory subjects.

Philodendrons are variable in shape and to some degree habit, but there are numerous aspects of culture in conservatory conditions that will apply to them all. The first prime requirement if they are to do well is to provide acceptable temperature and the minimum for the winter months ought never to be less than 16 °C (61 °F), with higher temperatures being a benefit rather than a problem. Being plants of the jungle they will also relish the prospect of growing in an environment that offers a high degree of humidity, and this will mean keeping the temperature up and ensuring that there is lots of moisture about in the conservatory. To achieve this, syringe the plants with water, quite heavily damping over the leaves with a hosepipe or by simply keeping the floor of the conservatory wet when temperatures are high.

They will also prefer shaded conditions to preserve the lusher colourings of the foliage – in bright sun they become very hard in appearance.

The philodendrons are all superb plants for growing in pots or large containers, and are generally better when handled in this way as opposed to planting out where they will tend to become much too robust. The larger leaved kinds, such as **P. hastatum**, will need half-barrel type containers once they have reached adult stage. For potting they will require a rich houseplant potting mixture, and this is a task that can be performed at any time provided conditions are agreeable – in particular reasonably high temperature.

Some plants are raised from seed, but most are from seed that is normally available only to the commercial grower. However, when getting started it is usually best to purchase young plants that are already started into growth and then pot them as necessary. Plants of specimen size can also be bought ready for important locations in the conservatory, but these are invariably costly.

**P. scandens** is well known by its common name of sweetheart plant which relates to its glossy green, heart-shaped leaves. This will climb, spread or trail, but it never really looks very happy when growing in a hanging container. To encourage them to climb they should have some form of support to which the developing growth should be tied. Of all the philodendrons, this one is also the easiest to manage, needing nothing more than the standard care set out above.

**P. erubescens** has larger glossy green leaves that are more elongated than the *scandens* variety, and the sort of plant that does well when its roots can find their way into a moss-covered support, or when the plant is against a damp wall. In recent years we have seen several cultivars of *P. erubescens*, notably **P. 'Burgundy'** and **P.e. 'Emerald'**; all of these are excellent plants for both conservatory and indoor decoration.

**P. bipinnatifidum** is a totally different style of plant with large finger leaves radiating all round from a robust central trunk. Not much of a plant to look at in its early stages when it is little more than a developing seedling, but once established it becomes a truly magnificent specimen. Alas, by then it is a plant that is only suited to the really large conservatory. In time it will need a very large container, and as it increases in size so the natural aerial roots of the plant begin to develop – the purpose of these is to spread out in search of moisture and nourishment for the plant and also to act as supporting 'struts' to keep the plant in position.

**P. melanochrysum** has leaves that are similar in shape to those of *P. scandens* but they are of velvety brown colouring with attractive venation, and it is a much more difficult plant to care for. Where most of the philodendrons would not object if some of the growing recommendations suggested earlier were not carried out to the letter, this is a plant that must be mollycoddled all the time, particularly in respect of both temperature and humidity. It is also a plant that should have a support, preferably a moss-covered one, so that it can in time reach the 2 m (6 ft) mark and, perhaps, be the prize plant in your collection.

There are numerous other philodendrons. They all need the same treatment in respect of feeding which should be given as a liquid fertilizer, once plants have become established in their pots and while they are in active growth, with larger plants needing a greater amount than the baby ones. If the growing conditions are agreeable and, in particular, if it is warm, plants may well grow right through the year, in which event they will also need a weak feed periodically in the winter.


## PHOENIX (*Palmae*) pigmy date palm

**Phoenix roebelenii** is the plant that bears the common name mentioned above and in tropical regions will develop into a palm tree with an attractive tuft of fine foliage. When grown as a potted specimen this foliage is an important attribute to this very stylish plant that provides attractive addition to the larger conservatory when it is placed as a solitary specimen to be viewed from all angles. Although in short supply, it is not impossible to obtain as a reasonably mature specimen, although the cost is usually high on account of the time taken for the plant to grow.

The other phoenix that you might find is *P. canariensis* which is much planted in the tropics for its ornamental value. It is, however, a rather different phoenix compared to the first mentioned in that it is much harder in appearance and it is also a vicious sort of plant with nasty spines which makes it difficult to handle. Space is the criteria – if the plant can be kept well away from passers by then it will make a stately addition to the appearance of the conservatory.

Not difficult to care for, they need average warmth, good light and ample watering and feeding once they have become established. They are essentially container plants that ought to be grown in half-barrels eventually. When potting on is needed, do it in the spring using a good loam-based mixture and do it with assitance and care!

## PHORMIUM (*Agavaceae/Phormiaceae*)
New Zealand flax

Not fully hardy, the plant mostly seen in gardens is *P. tenax*, but there are now many superior varieties in respect of colour if not in durability. Plants can remain outdoors during the summer months but are better under the protection of a glassed area in winter in colder climates. This can mean lifting plants from the garden and potting them each autumn – a daunting task as plants increase in size. It is generally better to grow them in containers permanently so that plant roots, hence plant growth is restricted. Some of the new introductions have very rich colouring that will do much to improve the appearance of the patio in summer months and the interior of the conservatory during the bleaker months of the year.

Comparatively easy to care for, they will just need the frost keeping out of the conservatory during the winter when they should also be watered sparingly. While in active growth they will obviously need additional water, and they will also have to be fed regularly. Good light is also essential and when potting on they will need to go into a good loam-based mixture. The surest and simplest method of propagation is to divide the roots into smaller sections and to pot them up in the early part of the year.

## PILEA (*Urticaceae*)
aluminium plant, artillery plant

These small plants mainly for the windowsill are grown almost entirely for their foliage colouring which is silvered in some varieties and attractively mottled in most. The most popular is *P. cadierei* (aluminium plant) which has silvered foliage and is grown from cuttings a few inches in length inserted several to each small pot filled with houseplant potting soil. Once they are prepared, cuttings are inserted to about half their depth and kept in warm and moist conditions. Rooting is very quick and once growth is under way the tops of all the cuttings can be removed to encourage a more bushy appearance. In the conservatory, as with many of these smaller plants, they are much more effective when several are grouped together, either in a planted bed or in a container.

*P. microphylla* (artillery plant) very conveniently propagates itself by means of seed that are sprayed in all directions when the seed pod explodes – hence the common name. However, this is one of its few interesting features, as the plant has little else to recommend it.

A plant not often seen is *P. peperomioides*, which is a bit of a tease plant when interested folk attempt to name it, as the plant has all the appearance from its leaf shape of being a peperomia. The rounded leaves are glossy green and attached to long petioles which is not unlike some of the peperomias, *Peperomia sandersii* in particular. The flowers are in themselves unattractive, but they are typically those of a pilea. Perhaps the most redeeming feature of the plant is its toughness, its ability to tolerate almost any conditions other than very cold. Where there is a growing table in the conservatory which is dark and inhospitable and where nothing ever grows, then this could be the plant that will tolerate these conditions.

In general, the pileas will do best in a lightly shaded location that offers a minimum temperature of around 16 °C (61 °F), and a houseplant mixture when potting on becomes necessary. They should be kept moist and regularly fed while in growth with little water and no feeding in winter.

## PITTOSPORUM (*Pittosporaceae*)
parchment-bark

Usually listed as half-hardy subjects, the pittosporums, with the exception of *P. tenuifolium*, will all succumb if planted in the garden and left to fend for themselves over a hard winter. These are much better grown in tubs or large terracotta pots so that they can be moved to a sheltered location for the winter.

For the conservatory that can offer generous space these are superb foliage plants for the winter months when colourful flowers are conspicuous by their absence. Some are more tolerant of colder conditions than others, but it is advisable to provide sufficient warmth to keep the frost out. Over winter the pittosporums will require full light in order to retain their bright colouring. While the majority of potted plants will do better if their roots are very much on the dry side over winter, it is not advisable to allow pittosporums to dry out too much as there will be a tendency for some of them to shed many of their leaves. Plants will not need any feeding from early winter through to the following spring.

Some could develop into shrubs that would be much too large for the average size conservatory, so it is important when procuring plants to ask the supplier about growth rate and eventual size. However, the growth of more vigorous plants can be restricted by keeping roots of plants confined to smaller containers and you can always trim or prune plants that are getting out of hand.

Some of the pittosporums are naturally short and compact in their habit of growth and one of the best in this respect is *P. tenuifolium* **'Tom Thumb'** which has glossy reddish bronze colouring on plants that will seldom attain more than 60 cm (2 ft) in height. There are several excellent plants in the medium size category and there are two good ones. *P.* **'Garnettii'** has glossy white and silver grey variegation, flushed pale pink. A further attribute of this splendid plant is that the stems are black, so setting off the variegation to perfection. The other in this size is *P.t.* **'Irene Patterson'** which has mature leaves that are pale green marbled white and beautiful new leaves that in their development stage are almost entirely white. Here again the black stems of the plant add much to the overall attraction.

Besides their decorative use as potted plants the foliage of the pittosporums when cut lasts well in water and is much used in flower arranging and floristry work in general.

When planting in tubs put some drainage material in the bottom of the container and use a loam-based potting mixture. The best time to carry this out is late spring when plants are beginning to perk up and get under way for the new season. For the summer months plants can occupy patio space out of doors when there are usually plenty of flowering plants for adding colour to the conservatory collection. A further plus with the pittosporums is that they are relatively free of pest problems.

Although they will be slow to produce roots, cuttings can be taken in spring or early summer and placed in a warm and shaded location in the greenhouse. The cuttings ought to be reasonably firm and some 10 cm (4 in) in length, and should be inserted singly in small pots filled with a peat and sand mixture. Keep them regularly misted over with a syringe or fine rose attached to a watering can to ensure that cuttings do not shrivel up as a result of excess transpiration.

These really are cut-and-come-again plants in that they thrive as a result of being regularly pruned. For the arrangement of flowers they are ideal, as foliage is available through the year regardless of whether the plant is indoors or out.

## PLATYCERIUM (*Polypodiaceae*)
stag's horn fern

In a well shaded conservatory maintained at not less than 16 °C (61 °F) with high humidity, ferns could well provide an absorbing interest. There will never be any flowers, but the many shades of soft greenery is to some folk more appealing than garish colours.

There are endless ferns that one may choose from, with the stag's horn being one of the most interesting of all with its prominent fronds that stand away from the main part of the plant like the antlers of a stag. Behind the stag leaves there are what are known as the anchor leaves which the plant utilizes for attaching itself to trees and such like when growing in its natural jungle habitat.

**Platycerium**
The distinctive stag's horn fern can become a magnificent plant when grown in a moss-lined hanging container – the latter is eventually lost within the plant.

These plants are often seen growing in conventional pots, but this is not the best way to present or display these fine plants. Rather than a pot they should be attached to a piece of tree bark to which they will quite quickly anchor themselves. However, the plant does need some initial encouragement as there is little chance of it performing in the conservatory what it would do naturally in the jungle!

You should first choose a piece of bark (a flat board will do it if bark is unobtainable) and lay it down so that a layer of moss can be placed on it, perhaps tied into position with plastic covered wire. The plant is then removed from its pot and a good thickness of fresh sphagnum moss is wrapped around the root before the root ball is laid on the moss and tied into position – a few nails may be needed at this stage. On completion you should see nothing of the roots of the plant. Finally the plant on its new bark anchorage should be submerged in a bucket of water to ensure a thorough soaking. You then hang your masterpiece on the wall in the shade where it will do fine if sprayed over regularly and taken down every few days so that the plant can be dunked in water to become really wet. The anchor roots will soon begin to spread and will in time completely envelop the bark or board to which it is attached. An odd thing about the platycerium is that when growing in a plastic pot the anchor fronds never grow onto the plastic – perhaps someone has told them something!

The plant most often seen for sale is ***P. alcicorne***, but there are other varieties, the most majestic being ***P. superbum*** (syn. *P. grande*) which produces quite wonderful fronds that may be all of 1 m (3 ft) long. To grow the latter well you really must have ideal conditions of good shade, warmth and humidity.

## PLECTRANTHUS (*Labiatae*) Swedish ivy

Not a bit like an ivy, this is a plant that is grown more extensively in Scandinavia than elsewhere, one that is easy to care for and very adaptable in its uses. Under the staging in the greenhouse or in the conservatory where there is little light and a tendency for neglect this is a plant that will do fine. It has a naturally spreading habit which will be an asset in respect of ground cover. Also, when under the staging the variety **P. oertendahlii** will be most attractive when producing its pale mauve flowers in the autumn – in better light the spires of flower will tend to be more pink in colour.

There are several other varieties including **P. coleoides 'Marginatus'** with attractively variegated foliage. Besides their lowly position in poor conditions the Swedish ivies make fine basket plants that will grow very full and lush if watering and feeding is attended to. They also need protection from strong sunlight.

Propagation presents no problem as almost any piece of stem will root in a peaty mixture if kept at reasonable temperature, several cuttings in each small pot. When potting on almost any prepared potting mixture will be suitable.

## PLEOMELE *see* DRACAENA

## PLUMBAGO CAPENSIS (*Plumbaginaceae*)
Cape leadwort

These are straggling, untidy plants with lovely bright blue or white flowers present over a long period of time during the summer months. Flowers are produced on the tips of the current year's growth, which means that fresh material is needed annually to get the best in the way of flowers. Drastic though this may seem, the best way of achieving this is to cut plants down to within one inch from their base when they have finished flowering. The result will be completely new growth that will flower much more freely.

Plumbago can be planted in the border or in tubs and ought to be close to a wall so that developing stems can be trained to a framework – growth will be considerable if plants are well maintained. Plants need good light with some protection from strong sun, and they should be amply watered during the spring and summer, giving less in the autumn and very little over winter. Feed regularly while plants are producing fresh growth. Any potting or planting should be done in early spring and a good loam-based mixture should be used. When planting beds or borders with plumbago, incorporate fresh soil mixture with the soil that is already there to give the plants a better chance of succeeding.

When flowers die cut the plants down as the flowers are covered in a sticky substance that results in the dead flowers attaching themselves to everything around them, including the handler! Pretty though they are the latter is one reason for not investing too heavily in plumbago plants.

Minimum winter temperature should be in the region of 7 °C (45 °F) for *P. capensis*, but there is also a red flowered variety that must have a temperature of not less than 16 °C (61 °F) at any time.

If available, plants can be raised from seed sown in high temperature in early spring, or they may be propagated from cuttings of young shoots, in small pots filled with peat and sand and kept at temperature of around 20 °C (68 °F). Cuttings should be taken from the first young growth of the year.

## PLUMERIA RUBRA (*Apocynaceae*)
frangipani

Bordering on being the most exotic of all flowers, the frangipani will need a minimum temperature of 18 °C (64 °F) and considerable care if it is to flourish in the conservatory. It is best to grow the plant in a tub in keeping with the overall size of the plant, and to use a rich loam-based potting mix when transferring plants to larger containers. Good drainage will also be important. Potting should be done in late winter/early spring.

Cuttings of frangipani are often seen being sold as material for propagation: they have the appearance of large and expensive cigars. If a high temperature of around 20 °C (68 °F) can be sustained over the period that the cutting takes to root then the chances of success are surprisingly high. Planted in a 13 cm (5 in) diameter pot in fresh peat the cutting will take some six weeks to develop roots and in six to eight months it will have developed into quite a substantial young plant. Unless growing conditions are exceptionally good it is probably best to leave the young plant in the same pot from the time of its propagation until the spring of the following year when it can be transferred to a slightly larger container using a reliable quality soil mixture. Plants must be watered with care over the winter period to ensure that the soil is not excessively wet; this could be fatal if temperatures are inadequate.

When will they flower is the big question and one can only say that it is a question of being patient and caring for plants well in order to get flowers with the most wonderful colour and fragrance at the earliest possible time. When feeding established plants it might be an inducement to flower if a high potash fertilizer such as tomato fertilizer is used.

## POLYSCIAS (*Araliaceae*) dinner plate aralia

At one time the polyscias were a very scarce commodity, but now that plants are being propagated and grown in tropical regions and flown to distant destinations they are more freely available. In the past the nurseries that needed heated greenhouses to bring on crops were reluctant to grow this plant on account of its very slow rate of growth. With the change in growing and handling arrangements plants are now much less expensive and they are available in a range of sizes.

Cuttings are rooted from mature pieces of stem of variable height with the result that they have an almost instant mature look about them. When obtained they are normally in small pots and might well need to be potted on almost immediately; after watering the need for potting ought to be checked, but if there are ample roots then the plant should be advanced to a slightly larger pot using a mixture containing a percentage of loam.

There are both green and variegated forms, as well as those with feathery foliage such as the ming aralia, **P. fruticosa**. Provide filtered light and cool, airy conditions for these to do well. Water well in the spring and summer, with less at other times, and ensure that reasonable minimum temperature of around 16 °C (61 °F) is maintained. These are reasonably interesting plants to have around, but their slow rate of growth can be a bit tedious if you are someone who likes to see plants growing and developing.

## POLYSTICHUM (*Dryopteridaceae*)
holly fern

Finding suitable plants for dark corners is often a difficult problem when it comes to furbishing the conservatory. Ferns in general are good value for darkish locations and the holly fern is no exception. As the common name suggests the fronds have a holly look about them and they are a lovely shiny green in colour which adds to their attraction. Plants should enjoy reasonable warmth and quite shaded location.

Propagation of new plants can be by spores sown on a surface of fine peat or, perhaps more easily, by dividing clumps of plants in the spring and potting them individually. Plants should be kept moist at all times and will benefit from damp surroundings.

## PORTEA PETROPOLITANA
(*Bromeliadaceae*)

This is an unusual member of the splendid bromeliad family, unusual in that the flowering bract is borne on a stem that is a little over 1 m (3 ft) in height. The narrow green leaves with barbs along their margin are of similar length and are arranged in a loose rosette. Unlike many of the more compact bromeliads, the leaves of the portea where they overlap at their base do not form a watertight 'urn', so there is a need to water the soil in conventional fashion. When watering it is best to give the soil a good soaking and to allow it to dry appreciably before repeating.

On account of the wide spread of foliage it will need ample space in which to grow, so is only suited to the larger conservatory. It is best suited among other plants where the barbs along the leaf margins will not inconvenience anyone making use of the conservatory. The bracts which are bright orange/yellow in colour with pale lavender flowers are the principal feature of the plant, as they will remain colourful for many weeks during the summer months. When the flowers have finished there will be further interest when colourful seed pods form and remain decorative well into the autumn.

In time plants will form large rosettes and will need to be potted on into pots measuring some 25 cm (10 in) in diameter. All the bromeliades need an open, well aerated mixture when potting. If a mix specially prepared for these plants is not available, then compromise by using an orchid mixture which will provide most of the plant's needs.

## PRIMULA (*Primulacaea*)

In the range of smaller plants for the cool conservatory there are few easier or more rewarding plants than the pot-grown primulas which flower over the bleaker winter and spring months of the year. The three species that are always available are **P. obconica**, **P. malacoides** (fairy primrose) and **P. sinensis** (Chinese primrose), and all of these will have been grown in cool conditions at every stage in their development from seed sowing to growing on. When introduced to the conservatory they should be offered cool, light and airy conditions and, in respect of care, do not let them dry out at their roots.

For raising plants from scratch, seed should be sown in late spring/early summer. Seed is thinly sown on the surface of a peat and sand mixture, either in seed trays or 13 cm (5 in) half-pots. When large enough to handle seedlings are transferred to individual small pots filled with a multipurpose mixture to be grown on until such time as they have become well rooted when they can be further potted on to 13 cm (5 in) pots which will generally be their final size. At all stages the growing conditions must be cool and airy, and the plants can either be in a cold frame or in a greenhouse. Keep the plants moist at their roots and fed at weekly intervals once established in their pots.

When in flower they can be moved to the conservatory where they will be ideal as windowledge plants or plants for grouping on a table. There is also much to be said for having shelves at a slightly higher level for accommodating plants such as the primula. Plants need good light in which to grow and over-winter should not need to be protected from the sun. Following flowering, it is general practice to dispose of them and to produce fresh plants from seed annually.

In terms of flowering period there are few plants that can compare with *P. obconia* which will flower almost through the year if conditions are to its liking and the watering and feeding aspect is not neglected. A drawback with this plant is that touching the leaves can cause a rash in sensitive skins. If one is particularly sensitive it is quite possible that a rash will develop simply as a result of being in the same room as the plant.

## PSEUDOPANAX (*Araliaceae*)

Indigenous to New Zealand, these are foliage plants best suited to the larger conservatory that offers ample space for the average 2 m (6 ft) height that the plants will attain when roots are confined to pots. Not fully hardy, the pseudopanax needs a minimum temperature of around 10 °C (50 °F), plus good light in winter and lightly shaded conditions during the hotter months of the year.

During the summer months plants need ample watering and weekly feeding, but less water and no feeding is required while plants are inactive. For potting plants on in the spring, a loam-base mixture should be used. Very large pots will only encourage excessive growth and this is really not the aim as they should be encouraged to develop as slender specimens as opposed to large clumps of foliage. Provided feeding and watering is attended to the pot size need never be larger than 25 cm (10 in) in diameter.

Perhaps the best of these plants for conservatory use is **P. lessonii 'Goldsplash'** which has yellow and green variegated foliage on pale green upright stems. This is a very durable plant which will tolerate much ill treatment and not seem to object unduly – a commendable quality if one does not have a lot of time for plant care. It is the sort of plant that the retailer is never quite sure about in respect of hardiness, with the result that the plant may be seen either in the outside or the inside sales area, sometimes in both departments!

If you have a very cool growing environment in the conservatory purchase plants from the outdoor area as these will take more kindly to conditions that are, if anything, an improvement.

## PTERIS (*Adianiaceae*)

These are ferns with attractively coloured, neat and compact foliage, ideally suited to shelves and table tops within the conservatory. The plant decorator also puts these to very good use when combining the pteris with other subjects in planted arrangements. In the conservatory that boasts a planted bed pteris can be planted at the front of the display. When displaying plants in this way it is general practice to remove plants from their pots and to plant them in the soil, but the pteris ferns might be a little too sensitive for this sort of treatment. The alternative is to arrange the plants in a shallow container in which the roots will be warmer, and partially bury the container in the bed of soil.

Minimum temperature should not be below 16 °C (61 °F), and there should be a humid feeling within the conservatory. As with all ferns, ensure that the plants are shaded from the sun if the foliage is not to shrivel and die.

In commercial establishments new plants are raised from spores sown on the surface of fine sand and peat in shaded conditions at a temperature of 20 °C (68 °F) at any time that spores and conditions are right for propagating. Fresh plants can also be propagated by dividing older clumps into smaller sections and potting them individually. Plants chosen for propagating in this way should not be too old and coarse, as these are less likely to provide attractive plants when compared to fresher material. For this and all potting operations a peaty houseplant mixture will give the best results.

## PUNICA GRANATUM (*Punicaceae*)
pomegranate

The best of the pomegranates for the conservatory is **P. granatum nana** which attains a height of some 2 m (6 ft) with its roots freely planted in a bed of soil, or about half this when the roots are restricted to a container. The plant forms into a reasonably neat bush with small, bright green leaves and salmon red flowers that are not unlike those of the fuchsia. It would be magical if plants bore pomegranate fruits but this, alas, is invariably a disappointment as fruits on pot-grown plants are generally small with a tendency to split their skins.

These are, nevertheless, interesting plants that will not be difficult to care for in cool, airy and lightly shaded conditions. Water should be given freely during the growing season, with feeding at weekly intervals, but no feeding and much less water at other times.

Plants can be propagated from seed sown in the spring if it is available. Alternatively, new plants can be brought on by inserting firm cuttings in a peat and sand mixture during the summer months of the year. When these are well rooted they can be potted on using a loam-based mixture, a mix that will apply at all further stages of potting on.

## PYROSTEGIA VENUSTA (*Bignoniceae*)
flame vine

For the owner of the conservatory with a lofty ceiling this is a plant that will be well worth seeking out. If provided with a wire, trellis or netting support, the flame vine will simply love to scramble to the highest point. In the smaller conservatory it can also be encouraged to fill in with growth at a lower level by training the tendrils in the desired direction as they develop.

Plants require good light and a minimum temperature in the region of 16 °C (61 °F), with frequent watering and regular feeding during spring and summer but much less water and no feeding while growth is inactive.

For planting in tubs or border, plants should have loam-based potting mixture that is free-draining. Place plants close to a wall so that they may be trained as soon as growth begins to develop.

Minimum winter temperature should be in the region of 16 °C (61 °F), with slightly higher temperature should propagation of new plants be the objective. To propagate, cuttings of young shoots a few inches in length should be inserted in small pots filled with a sandy mixture; place the cuttings in a propagator in a lightly shaded greenhouse.

Flowers are reddish orange in colour and are borne in pendulous clusters of slender tubes, produced over a lengthy period.

## RHAPIS (*Palmae*) lady palm

There are three of these attractive palms that one might be able to obtain for growing in the lightly shaded conservatory, all of them attaining a height of just over 1 m (3 ft) when roots are confined to a container. The most robust of the three is **Rhapis excelsa** (large lady palm) which produces clumps of canes from soil level not unlike bamboo and with segmented glossy green leaves of leathery appearance. The variegated form, **Rhapis excelsa variegata**, is a very attractive plant originating in Japan and having ivory white and green variegation on plants that remain compact and easy to accommodate. The plant considered to be the better of the three is **R. humilis** (slender lady palm) which is, as the common name suggests, a more graceful plant. Growing in similar fashion with bamboo-like canes developing from soil level this is an ideal plant for placing as an individual in an important location within the conservatory.

Lightly shaded conditions will suit all three, as will ample watering from spring through to the end of the summer with appreciably less in winter. Plants should also be regularly fed with a liquid fertilizer while in active growth, and an old recommendation for retaining the deep glossy green colouring of foliage is to place a piece of sulphate of iron on the surface of the soil in the pot.

When plants are potted on, a rich mixture should be used, but plants never need to go into containers that are very large: an 18 cm (7 in) pot is sufficient as a final pot if feeding is not neglected.

Seed is invariably difficult to obtain, but if it can be acquired it should be sown in a peat and sand mixture in early spring. Alternatively, fresh plants can be obtained by removing suckers with a little root attached.

## RHIPSALIDOPSIS GAERTNERI
(*Cactaceae*) Easter cactus

These are succulent plants that have gone through numerous name changes, with the common name of Easter cactus being the one that may be more readily recognized. These are low, spreading plants that in time will develop into clumps of reasonable size when plants are potted either into reasonably large pots, or when they are growing in hanging containers. They make fine hanging container plants with slightly pendulous foliage setting off colourful flowers when the plant is raised to a higher level.

During the summer months plants can be placed out of doors in a sunny location where the normally green foliage will take on a reddish bronze hue. Plants treated in this way may be inclined to flower more freely when the following spring comes around. The leaves are, in fact, pads of growth that grow one from the other, on the ends of which hose-in-hose flowers appear. The common name of Easter cactus refers to the time of flowering, but this can be variable depending on the cultural conditions that prevail.

They are particularly easy to propagate, as almost any piece of leaf removed and placed in sandy mixture will produce roots. The best way to start new plants is to fill a pot with a mixture containing loam, sand and leafmould and to place up to six cuttings around the edge of an 8 cm (3 in) pot. Once rooted through to the side of the pot the plants can be transferred to a larger container using the same sort of mixture. Alternatively, the potful of cuttings can be planted in a hanging planter to grow on and flower.

Children will be interested in the Easter cactus and it may encourage them to become plant minded; adults should provide the propagating soil and the advice, but allow the youngster actually to insert the cutting. When it produces roots and growth as it almost invariably will the child will take an uncommon amount of interest in its own plant.

Care is needed when watering, as too much will result in roots rotting and excessively dry conditions will result in the foliage shrivelling. Keep the soil just moist, using care to avoid very wet conditions in winter. Feed with a weak liquid fertilizer when growth is evident.

## RHODOCHITON ATROSANGUINEUS
(*syn. R. volubilis*) (*Scrophulariaceae*) purple bellerine

This is a vigorous climber that will attain a height of some 3 m (9 ft) during the course of one season. Plants are grown from seed and are best treated as annuals with fresh plants being raised each year. Leaves are heart-shaped and flowers are dark red in colour and naturally pendulous. Plants should be placed close to a wall if they are to go into a prepared bed or containers. A framework of some kind is then necessary to which the twining petioles can attach themselves.

Plants can be raised from seed sown in conventional fashion in the spring, the temperature to be in the region of 16 °C (61 °F). Plants should be potted on as they fill their existing pots with roots until such a time as they are in 25 cm (10 in) pots where they can be sustained by regular feeding. Plants being saved from one year to the next, as opposed to treated as annuals, should all have weak growth removed in late winter, and all other shoots ought to be shortened, but not too drastically. If the latter practice is opted for, then firm young shoots can be propagated in cool conditions in early spring. As cuttings and seedlings become well rooted they should be progressively potted on using a loam-based potting mix.

Plants should have a lightly shaded location in which to grow and cool conditions where the temperature minimum should be in the region of 10 °C (50 °F). They will require ample watering during the summer months with much dryer, but not bone dry, conditions while growth is inactive. It is not necessary to feed plants while growth is inactive.

## RHODODENDRON (*Ericaceae*)
(including azaleas)

This is an acid-loving garden plant that will do well when carefully grown in larger containers; if you live in an area where the garden soil is very alkaline then tub growing is the only practical answer. Many are too large for tub culture and would be out of place in all but very large conservatories. However, there are now many splendid compact varieties and it is advisable to impress upon the supplier when acquiring plants that they are wanted for tub growing and must be of more dwarf habit. It is also wise to stress that compact plants as opposed to those of more straggling habit are required.

These are not the sort of plants that can be accommodated in the conservatory the year round – they should be planted in tubs that are not too large and difficult to move around as plants will have to be in their tubs in the garden for the greater part of the year and brought into the conservatory some weeks before their natural garden flowering time. The result of this will be that you will have rhododendrons in flower indoors some time ahead of similar plants outside. Using plants in this way is one of the great advantages of the conservatory, and one of the ways of continually ringing the changes.

While being brought into flower, plants will need gentle heat, but at all other times they must be in cool and airy conditions where there is ample light. They must also have ample feeding. When plants are in need of potting on, which is not often once they are in pots of good size, they should be potted into an ericaceous mixture.

There are tender species that need winter protection from the elements, but these are not really suited to the average conservatory as they are too demanding on space, so it is much better to have plants indoors only while they are in flower, as the foliage of these plants will do little to improve the conservatory display.

*R. indicum* (florist's azalea) are wonderful plants for flowering over autumn and spring months of the year, preferring cool conditions to be at their best. Glossy evergreen foliage is topped by a wealth of flowers in various colours ranging from the purest white to the deepest red. To really see what can be done to get an amazing result from growing these plants, it is almost obligatory to visit the five-yearly Ghent Floralie in Belgium where plants can be seen growing as conventional bushes, pyramid shapes and breathtaking mop-head standards.

Essential requirements of these plants are cool growing conditions and permanently wet roots – any drying out and there will be a dramatic loss of leaves and total deterioration in the appearance of the plant.

The principal care time is after the plants have flowered (the time when they are generally neglected through having lost their flowers), when old flowers should be carefully removed so that new growth immediately below the flowers is not damaged. This is a good time too to consider potting plants on into slightly larger containers using an ericacious potting mix – specifiy this requirement when purchasing. Avoid getting plants frosted, but get them outside as soon as possible for their non-flowering period. Plunge their pots to their rims in a bed of peat if this is a practical possibility. While outside keep them well watered and sprayed over regularly, particularly during warm periods. They will also benefit from weekly feeding with a liquid fertilizer while outside and producing new growth. Fetch plants in before frosts are likely and house them in cool conditions until flower buds appear when they will appreciate slightly higher temperature to get the flowers under way.

What ever else may be said about these fine plants it is the summer care (watering, feeding, cool shaded location) that is the most important if plants are to go on giving pleasure over the year. Bothered by few pests these plants will occasionally develop galls or misshapen tip growth. The answer is to simply cut out any offending pieces.

**RHOEO DISCOLOR** *see*
TRADESCANTIA

**RHOICISSUS RHOMBOIDEA** (*Vitaceae*)
grape ivy

An old favourite and one of the most durable of all the foliage plants that come under the general heading of houseplant, this is a natural climber with fresh green segmented leaves which have a natural gloss to them. In respect of height and spread, it can go on growing forever if space is available and growing conditions reasonable. If provided with some means of support it will provide a fine background of greenery that is of pleasing colour throughout the year.

In strong light the colouring of the leaves will harden and will lose much of the fresh greenness. This, in fact, is one of those rare plants that seem to do better in both growth and colour when growing in poor light, so a dark corner could well be the answer.

Feed and water them well during the spring and summer and water less and discontinue feeding during the winter, with a gradual easing of watering during the autumn. When potted on, plants will prefer a good houseplant mixture, but potting is something that need not be done too often. An 18 cm (7 in) container will be large enough for most plants as a final pot if feeding is not neglected, but plants that are growing well against a wall and developing lots of leaves may well need to be eventually in pots of 25 cm (10 in) diameter. Minimum temperature of not less than 10 °C (50 °F) should be the aim, and a higher temperature will be preferred.

Besides being good wall plants, the grape ivy can also be grown as an upright plant trained to a support so that it can be more of an individual specimen. Just to prove its versatility it can also have its foliage spread out on the floor in a display bed, and will not take too unkindly to being planted in a hanging basket to become an effective green trailing subject.

There is also an attractive Danish cultivar with more interesting foliage that goes under the name of *R.* **'Ellen Danica'** which needs the same attention as the first mentioned.

**RICINUS COMMUNIS** (*Euphorbiaceae*)
castor oil plant

Whereas the ricinus will grow to tree proportions in the tropics, in pots it is generally grown as an annual plant raised fresh from seed annually. The greenish purple palmate leaves sprout from an upright stem which can attain a height of between 1 and 2 m (3–6 ft).

This is a very easy plant to manage and will make a pleasing contrast to other foliage when grown in a mixed arrangement. The seed is hard and should be soaked in warm water for a few hours before being sown in a sandy mixture in warm conditions in the spring. When seedlings have produced two or three leaves they should be planted into small pots using a loam-based mixture, and should subsequently be potted on until such time as the plants are in 18 cm (7 in) pots where they can remain until the end of the season when they are disposed of. When established plants will need ample watering and frequent feeding in order to do well.

**ROCHEA COCCINEA** *see* CRASSULA COCCINEA

**SAINTPAULIA IONANTHA** (*Gesneriaceae*)
African violet

This is another plant that could well form a collection on its own for the enthusiastic grower, and there is no shortage of supporters as far as these plants are concerned. The first of these were discovered by a Baron St Paul in what was then known as German West Africa and is now Tanzania. Compared to the vastly improved plants that are available today the original introductions would have been rather weedy plants of little merit. With the passing of years, enthusiasts and hybridization of plants has wrought many changes, with the result that the violets of today bear no comparison with the original discoveries. Not only have the flowers of these plants improved in colour, shape and size, the plants themselves are much more robust in both habit and appearance. The commercial plant producer is forever on the lookout for improvements in plants: plants that will give a good account of themselves on the growing benches as well as plants with the prettiest flowers. The result is that the saintpaulia for the house is much more tolerant of room conditions. It is obviously possible to purchase the less usual plants from the more specialized grower, but these less usual subjects will often need better growing conditions in the home, and a greater degree of skill on the part of the custodian.

There are now endless varieties of saintpaulia with flower colouring ranging from the purest white to the deepest red with many bicolours, double flowers, flowers with frilled edges, even trailing saintpaulias. Besides these there are also delightful miniature forms that will enable the enthusiast with limited growing space to accommodate a much greater number of plants.

The conservatory owner has in many ways got the edge over the person who can only offer room conditions. An important requirement of saintpaulias wherever they may be grown is adequate light, and the conservatory will normally have light in abundance, so much in fact, that some form of shading will be needed during the summer months if saintpaulias are to do really well. In normal room conditions plants ought to have a light window location during the day and a location under a fairly bright light fitting in the evening. Provided the light can be left on for some twelve hours in every twenty-four, the saintpaulia will do very well without natural daylight. In the conservatory filtered light is the ideal: the amount of available light should be controlled with blinds, curtains or shading applied to the outside of the glass, but one must ensure that the room does not become too dark. Some form of portable shading will be the best investment as it can be removed or drawn to one side on days when the sun is not in evidence.

Besides good light, the other important requirement is warmth: it will be impossible to grow these plants successfully if the temperature in the conservatory is frequently below 16 °C (61 °F). Minimum temperature of around 19 °C (64 °F) is what you should aim for. Maintaining a conservatory at this level will be an expensive business, but it can be eased somewhat by fitting the conservatory with thermal screens or blinds that will help to reduce the heat loss. Alternatively the saintpaulias and other small plants in need of higher temperature can be housed in heated glass cases within the conservatory so that only a small area of higher temperature is required. (More about this aspect can be found on pp. 105–6.)

When watering it is important to ensure that water does not get onto the foliage as this can cause unsightly damage, a problem that will be much aggravated should the sun be on the leaves at the time of watering. There are all sorts of suggestions put forward for the watering of these plants and the favourite seems to be that the plant pots should be placed in a dish of water so that moisture is drawn up by capillary action into the soil in the pot. There is no question that plants can be effectively watered in this way, but it is of extreme importance to ensure that plants do not stand in the dish of water for too long, as very wet conditions will almost certainly put paid to saintpaulias. In continually wet conditions the roots of the plant will rot as a result of poor circulation of air around the roots. Perhaps the best method to employ when watering these plants is to have a small watering can with a narrow spout that can be carefully directed under the leaves so that water if poured onto the surface of the soil, giving sufficient to ensure that surplus water is seen draining through the holes at the bottom of the container. The watering exercise is repeated as necessary but, whatever method is employed, it is important to ensure that before any further water is given the leaves of the plant should feel just perceptibly limp to the touch. Use of very cold water direct from the kitchen tap is also detrimental to plants. Cold water should have a little hot water added to it, or the watering can should be filled after each watering session so that the warmth of the room will take the chill off so leaving the can ready for use.

African violets can be raised from seed in warm conditions with results that can be interesting if unpredictable in respect of flower colourings. To produce young plants with all the characteristics of the parent plant it is necessary to propagate plants vegetatively form leaves. A lot of mystique surrounds this exercise but, given reasonable conditions, they can be persuaded to root with very little trouble. As with all propagating from sections of the plant you must begin with healthy propagating material, removed from healthy plants – poor, weedy pieces will simply produce poor, weedy results.

Before removing any propagating material you should first think about the materials and conditions that the leaves of the plant will need in order to produce roots of their own. First and foremost is temperature, and this should be set to remain at 18 °C (64 °F) or above, which will almost certainly necessitate the use of a propagating case with temperature controls. The next requirement will be fresh peat that has moistened sufficiently for moisture to ooze gently from between the fingers when a handful is compressed. The peat is loosely placed into pots of no more than 8 cm (3 in) diameter. An entire healthy leaf should be removed from the plant so that there is no piece of stem left that will in time rot and cause damage to the parent plant. The leaf stalk will probably be too long as it is; therefore, use a sharp knife to reduce the length of the stalk to about 4 cm ($1\frac{1}{2}$ in). Three or four holes, depending on the size of the leaves, should be made with a pencil around the edge of the pot and the leaf cuttings should be inserted in the holes so that the end of the leaf stalk is touching the peat in the bottom of the hole. (If desired the cutting can be treated with a rooting powder or liquid, but this is not normally essential.) The leaves should face inwards so that the young plants when they appear come up into the light. If there is filtered light, sufficient warmth and conditions that are agreeably moist (not wet) there will be no difficulty in encouraging leaves to produce roots and small plants. New growth will appear as a cluster of baby leaves around the base of the leafstalk, and these should be left undisturbed until they have become well developed.

The next stage of handling is the one that can make all the difference between good and bad saintpaulias. If the clumps of leaves are lifted and potted on into larger pots as they are, then a plant that will be all leaves with little style will be the result. When well rooted the trick is to remove the cuttings from their original pot and to tease the clump of leaves apart – on doing this it will be found that the clump is actually composed of lots of baby plants that are crowded together around the parent stem. If these are separated and potted individually into small pots filled with peaty multipurpose mixture they will, in spite of their apparent weakness, soon perk up and begin to grow of their own accord. The benefit of this part of the exercise is that you will have what is known as a single crown plant, one with all its leaves radiating from a central point. Such plants are much more attractive than the clumpy ones, and when the flowers appear they will be set off to perfection against the symmetrical background of greenery. From this stage one has simply to provide the essentials of warmth, light and a controlled amount of moisture to be able to grow saintpaulias like the proverbial weed.

## SANCHEZIA NOBILIS (*Acanthaceae*)

This is a plant for the warm conservatory where the temperature does not fall below 16 °C (61 °F). Besides warmth the sanchezia will also have to be grown in a humid environment where it can be protected from bright sunlight. Plants should be kept moist and fed weekly with liquid fertilizer during the growing season, needing less water and no feeding at other times. A peaty houseplant mixture should be used when potting plants on.

This is a handsome plant growing to a little over 1 m (3 ft) in height and having the dual qualities of decorative foliage and flowers that are papery in texture and orange-yellow in colour. Flowers are colourful over a long period during the summer months.

New plants are made from cuttings inserted in fresh peat during the spring months of the year. The chances of cuttings rooting will be improved if they are placed in a heated propagator that is placed out of direct sunlight. Frequent misting of the foliage with tepid water will also help to keep the cuttings fresh which will be an inducement to rooting.

## SANSEVIERIA TRIFASCIATA
(*Agavaceae*) mother-in-law's tongue

In some parts of the world the common name of **S.t. 'Laurentii'** may well be variegated snake plant which relates to the colourful mottled pattern in the centre of each leaf. The leaves also have an attractive wide margin of yellow along their enture length, but this margin is strangely absent from plants that have been propagated from leaf cuttings. The leaves of mature plants attain a height of approximately 1 m (3 ft) and form in tightly clustered rosettes at soil level. Mature plants will usually flower during the summer, the flower being a dull yellow like a hyacinth with widely spaced florets.

For the conservatory with little or no shading and a custodian with little time for plant care, the sansevieria could be the ideal plant as it thrives on neglect and does not take too unkindly to being exposed to bright sunlight. The leaves are succulent and capable of storing a lot of moisture, hence the ability of the plant to survive long, dry periods. A good watering once each fortnight during the summer will be adequate for their needs, and they will not suffer unduly should they be given no water whatsoever during the winter. It is much better to have plants in dry soil in winter if temperatures are unavoidably low, rather than that they should be wet at their roots. Combination of wet and cold is a perfect recipe for failure as far as these plants are concerned. Occasional feeding of established plants during the summer will be beneficial, but it is not desperately important.

Potting on can be left until plants actually break the pots in which they are growing, and when this happens the plant can be advanced to a slightly larger container using a loam-based mixture. They can become top heavy with their weight of foliage so it is advisable to use terracotta pots when potting on.

New plants can be propagated by cutting up mature leaves into sections some 8 cm (3 in) in length and inserting them in sandy mixture in warm conditions. As mentioned above the resultant plants will not have the attractive yellow margin of the parent plant. To produce plants of the same colour it is necessary to remove smaller plants that are developing at the base of the parent plant and to pot these individually. This is by far the best method, and if the small rosette is removed with some root then the success of the exercise is a foregone conclusion.

There is also a green mottled form (**S. zeylanica**) with similar habit, but it is a much less attractive plant. With low-growing, star-shaped rosettes, **S.t. 'Golden Hahnii'** is an attractive plant for placing on windowledges or for including in displays of cacti and succulents.

## SARRACENIA (*Sarraceniaceae*)
pitcher plant

Carnivorous plants are gaining in popularity, and these are especially attractive with their tubed pitchers which are either erect or prostrate and pleasantly coloured in shades of green and yellow. For the conservatory capable of maintaining just a modicum of warmth these could be interesting plants to specialize in, along with the other carnivors available. Cool and airy conditions in good light will suit them well, provided the surroundings are moist.

When plants are being potted they must go into containers that are well provided with drainage, and the potting mixture should consist of fresh sphagnum moss with fresh peat worked into it to provide something that is very open and spongy. If there are only a few plants in the collection the plant to be potted should be placed in another, larger pot with sphagnum moss packed around in the area between the two pots. The more ambitious person may well experiment with a moss bed into which the plants in their pots can be plunged. Feature beds of this kind can be very attractive if one uses pieces of tree bark or similar natural material around which the fly eaters can be planted.

Propagating fresh plants will not be difficult as it simply entails the splitting up of mature clumps of growth and potting them individually in the moss mixture.

## SAXIFRAGA (*Saxifrageaceae*)
mother-of-thousands

Among the saxifrages the most obvious choice for the conservatory is **S. stolonifera** (syn. *S. sarmentosa*) and its tricolor form. These have the common name of mother-of-thousands which relates to the numerous plantlets that hang from slender pendulous stems when the plant is growing in a hanging container. These babies can be detached when of manageable size and potted individually into small pots filled with houseplant mixture.

Offer lightly shaded conditions and a temperature minimum in the region of 16 °C (61 °F). Keep plants moist during the spring and summer, but avoid getting them too wet at their roots for long periods – in winter very much less water is required. Weekly feeding with weak liquid fertilizer will suit them while in active growth but none should be given at other times.

For the cold conservatory there are other saxifrages that will provide a very fine show. Those with hard, crusty foliage are decorative in themselves, but they can be particularly attractive when their flowers appear in the spring.

These plants ought to be grown in shallow terracotta pans using a gritty, free-draining alpine potting mixture. They need cool, airy and light conditions in order to do well, also careful watering to ensure that roots never become waterlogged.

Besides the crusty varieties there are also mossy saxifrages which form clumps of tight green rosettes with white, pink or red flowers appearing in the spring. These prefer moist and shaded conditions in which to grow. Both kinds will also prefer to be out of doors on a hard-standing ground during the summer months. While the saxifrages and alpines are holidaying in the garden, the conservatory can be filled with spring and summer flowers!

## SCHEFFLERA ARBORICOLA
(*Araliaceae*) parasol plant, umbrella tree

*Schefflera arboricola* and *Heptapleurum arboricola* are very similar in appearance but the heptapleurum will always have smaller fingered leaves than the schefflera, although they have now been classified together. The former *Brassaia* has also been reclassified here.

Initially there was only the green form of parasol plant to choose, but there are now several different cultivars available. The greatest improvement has been seen in the variegated forms, such as **S.a. 'Capelle'**, which is an especially fine plant. All of them produce upright stems with attractive finger leaves radiating from them. Plants can attain a height of some 3 m (9 ft) when roots are confined to a pot, and a lot of space will be required to accommodate their size. They are essentially individual plants seen at their best when growing in a container where they can be given reasonable space in which to develop their all-round habit of growth. Young plants are normally bought as individuals with one stem in the pot, but when larger and more expensive plants are acquired it will be found that there are several stems in the pot with the result that plants of much more stature develop as they age.

One of the main reasons for the greatly increased popularity of this plant is that it is very tolerant of variable conditions that may range from very warm to surprisingly cold. It is not generally appreciated but plants can easily come down to temperatures of 5 °C (41 °F) minimum in winter provided the change from very warm to cold is not too sudden. If the soil in the pot is kept very much on the dry side they will, in fact, tolerate a few degrees of frost with only odd leaves being damaged, so it can be very useful in the cooler conservatory during the winter months when there is not a lot of tolerant material to select from.

To get the best from them, however, they should enjoy temperatures of not less than 16 °C (61 °F) and light shade and lots of fresh air. Being active plants they will need frequent watering during the spring and summer with a good deal less in winter, particularly if temperatures are to be unavoidably low. Regular feeding with weak liquid fertilizer will suit them while they are in active growth. Having a slight gloss to the lush foliage they will also benefit from regular cleaning of the leaves, but too frequent use of chemical cleaners should be avoided.

Any potting on that may be thought necessary should be undertaken in the spring and a good houseplant mixture should be used to pot plants into slightly larger containers. Following potting, plants should be well watered and placed in a shaded location for a few weeks until they settle down and begin to root into the fresh mixture.

New plants can be propagated from single leaves with a piece of stem attached or from the top section of the stem with three leaves attached. The bother with propagating in this way is that the plant used for taking cuttings will become much less attractive until such time as new growth develops. Very old plants with mature stems are not very suitable for propagating material. Propagation from seed is also possible, sown at any time of year when conditions are suitable.

## SCHIZANTHUS (*Solanaceae*)
poor man's orchid

These annual plants have a wonderful range of flower colouring, from pink and salmon to yellow and cream. They are comparatively easy to grow if you take care with both watering and feeding. The flowering season for plants in the conservatory can be extended from spring through the summer if the sowing of seed is staggered.

For spring flowering seed should be sown late in the previous summer, in a sandy mixture in either trays or pots. A cold greenhouse or cold frame will be fine for starting them off, and once mature enough to handle the small plants are transferred to 8 cm (3 in) pots where they are grown on in a temperature of not less than 10 °C (50 °F) until the following winter when they should be potted into larger containers using a loam-based potting mixture.

Plants should eventually be in pots of 18 cm (7 in) diameter, and they ought to be carefully staked so that they look their best when flowers are present. For flowering later in the year, seed is sown in the same way in mid winter, but the temperature needs to be set at a minimum of 16 °C (61 °F).

Once under way keep schizanthus well watered and regularly fed and they will provide a very colourful display that, other than one's time, will have cost comparatively little. When plants have finished flowering they should be disposed of.

**SCINDAPSUS AUREUS** *see*
EPIPREMNUM AUREUM

**SELAGINELLA** (*Selaginellaceae*) bun moss

The majority of these plants form low mounds of greenery that would, if anything, be a little lost in the conservatory. However, they have their uses and can be very attractive when seen growing in terrariums and bottle gardens planted up with care.

The plant most likely to appeal to the conservatory owner is *S. martensii* **'Variegata'**, which has pleasant green leaves attractively tipped white. It has a more open habit, and in time will develop stilt roots that are both interesting and attractive. These roots are produced in great number and have the appearance of supporting the plant in its growing position. The plant would look well in a collection containing ferns as they both prefer the same shaded, warm and moist conditions.

Plants are propagated from small sections of stem inserted in a peat and sand mixture in a propagator which should be maintained at a high temperature until such time as the cuttings are seen to be rooted. When potting these or any other of the selaginellas, a peaty houseplant mixture should be used.

**SENECIO MACROGLOSSUS**
**'VARIEGATUS'** (*Compositae*)
variegated wax vine, Swedish ivy

The common name of Swedish ivy is misleading as the plant belongs to the daisy family, which is obvious when the small yellow and white daisy flowers appear. Although the flowers are attractive they are very small and are produced in no great number.

However, the leaves are not unlike those of the smaller leaved ivies, although they are glossy and very much brighter. The cream and green colouring also adds much to the appearance of the plant. Something else that might be considered a benefit is the prodigious rate of growth during the summer months when the plant will twist and climb in all directions. It is debatable whether or not this is a good thing in the small conservatory where ceilings are low and space is limited, but it could be one way of covering a wall with reasonably attractive foliage in a comparatively short space of time. Plants would have to be provided with a framework onto which it will naturally cling and climb to the upper reaches.

Aphids can become a problem and should be watched for. Use a suitable insecticide as soon as detected. There is little difficulty in propagating the plant from stem cuttings that can be taken at any time during the spring and summer. Take any piece of stem with a mature leaf or two attached and insert five or six of these in small pots filled with peat or a houseplant mixture. In a heated propagator they will root fairly readily and can be removed and progressively potted on as they fill their existing pots with roots.

**SETCREASEA PURPUREA** *see*
TRADESCANTIA PALLIDA

**SINNINGIA** (*Gesneriaceae*) gloxinia

Much better known by its common name, these are summer flowering plants that in recent years have lost much of their popularity, due perhaps to the fact that a much greater range of easy care potted plants is now available from an assortment of plant retailers. This is not to say that these are not superb plants which will give a spectacular summer display of plants when they are properly grown. This starts with saving the best flowering corms from one year to the next and growing them on.

The commercial practice is to sow seed in early spring in warm conditions and to push the plants along as quickly as possible to flowering time when they will be sold. Herein might lie a reason for plants being less popular: the plants are of poor quality and unacceptable to the would-be purchaser. There is no reason, however, why you cannot make a start with growing gloxinias by purchasing seed and growing plants on for one season so that the corms producing the best quality flowers can be saved for growing on in future years.

In the conservatory plants will not be difficult to manage in cool, airy and lightly shaded conditions. Watering should be done with care, avoiding the temptation to be too generous, and ensuring that the area surrounding the plants is kept moist. On healthy plants flowers are produced in abundance and are generally large and brilliantly coloured. While in flower, plants should be fed with something akin to a tomato fertilizer.

Following flowering the plant will begin to die back naturally and this should be a sign to reduce watering, and eventually stop altogether so that the corm can be stored warm and dry until the following year when corms are started into growth. The first three months of the year will be the time for fresh activity when corms are planted in 8 cm (3 in) pots of peaty mixture with the corm just buried below the surface of the soil – large corms might need slightly larger starting pots. At this stage the plants will be better if housed in warm and moist conditions in a greenhouse with a minimum temperature of not less than 16 °C (61 °F). During this stage in their development plants must be kept on the move, and this will mean potting them on as soon as their existing pots are filled with roots, or applying weak liquid fertilizer if the potting operation has to be delayed. Plants grown in this way will be much more robust than those that are raised in their first year from seed, and pots of 18 cm (7 in) will be needed for plants that are growing well.

Ideally a feeder greenhouse is useful for bringing on such plants so that they can be moved to the conservatory and enjoyed to the full when flowers are at their best.

When it comes to propagation the gloxinias are particularly obliging as almost any piece of leaf or growth will produce roots and eventually make a plant. Young shoots can be taken and planted; young leaves with their stems can be pushed into the propagating mixture; or complete large leaves can be removed and the underside of the midrib can be cut along its length before being laid flat on a bed of peat and sand mixture. For all of these methods a heated propagator will be needed and the location should be shaded and moist. Propagating new plants from leaves and stems will

be a useful method for increasing stock of plants that are of special merit, besides being a sort of fun exercise that will impress the visitors!

## SMITHIANTHA (*Gesneriaceae*) temple bells

Mention has been made (p. 191) of the possibility of specializing in plants of the family Gesneriaceae, and the smithiantha is a fine example of the sort of plant that you can look out for to include in the collection. By regulating the time of planting of tubers these plants can be had in flower over three seasons of the year.

Plants can be propagated from seed sown in peat and sand mixture in late spring, but it is necessary to maintain a temperature in the region of 24 °C (75 °F) to be reasonably sure of success. At the same time of year it is also possible to root firm cuttings in peat and sand in similar temperature. A third, and possibly the surest method of propagating is to divide the clumps of tubers at potting time and to pot them individually into pots just a little larger than the tuber using a peaty mixture.

Plants must have warmth, shade and humidity if they are to succeed – while in growth the minimum temperature should be in the region of 18 °C (64 °F). In the early stages of growth water with care, but as growth develops so the amount of water can be given more generously, not forgetting the importance of keeping the area surrounding the plant as moist as possible in order to increase the humidity level.

There are several varieties to choose from, but acquiring plants or seed will usually mean going to a specialist grower. Average height is just under 1 m (3 ft), with plants having beautiful velvety leaves and nodding bell flowers in many colours from yellow through to red.

In order to enjoy these plants in flower over the seasons it is necessary to stagger the times of starting tubers into growth. For plants to flower over the summer the tubers should be potted in early spring; for autumn flowering they should be started in late spring and to have winter colouring the starting time is early summer. For such activity one will clearly need the back-up facility of a greenhouse, a heated greenhouse being an almost indispensable part of a well-managed conservatory.

When the foliage of the smithiantha begins to die down naturally so the amount of water given should be gradually reduced until such time as the soil is bone dry. For storage purposes the heated greenhouse again comes into its own, as the procedure for storing is to lay the pots on their sides under the staging of the greenhouse so that no water can get into the pot – the temperature for storing tubers should be in the region of 13 °C (55 °F) as a minimum. When it comes to starting the tubers into growth for the new season, the tubers should be removed from their pots so that much of the soil can be removed before the tubers are replanted in the same container using fresh mixture. These plants like an open, spongy mixture in preference to the all-peat concoctions that are generally offered today. It will be well worth the trouble of acquiring good loam, fresh peat and leafmould and mixing equal parts of these ingredients together with the addition of a little sharp sand. As plants increase in size so they can be potted into slightly larger containers using the suggested potting mixture.

## SOLANUM (*Solanaceae*)
winter cherry, potato vine

Known to everyone, **Solanum capsicastrum** is raised from seed sown in warm conditions in late winter, being potted on and gradually introduced to cooler conditions as plants develop in size. The tips of young shoots need frequent pinching out in order to encourage a more bushy habit of growth. When properly grown these plants develop into compact bushes of dull green foliage of little distinction. It is only when the green berries appear that they become more interesting, with the berries turning to orange red for Christmas making them the popular plants that they are.

To grow these from seed would mean many months of regular daily attention and much space used for housing them. Even then the result of growing a small batch of plants could well fall far short of expectations. For the conservatory owner it is very much better to purchase plants that are covered in berries as a result of growing expertise of the commercial grower.

The cool conservatory offering abundant light will be the ideal location for these plants which, at little cost, do much to brighten the Christmas scene. Plants can be saved and grown from one year to the next, but it is really very much better to dispose of them when they have lost their attraction.

**S. jasminoides** (potato vine) is more suited to the conservatory, but ample space will be needed for the vigorous climbing growth which will require some form of support. It will quickly fill a wall space and can be grown in a container or free-planted in a border.

They are half-hardy only requiring sufficient heat to keep out the worst of the weather. They should also have a lightly shaded location to provide some protection during the sunnier months of the year. Water should be given generously while the plant is active, and regular weekly feeding will not come amiss. During the winter less water and no feed is needed. In the early part of the year any weak, soft or unwanted growth can be cut back to improve the appearance of the plant.

White, flushed blue, star-shaped flowers with yellow centres are borne in clusters, appearing over the summer months. There are other colours, including blue, but the white form (the 'potato' vine) offers the best value. New plants can be propagated from firm cuttings inserted in peat and sand mixture in cool conditions during late summer.

## SOLEIROLIA SOLEIROLII (*Urticaceae*)
baby's tears

The former name for this plant, *Helxine soleirolii,* is the more popular and one wonders why the name of such a humble plant should be tampered with at all, as it really is little more than a cultivated weed! One reason for including the plant here is so that the beginner may be warned against doing anything with it other than grow it in a plant pot where it can be kept under control. It is a plant that is sometimes described as ground cover which, no doubt, it is, as it will cover all the available ground in an amazingly short space of time. Not only will it invade the area of every corner of the planted bed in the conservatory if given the chance, it will also do likewise if you are foolish enough to plant it in the garden.

It has small, fresh green leaves and is also available in gold and silver forms. It propagates itself from virtually every piece that falls where the merest crumb of soil may happen to be. Caring for these plants amounts to nothing more than providing water to prevent the soil drying out. Dry soil will result in dry and shrivelled foliage.

One of the many suggestions in respect of this plant is that it makes an ideal inhabitant for the bottle garden or terrarium. As far as baby's tears is concerned this might well be so as it will thrive beyond belief to the point whereby it will in little time completely smother all the other unfortunate occupants of the bottle!

## SOLENOSTEMON (*Labiatae*) flame nettle

For anyone on a low budget wishing to introduce some colour to the conservatory scene, the flame nettle (formerly *Coleus*) grown from seed could be a good proposition. Seed can be sown in warm conditions in early spring (earlier the better). When of manageable size the seedlings can be potted up and when plants have developed their true colours it is wise to go through them so that the inferior ones can be eliminated. The best can be planted into pots of reasonable size as soon as plants are sufficiently rooted in their existing containers. They are greedy plants and will respond well to potting into a rich mixture containing a proportion of loam. As plants develop those of poor colour can be further weeded out, and any plants of particular merit can have cuttings removed with a view to increasing their numbers.

Plants from seed tend to produce rather too many run of the mill plants, and if one is keen to introduce really fine coloured plants to the conservatory then it is advisable to procure named varieties as they will be much superior to those that are raised from seed. There are specialist growers who can supply named varieties and these will add interest particularly if some plants are grown as standards.

Plants appreciate good light in which to grow and ample watering and feeding during the spring and summer months.

## SPARMANNIA AFRICANA (*Tilaceae*) wind flower, indoor lime

For the conservatory able to accommodate a free-standing small tree, the sparmannia is well worth considering, as it is reasonably quick and easy to grow. The large, pale green leaves are borne on stout stems which radiate fom the central slender stem of the plant and have a lovely cool freshness about them.

A minimum temperature of 16 °C (61 °F) should be the aim, although plants will tolerate less if the roots are kept on the dry side. Shade will suit them better than bright sun, but they must not be located in very poor light.

During the summer months plants will need ample watering and weekly feeding with a balanced liquid fertilizer. Less water is needed in winter, but plants should at no time become dry. Feeding should stop in the autumn and start again when new growth is evident in the spring.

Plants do not come into their own until they are growing in pots of at least 25 cm (10 in) diameter and are beginning to take on tree proportions. Potting plants on can be undertaken at any time other than during the winter, and a loam-based potting mixture will be the most suitable for the job. Plants can be propagated from pieces of stem with two leaves attached, smaller leaves being preferable should there be any on the plant. Place cuttings in a peat and sand mixture and keep them moist in a heated propagating case shaded from direct sunlight.

The common name of windflower relates to the prominent yellow filaments in the centre of white petals; the filaments open outwards when disturbed by the wind. Indoor lime relates to the similarity the plant bears to the lime tree (on the continent, Germany in particular, the plant is known as the *zimmer linden*).

Plants which become too large for their allotted space can be cut back at any time of the year; this is sometimes necessary to improve the shape of the plant which can become lopsided when old branches grow too vigorously.

## SPATHIPHYLLUM (*Araceae*) peace lily

Worldwide the two most popular of this genus are **S. *wallisii*** and **S. 'Mauna Loa'**, both plants sharing the common name of peace lily. Both have white spathe flowers that are long lasting and produced almost throughout the year on healthy plants growing in agreeable conditions. *S.* 'Mauna Loa' is much the larger plant of the two. Dark, glossy green leaves grow on long petioles tightly grouped at soil level so that compact and attractive plants are the result.

There is little doubt that this is the best flowering plant for locations in poor light, which is good reason for their extensive use by landscapers in public buildings. In the conservatory they will have to be grown in fairly heavy shade if deep green colouring of leaves is to be retained. A minimum temperature of 18 °C (64 °F) should be the aim and the general feeling within the conservatory should be humid.

Plants can be potted at almost any time of the year if the growing conditions are agreeable, and a rich mixture will be needed. Plants are propagated by dividing older clumps and potting them individually; do this by giving the soil in the pot a thorough watering before separating the roots.

Plants can be grown as specimens in large containers, or as part of the scheme when display beds are being planted out. Flowers turn from white to washed out green before they die, but there are almost always new flowers coming to replace those that have gone over.

## STEPHANOTIS FLORIBUNDA
(*Asclepiadaceae*) Madagascar jasmine

A puzzling plant which either grows with rampant freedom in the conservatory, or collapses, hangs its head and dies for no apparent reason. When growing well it will produce strands of growth that seem to go on forever – 5 m (16 ft) is often quoted as ultimate length, but it can be much more than this. The leaves are of leathery texture, evergreen and attached to twining stems, the tips of which will curl around very securely to anything that will give the plant some means of support. The flowers are tubular and borne in small clusters, white in colour and very fragrant. If the door to the conservatory is open when plants are in flower the fragrance will permeate through to every room.

To do well they should be planted in a good, loam-based mixture, either in tubs or in the planted display border. There is no reason why they should not be planted in a corner of the conservatory as individual plants. Lightly shaded conditions in sunny weather will suit them with clear glass to give additional light over winter. Watering needs to be done with care as plants are inclined to collapse dramatically if the soil in which they are growing becomes excessively wet for long periods. The winter months are especially difficult when water should be given very sparingly. Feeding of established plants is only necessary while there is new growth in evidence. Plants will generally tolerate widely fluctuating temperature levels, but a minimum of 13 °C (55 °F) should be the aim.

Why should they die so miserably for no apparent reason, and often soon after purchase? The reason is that many of the plants sold by the retailer are grown in very soft conditions – warm greenhouses with artificial lighting to encourage them to produce flowers out of season. When such plants are handled by a retailer with poor plant-keeping facilities, and are subsequently introduced to the conservatory, the plant is often half way to the grave! It is very much better to buy plants during the summer months of the year and to choose those that have a robust look about them, as opposed to weaklings with droopy leaves and a lifeless feel to them. The initial purchase will usually indicate the eventual quality of the plant.

When growing well plants need some sort of frame to which they can be trained. To prevent plants developing as long, thin strands of growth it is advisable to train the growth so that fuller and more attractive plants are the result.

Plants can be propagated from cuttings prepared from a piece of stem with two opposite leaves attached; these go into peat and sand in a heated propagator. Rooting will be a slow business. Plants can also be grown from seed but this takes even longer before they develop reasonable size. An interesting aspect of the seed is that the stephanotis will sometimes produce a fruit that is the size of a large plum, and green in colour, turning to pale brown as it ripens. When it splits the black seeds attached to white silky 'parachutes' will appear like gossamer to drift away on the wind. Just to see how beautiful seeds are at this stage would be worth your while trying to pollinate the stephanotis flowers. Seed can be sown on the surface of a peat and sand mixture with just a sprinkling of sand over them to complete the job – a heated propagator in a lightly shaded location should ensure that the seed germinates.

## STEREOSPERMUM CHELONOIDES
(*Bignoniaceae*) snake tree

A large name for a plant previously known as *Radermachera* when it first came on the scene as a potted plant. With a central stem from which grow dense, pale green leaves, it is not the sort of plant that will set the world on fire. There is also a variegated form with washed out pale green leaves that does nothing to improve the chances of this plant becoming a best seller. A possible argument in favour of the snake tree is that mature plants have a wide spread of foliage.

In the conservatory it will need a lightly shaded location and regular watering and feeding during the spring and summer with careful watering and no feeding while the plant is resting. It is not the best of plants, and will have a marked tendency to shed lower leaves no matter how well it is cared for. Any potting on that might be required should be done in the spring using a houseplant soil. Cold and wet conditions will be detrimental, so a minimum temperature of 16 °C (61 °F) should be maintained.

## STRELITZIA REGINAE (*Strelitziaceae*)
bird of paradise

Seen in their native South Africa, these are field-grown plants cultivated for their exotic flowers which are long stemmed with boat-like bracts from which emerge the colourful orange and blue flowers. Here they are grown with ample space around them and that combined with continuous bright sunlight ensures that plants will produce flowers in reasonable time, which makes these plants an economical crop to manage.

Mature plants attain a maximum height of just over 1 m (3 ft) when grown in a pot, and produce a considerable number of leaves which are oblong in shape and attached to stout petioles. In the conservatory they will do best in full sun and should be freely watered during the spring and summer, giving less in the autumn and very little water over the winter period. Plants can be fed during the growing months of the year when other plants in the conservatory are being similarly dealt with. However, it is not wise to be over-generous with either feeding or potting on as plants will often respond better in the way of flower production if they are well rooted in their containers and a touch neglected.

How long it will be before seed-grown plants come into flower is a question frequently asked; the answer is about eight to ten years and, sad to say, the flowers that do develop are frequently inferior to those normally associated with this plant.

Seed is sown in the spring in warm conditions where the temperature does not fall below 20 °C (68 °F) and should not be difficult to germinate. When large enough to handle the seedlings are transferred to small pots filled with a standard potting mixture. Thereafter it is simply a question of potting them on as needed using a loam-based mixture, and ensuring that plants have ample sunlight and moisture while they are actively growing. Alternative methods of propagation are to remove suckers from around the base of the plant in the spring and to pot these individually. The suggestion is often made that plants can also be increased by division, but this could be a daunting task and a traumatic experience for the plant: strelitzias as mature plants have many solid roots making separation extremely difficult, but it may be possible with younger plants.

Be warned that these plants are very easy to grow, but they take up a great deal of space in the conservatory, and caring for them over the years might not really be worth it in the end!

## STREPTOCARPUS (*Gesneriaceae*)
Cape primrose

Indigenous to South Africa, there are now lots of superb hybrids of these fine plants – plants that with only moderate care will go on flowering for months on end.

Plants are generally of compact habit and should be grown in a lightly shaded location at a minimum temperature of around 10 °C (50 °F). Feed them weekly with a liquid fertilizer and when potting plants on use a recognized houseplant mixture. The atmosphere in the conservatory should be moist, but care must be taken not to overdo watering.

Besides the many hybrids there are also the old-fashioned kinds, such as the blue and the white flowered forms of **S. 'Constant Nymph Seedling'**, the flowers being smaller and more delicate than the hybrid forms. Stiff green leaves do little for these plants and are easily broken if carelessly handled. The breaking of leaves can turn to your advantage as the streptocarpus is one of those plants where every section of leaf removed and placed in potting mixture will produce roots. Mature leaves can be removed and cut along their midrib for their entire length so that you have two halves. If the leaf is placed on its side with the midrib pushed gently into potting compost, it will not be long before baby plants are clustering around the parent half-leaf. A propagator and modest warmth and moisture is all that is needed to ensure success.

The streptocarpus belongs to the splendid Gesneriaceae family and can be put to many uses in the conservatory. Planting in decorative hanging containers, for example, will ensure they have ample air and light and in return they will provide colour right through spring, summer and into autumn.

## SYNGONIUM PODOPHYLLUM
(*Araceae*) goosefoot plant

Belonging to the Araceae family, there are numerous hybrids with slight variation to the arrowhead-shaped leaf and with varying degrees of leaf colouring. As with all members of this family, the syngonium must have moist, shaded and warm conditions in order to succeed – minimum temperature should not fall below 16 °C (61 °F).

Plants are grown entirely for their foliage colouring and may be used as ground cover in a planted bed in the shaded conservatory, in hanging containers if the atmosphere is not too dry, or they may be utilized as wall plants. In the moist, humid conservatory the latter option would suit them best if plants can be trained to grow against a solid wall and can be kept moist to encourage growth and production of aerial roots. Large tubs, or planted beds with warming cables will suit them fine; in such conditions if the temperature can be maintained at a few degrees above the recommended minimum the plant will produce larger and more attractive leaves. Never allow them to dry out and feed only during the spring and summer.

## TETRASTIGMA VOINIERIANUM
(*Vitaceae*) chestnut vine

This one must be the ultimate in free-growing plants for the conservatory that can be maintained at minimum temperature of 18 °C (64 °F) with high level of humidity. In these conditions it is an ideal plant for covering a large wall area in the shortest possible length of time – you can almost see it grow. On a stout wire framework the plant will utilize its coiling tendrils to climb and spread in all directions. They must have large pots, ample watering and regular feeding to sustain the clambering growth. The segmented leaves are an attractive soft green in colour, but there are no flowers.

Soft, pale green fresh leaves must have protection from direct sunlight if they are not to suffer scorch, so light shading of the conservatory ought to be the aim, with less in winter than in the summer.

**Tetrastigma**
A rampant, natural climbing vine that will cover wall and overhead space in remarkably little time, but needs good growing conditions.

## THUNBERGIA ALATA (*Acanthaceae*)
black-eyed Susan

The common name refers to the flower which has a jet black centre, surrounded by attractive single petals of orange colouring. They can trail or be encouraged to climb.

Very easy to manage, new plants can be raised from seed each year in warm conditions in late winter. When seedlings have produced two or three leaves they should be carefully handled and potted individually into 8 cm (3 in) pots using a houseplant mixture. Thereafter, pot on as they fill their pots with roots until such time as plants are in pots of 18 cm (7 in) where they can be sustained by regular feeding. These are easy-care plants that will tolerate a wide assortment of conditions without coming to any real harm.

## TIBOUCHINA (*Melastomataceae*) glory bush

Native to Brazil, several of these would make an attractive addition to the range of plants grown in the conservatory. Depending on where they are grown and the attention given, plants will attain a height of between 2 and 3 m (6–10 ft). The majority have violet-blue flowers in evidence from mid summer through until the autumn.

A lightly shaded location will suit them best, and plants can be grown either in tubs or planted in a display bed. Use a loam-based potting mixture when potting on, and when planting in a bed it is advisable to incorporate good potting soil to get them off to a good start. Ample water is needed from spring through until the autumn when the amount of water should be reduced for the inactive winter months.

Plants can be raised from seed sown in warm conditions in the spring, or from firm cuttings a few inches in length taken at any time during the spring or summer. Individual cuttings should be inserted in a peat and sand mixture in an 8 cm (3 in) pot to be maintained at a temperature of around 20 °C (68 °F) in moist, lightly shaded conditions. Once rooted the small plants will quickly get away and should be potted on as necessary using a loam-based potting mixture. In time plants will form into neat bushes that can be kept in shape by pruning after it has finished flowering.

## TILLANDSIA (*Bromeliaceae*) air plant

These plants belong to the bromeliad family and are indigenous to tropical South America; there are many varieties and all of them extremely durable. In recent years they have come to prominence as 'air plants', sold for decorating shells, driftwood and such like. Most of them develop into small rosettes of grey foliage that needs little more than warmth and moisture sprayed onto the foliage to keep them in reasonable trim. For small bromeliad trees they are the perfect plants for fitting into clefts and tying onto branches. Baby rosettes will in time form around the base of the parent, and these when of reasonable size can be removed and planted in small pots using an orchid mixture or they too can be fixed to branches where they will usually flower when of sufficient age. The growing temperature can be very variable and do no real harm, but where possible a minimum of 13 °C (55 °F) should be the aim. Filtered light will be the most suitable and when potting plants on they should go into an orchid mixture if there is not a special bromeliad soil available, but it must be said that tillandsias are plants that never need to be potted into larger pots. When fixing them to bromeliad trees the pots are removed and the roots of the plants are wrapped in fresh sphagnum moss before the plant is secured.

## TOLMIEA MENZIESII (*Saxifrageaceae*)
piggy-back plant

These are fun plants that will grow with little bother in the cold conservatory. They will need filtered light and moist conditions. The fun relates to the odd way in which mature leaves produce perfectly shaped miniature plants on the back of the parent leaf close to the petiole. When of reasonable size the leaf and its baby can be removed and planted in small pots filled with a houseplant mixture where they will grow away to become sizeable plants in no time at all.

Leaf colour is yellowish green and the plant forms into a loose rosette of foliage that can be potted conventionally, planted in a display bed, or suspended from the ceiling in a hanging container. A good houseplant mixture will be suitable at all stages of both propagating and potting on.

## TRADESCANTIA (*Commelinaceae*)
wandering jew, wandering sailor, purple heart, three men in a boat, inch plant

These humble plants are often underrated, considered cheap and of little importance for interior decoration. There are, however, many fine varieties with a splendid colour range from silver through gold to deep maroon. Where most people go wrong with these is that the plants are looked upon as cheap and easily replaceable, so they are neglected in favour of other plants in the collection. There is also the old adage that these are plants that do better when neglected in respect of feeding and potting on, and nothing could be further from the truth.

Cuttings can be taken at any time of the year and should be firm and prepared from the top section of the stem, a piece some 10 cm (4 in) in length. The lower leaf is removed and up to seven cuttings should be firmly inserted in 8 cm (3 in) pots using a houseplant mixture. Kept moist in a lightly shaded location, cuttings will root in two to three weeks. When they begin to grow, the tips of all the cuttings should be removed to encourage the plants to branch – this will result in more attractive plants at a later stage. The potful of cuttings can later be potted on into 13 cm (5 in) pots where they will make fine plants for all sorts of uses in the well stocked conservatory.

An alternative to pots would be to put several of the pots of cuttings into a hanging basket of generous size and to keep the soil moist and fed once plants have become established. The purist may disagree, but a very pleasing effect can be obtained by planting several different varieties of these plants in the same container, so that you have silver, green, gold, pink and wine shades to liven up the conservatory. Where space is limited this is one way of displaying several varieties to very good effect. It is said that tradescantia leaves will turn green if the plants are fed, but this is nonsense. Green leaves will periodically appear no matter what the growing treatment may be, and the simple answer to green growth is to pull it out otherwise it will dominate and spoil the appearance.

When tradescantias inevitably take on a tired look, be ruthless and dispose of them, but have back up plants ready for planting so that they fill the gap.

*T. pallida* (purple heart, formerly *Setcreasea purpurea*) derives its common name from the bright colouring of the purple foliage, particularly striking when seen in bright sunlight; both leaves and stems of the plant have similar colouring. This is not a commercial pot plant for the simple reason that the plant has very untidy habit of growth, with stiff stems and

247

leaves pushing out in all directions. Although the commercial grower likes his plants to be well controlled, the interested plant person is not so particular and willingly accepts either cuttings or plants from acquaintances knowing that the plant will attract a deal of attention when sitting on its sunny windowsill. Pinch out the tops of all young plants (to make more plants!) so that the pieces remaining in the container will branch out to make a full and handsome plant. It is well worth taking this amount of trouble at the outset as these are evergreen plants which will be an attraction throughout the year. In time they will produce small but attractive pink flowers. Give it reasonable warmth, good light and a watering programme that errs on the side of dryness; this is particularly important over the winter months. Plants can be fed occasionally while in active growth, but feeding is not really an important need.

For the warmer conservatory, *T. spathacea* (three men in a boat, formerly *Rhoeo discolor*) forms neat rosettes of metallic green leaves which are purple on the reverse. The leaves are lance-shaped and upright, growing from a central stem from which young plants will be produced at the base. An interesting feature of the plant is the odd boat-shaped bract, in the middle of which are small white flowers said to resemble three men in a boat – hence the common name. (In some parts of the world it may be called Moses in the cradle.)

When grown in the conservatory these plants will require a minimum temperature of not less than 16 °C (61 °F), and should have lightly shaded location. Moist conditions will also suit them, and this means moisture at their roots and in the atmosphere. A little less water is needed in the winter, but plants should not be allowed to dry out too much. Feed should be given during the spring and summer but none in the winter. Although plants will never need to go into very large pots, any potting that is considered necessary should be undertaken in the spring and the mixture should be a loam-based one. The small rosettes of leaves that develop at the base of the parent plant should be allowed to develop to reasonable size before they are potted separately into small pots of houseplant compost to make new plants.

*T. zebrina pendula* (inch plant) is usually passed over as being very ordinary, but when a leaf is removed and inspected it will be found that it is indeed a very colourful plant, with green and purple base colouring, and a beautiful silver sheen. The undersides of leaves are bright purple, which is a good reason for ensuring that these plants are grown in hanging containers where all these features can be appreciated to the full. The small purple coloured flowers are insignificant compared to the foliage and are not much in evidence in healthy plants. When flowers in any quantity appear on the zebrinas it is often a sign that the plant is ailing. The succulent stems are rigid and upright initially, but these will droop gently with the weight of foliage as the plant increases in size.

Take cuttings as previously described. Hanging containers can be planted with several potfuls of cuttings so that a reasonably full plant is the immediate result. After potting the soil should be given a good watering and the container should be placed on a bench in the greenhouse for the first few weeks so that it will be easier to water and look after generally. When hanging it up resist the temptation to suspend it from the highest location in the conservatory: plants will be easier to water and check on when they are hanging at about head level.

There is also a more choice sport and that is *T. zebrina* 'Quadricolor' which, besides having all the attributes of its parent, has white pink and red in its multicoloured foliage. It is a little more difficult to manage, and needs care to select only the best coloured pieces of stem when propagating plants.

Tradescantias may be last on the list, but they really are worth a second look, as they can be colourful throughout the year.

## TULIPA (*Liliaceae*) tulip

It is really quite easy to have a tulip in flower in the conservatory some time before they are seen in the garden. Choose good quality bulbs, not forgetting some of the lovely short species types that come in a wonderful array of colours. (Groups of these will be ideal for planting in the rock garden following their spell indoors.)

Bulbs should be planted fairly close together in bulb fibre, just below the surface of the soil. This should be done in late autumn, the pots completely covered over with peat in a cold frame (in the garden if there is no cold frame), and must be left at least eight weeks to fill their pot well with roots. During this period the soil must be kept moist, and once growth is visible the pots can be lifted, cleaned and put on display for the flowers to appear soon after, and way ahead of those in the garden.

## VALLOTA SPECIOSA *see* CYRTANTHUS PURPUREUS

## VELTHEIMIA CAPENSIS
(*Liliaceae/Hyacinthaceae*) forest lily

Tender South African bulbous plants producing attractive tubular flowers in clusters on stems that are some 45 cm (1½ ft) in length. Bulbs should be firmly planted just below the surface of the soil which must be rich and contain a proportion of loam. During the early stages water must be given sparingly, but should be increased when the plant is well furnished with leaves. When the leaves die down naturally the soil must be kept almost dry and the bulb should be stored at a temperature of not less than 5 °C (41 °F). During the growing season plants prefer cool, airy and lightly shaded conditions, and should be fed each week with a liquid fertilizer.

Plants can be propagated by removing offsets from around the base of the parent bulb and planting them in small pans or seed trays to get them under way, potting them into individual pots as they become established. Plants can also be increased from seed, or by peeling off the leaves close to the bulb and inserting them upright in peat and sand in a warm propagator.

## VRIESIA (*Bromeliaceae*) flaming sword

There are lots of species, the best known being

*V. splendens* (flaming sword), a plant with an attractively marked upright rosette of leaves and a red bract, very descriptive of the common name. Orange-yellow flowers appear over a period of time from either side of the bract starting at the bottom. Flowers are not a significant feature of this fine plant.

Requiring a minimum temperature of around 16 °C (61 °F) it should be watered by filling the rosette 'urn' with water but be very sparing when it comes to applying water to the soil. Young plants are sometimes available and these can be grown on in small pots using an orchid mixture that is open and free draining.

There are numerous other compact vriesias that are equally easy to care for, but if you desire something really spectacular to brighten the plant collection there are two vriesias that might fill the bill: *V. fenestralis* (netted vriesia) and *V. hieroglyphica*, the latter having the honour of being named 'king of bromeliads', a grand title when one thinks of the many fine bromeliads that there are. It produces a very large rosette of broad leaves with hieroglyphic markings of greenish yellow colouring. It will require ample space and takes several years to produce its tall branched flower spike; compared to the foliage the flowers, when they arrive, are a touch disappointing.

*V. fenestralis* also produces a very large rosette of leaves which are beautifully marked with a network of light and dark lines on a yellow-green background.

Both these are invariably in short supply, and would only be suited to the connoisseur's collection. They need a warm, humid and shaded (but not dark) situation and this can only be achieved if there are lots of plants in the conservatory contributing to the general atmosphere, an atmosphere which the true plantsman just knows instinctively is right for his plants. In your efforts to produce the right 'feeling', you need to damp down the floor and around the plants at regular intervals to ensure that there is no excessive drying out. This does not mean that you have to be forever watering the pot in which the plant is growing – by regularly damping the surroundings there will be very much less need for actually watering the pot itself.

## XANTHOSOMA (*Araceae*) Indian kale

The common name suggests a plant of little consequence, but the arrow-shaped, large leaves of the xanthosomas are among the most beautiful of all foliage plants. The leaves are of superb colouring with attractive venation and grow either from a rhizome or a short trunk.

They need special conditions if they are to succeed, and there will be little hope for the plant acquired simply to stand in a corner to improve the appearance of the conservatory interior. To manage these well you need shaded, warm and humid conditions, plus a deal of expertise in the care of more demanding plants.

Watering and maintaining humidity will be important factors while plants are in leaf, and this will mean daily attention to ensure that the entire floor area of the conservatory, both display beds and paths, is kept moist by damping the area with a watering can or hose-pipe with a fine rose attached. Getting the correct feeling in a conservatory that houses a collection of exotic plants is something that comes with experience – you just know that everything is in order and right for the plants when you step over the threshold. Syringing of foliage of more exotic plants that are growing in warm conditions will also benefit in respect of humidity and will discourage such pests as red spider mites. The xanthosomas belong to the Araceae family, all of which fare better if grown in the warm and humid conditions recommended here.

Plants will normally be bought in leaf, but it may also be possible to acquire rhizomes, in which case these should be potted in late winter. Use a houseplant mixture in pots that are only just large enough to accommodate the rhizome. In the warm and shaded conservatory or greenhouse growth will be fairly rapid and you will be able to pot the plants on into larger pots in only a matter of weeks following initial potting. This will be a critical stage in the development of the plant so it must have every consideration in respect of watering, feeding and warmth. Plants must be kept moist during the summer months with a gradual reduction towards autumn so that over winter they are kept dry.

It may seem a great deal of bother keeping such plants in good order, but when grown with similar exotics in the conservatory devoted to tropical plants, the xanthosomas will be very rewarding. New plants can be made in late winter by removing rhizomes from their pots and dividing them into sections to be potted separately.

## YUCCA ELEPHANTIPES (*Agavaceae*) spineless yucca

There are numerous other yuccas, but not all are suitable for growing in the conservatory where there are lots of people moving around. The Spanish bayonet, *Y. aloifolia*, has leaf tips that are as sharp as the common name suggests, sharp enough to draw blood should skin come into contact with the plant. Much more worrying is the prospect of getting one of the stiff needle points in one's eye when inadvertently coming into contact with the plant.

The plant most freely available is *Y. elephantipes* and this is the plant that should be chosen as it is quite harmless and, surely, one of the most durable plants for the conservatory. In nature the stout stems of this yucca will emerge from a swollen base, but when bought as a potted plant they will usually have one or several stems in the pot with fresh green rosettes sprouting from the top or sides of each stem.

Plants are grown in tropical regions where the stems are cut to precise lengths to be shipped to commercial nurseries around the world. The stems are placed in heated propagating beds filled with moist peat in order to root. These stems might be 8–10 cm (3–4 in) in diameter and not seem to be very suitable material for propagating purposes, but it says much for the yucca's tough disposition when you learn that these tree-like cuttings root at 100% rate!

Purchase plants which are firm in their pots, as opposed to those that feel loose when the stems are moved from one side to the other. It is also wise to buy plants with unblemished foliage. as marked leaves or leaves that have become discoloured will be indications of indifferent attention in respect of watering:

yuccas too wet at their roots for lengthy periods, particularly in winter, will be at risk.

Having chosen a quality plant, offer it a light location at modest temperature for it to do well. It is important never to overwater these plants, particularly so during the winter months. A firm loam-based mixture should be used when potting, but frequent potting of these durable plants is not necessary.

## ZANTEDESCHIA (*Araceae*) arum lily

These range in height from 13 cm (5 in) in **Z. rehmannii** to just over 1 m (3 ft) in **Z. aethiopica** and **Z. elliottiana**, all having glossy green leaves. Depending on the species, plants can be had in flower from spring through summer. *Z. rehmannii* is rosy purple in colour, *Z. aethiopica* is white and *Z. elliottiana* yellow. There are other forms but *Z. aethiopica* is probably the best known.

Plants can be propagated from seed sown in warm conditions in the spring, or they can be increased by dividing clumps of growth when plants are being potted. Another method is to remove suckering young plants from the base of the parent plant, also at potting time, and to plant these in 13 cm (5 in) pots. For all operations a loam-based mixture should be used.

Following potting or propagation it is important to water sparingly until plants are obviously under way with fresh growth. While plants are actively growing and in flower they should be fed regularly. Following flowering the amount of water should be reduced and the plants should go out into the garden in a sunny location until the autumn when they should again be brought inside. The large leaves of these plants are of little attraction while there are no flowers present, which is a good reason for having a feeder greenhouse where plants can be stored; they then occupy valuable conservatory space only while they are in flower.

## ZEBRINA PENDULA *see* TRADESCANTIA ZEBRINA

# Index